CAVALIER POETS

CAVALIER POETS

Selected Poems

Edited with an Introduction and Notes by
Thomas Clayton

1478
1978

OXFORD UNIVERSITY PRESS

OXFORD   LONDON   NEW YORK

Oxford University Press, Walton Street, Oxford OX2 6DP

OXFORD LONDON GLASGOW NEW YORK
TORONTO MELBOURNE WELLINGTON CAPE TOWN
IBADAN NAIROBI DAR ES SALAAM LUSAKA
KUALA LUMPUR SINGAPORE JAKARTA HONG KONG TOKYO
DELHI BOMBAY CALCUTTA MADRAS KARACHI

Casebound ISBN 0 19 254171 4
Paperback ISBN 0 19 281204 1

© Thomas Clayton 1978

*The texts of the poems are based on those published in the Oxford
English Text series by the Clarendon Press, Oxford: Carew, ed.
R. Dunlap, 1949, corr. rpt. 1957; Herrick, ed. L. C. Martin,
1956, corr. rpt. 1963; Lovelace, ed. C. H. Wilkinson, 1930,
corr. rpt. 1953; Suckling, ed. T. Clayton, 1971.*
*This composite edition first issued in the Oxford Standard
Authors series and simultaneously as an Oxford Paperback 1978*

British Library Cataloguing in Publication Data

Cavalier Poets. – (Oxford standard authors).
  1. English poety – Early modern, 1500–1700
  I. Clayton, Thomas   II. Series
  821'.4'08   PR1209   77–30071

  ISBN 0–19–254171–4
  ISBN 0–19–281204–1 Pbk.

PRINTED IN GREAT BRITAIN BY
THE BOWERING PRESS LTD
PLYMOUTH

For
ROBERT *and* VIDA SWOVERLAND CLAYTON
(My Father *and* Mother)

PREFACE AND ACKNOWLEDGEMENTS

I undertook to prepare this edition because I wanted to share with others the pleasure and interest I have in reading these Cavalier poets, who except for Herrick have seldom received their due of attention and appreciation, owing partly to the lack of an up-to-date annotated and reliable modern-spelling text of a substantial body of their verse in a single convenient collection. Thus I hope to supply what seems to me a genuine need with this edition, which brings together over a fifth of the 1,130 secular poems of the prolific Herrick, nearly half of Carew's and Lovelace's, and over a third of Suckling's, and combines their best and most important with other especially characteristic and interesting poems, many of them not previously anthologized, to present a corpus for each poet that allows him to be seen both at his best and as he is.

My greatest scholarly obligation is to the editors of the Oxford English Texts of the Cavalier poets, without whose prior editorial work I should not have undertaken mine here, where I have edited Suckling for the second time, though in very different form from my OET old-spelling text of *The Non-Dramatic Works*. Mr. John Buxton read the entire book in typescript and shared with me his fine scholarship in the form of many valuable suggestions prompted by an extraordinarily careful and learned reading, but I cannot hold him responsible for surviving faults. And I owe a special debt to my Oxford University Press editors, Mrs. Carol Buckroyd, whose valuable advice guided me in the compression of my Introduction and Notes, and Miss Robyn Swett, whose keen and comprehensive therapeutics contributed much to what is viable in the present edition.

We learn not only from other scholars, colleagues, and editors but from the students who will or could become scholars themselves, and I wish to express indebtedness for seventeenth-century edification to Linda Anderson, Carl Buchin, Roger Conover, Dr. David Farkas, Gayle Gaskill, Bruce Haber, Peter Isackson, Michael Levy, Mark and Carol Gilbertson Muggli, John Sullivan, and Dr. Arthur Walzer. I have also to record special thanks to Virginia Hansen for extensive bibliographical, critical, and typing help during the early stages of my work.

Of my many debts to the University of Minnesota, the most obvious are those to the Graduate School for grants in aid of research, and to the Department of English and the College of Liberal Arts for two single-quarter leaves that enabled me to begin and to complete this edition.

How very much I continue to owe my parents, to whom this book is dedicated, I trust they know.

Last and never least, I owe my wife Ruth the usual debt for good company and thoughtful reading: whatever I write is the better on those accounts, and the worse remains at my charge.

St. Paul, Minnesota   T.C.
March 1977

CONTENTS

ABBREVIATIONS

Obvious titles like those of books of the Bible and plays by Shakespeare are abbreviated without being 'keyed' in the list of Abbreviations. (I have used the Authorized Version of the Bible and Peter Alexander's one-volume edition of Shakespeare's *Complete Works*, 1951.) Further details of books in this list are given in the Select Bibliography (p. 333).

Abbott	E. A. Abbott, *A Shakespearian Grammar*, 3rd revised edition (1870; rpt. 1966)
Brewer	*Brewer's Dictionary of Phrase and Fable*, Centenary edition (1970; corr. rpt., 1974)
Broadbent	*Signet Classic Poets of the 17th Century*, 2 vols., edited by John Broadbent (1974)
C	Carew
CE	*College English*
Clayton	Editorial matter, OET *Suckling*
CP 40	Carew, *Poems* (1640)
CP 42	Carew, *Poems* (1642)
Dunlap	Editorial matter, OET *Carew*
ELH	*ELH, A Journal of English Literary History*
ES	*English Studies*
FA 46	Suckling, *Fragmenta Aurea* (1646)
FA 48	Suckling, *Fragmenta Aurea* (1648)
G	Glossary (pp. 339–44 of this edition)
H	Herrick
H 48	Herrick, *Hesperides* (1648)
Howarth	*Minor Poets of the Seventeenth Century*, edited by R. G. Howarth (Everyman's Library, 1931; rev. rpt., 1953)
L	Lovelace
L 49	Lovelace, *Lucasta* (1649)
LP 59	Lovelace, *Lucasta. Posthume Poems* (1659)
LR 59	*The Last Remains of Sir John Suckling* (1659)
Martin	Editorial matter, OET *Herrick*
MLN	*Modern Language Notes*
MLR	*Modern Language Review*
N & Q	*Notes and Queries*

NRC	Note on Renaissance Cosmology (pp. 337–8 of this edition)
OED	*Oxford English Dictionary*
OET	Oxford English Text
OPET	Oxford Paperback English Text
Oxford Proverbs	*The Oxford Dictionary of English Proverbs*, edited by F. P. Wilson, 3rd edition (1970)
Patrick	Editorial matter, *Complete Poetry of Robert Herrick*, edited by J. Max Patrick (1963; corr. rpt., 1968)
Pollard	Editorial matter, *Robert Herrick: The Hesperides and Noble Numbers*, edited by Alfred Pollard (Muses Library, 1898)
PQ	*Philological Quarterly*
REL	*Review of English Literature*
RES	*Review of English Studies*
S	Suckling
SEL	*Studies in English Literature*
SP	*Studies in Philology*
Tilley	Maurice P. Tilley, *A Dictionary of the Proverbs in England in the Sixteenth and Seventeenth Centuries* (1960)
TSLL	*Texas Studies in Language and Literature*
Weidhorn	Manfred Weidhorn, *Richard Lovelace* (1970)
Wilkinson	Editorial matter, OET *Lovelace*

INTRODUCTION

CAVALIER POETS

Herrick, Carew, Suckling, and Lovelace share a continuing
appeal that continues also to change as the times change. They
are 'for all time', as Ben Jonson wrote of Shakespeare, but they
are also much more 'of an age'; hence their varying critical
fortunes with ages and audiences like and unlike theirs. They have
always found most favour with those who prefer their poetry first
to be poetry ('creation through words of orders of meaning and
sound', as the late Reuben Brower once put it), and who recognize
'high seriousness' as not necessarily to be demanded everywhere
in the same measure, kind, and character. Not that these poets
don't speak to the human condition. They do. But heirs of the
opposing puritans have difficulties with the Cavalier perspective,
for reasons suggested by Hume in his assessment of relations
between art and society: 'in a republic, the candidates for office
must look downwards, to gain the suffrages of the people; in a
monarchy, they must turn their attention upwards, to court the
good graces and favour of the great. To be successful in the former
way, it is necessary for a man to make himself *useful*, by his
industry, capacity, or knowledge; to be prosperous in the latter
way, it is requisite for him to render himself *agreeable*, by his wit,
complaisance, and civility. A strong genius succeeds best in
republics, a refined taste in monarchies. And consequently the
sciences are the more natural growth of the one, the polite arts
of the other' ('Of the Rise and Progress of the Arts and Sciences',
1742).

For better as well as for worse 'the protestant ethic and the
spirit of capitalism' have given us much of the modern West, but
it is still not for nothing that the puritans have also given their
name to stern-faced repression in the parsimonious interests of a
theocratic millenium. And it was the puritans who closed the
theatres, restricted sports and pastimes, took the land by force and
violence, and beheaded the Archbishop of Canterbury and the
King—a course of national and international events that brought
about Suckling's death in 1641 and possibly Carew's in 1640, and

that Lovelace and Herrick saw most feelingly, Lovelace on occasion as a political prisoner and Herrick by expulsion from his parish living in Devon. Herrick expresses a keen sense of the times' universal upheaval in 'Farewell Frost, or Welcome the Spring': rejoicing over the turn of the greening season, he hopes that,

> . . . when this war (which tempest-like doth spoil
> Our salt, our corn, our honey, wine, and oil)
> Falls to a temper, and doth mildly cast
> His inconsiderate frenzy off at last,
> The gentle dove may, when these turmoils cease,
> Bring in her bill, once more, *the Branch of Peace*.

Here Herrick speaks plaintively and forcefully for the free-from-party-coloured heart, although the cast of his allegiance is clearly in evidence when 'the palms put forth their gems, and every tree / Now swaggers in her leafy gallantry.'

Carew and Suckling were close friends, and they were certainly acquainted with their younger contemporary, Lovelace. All three served in the first Bishops' War in 1639, and Suckling and Lovelace served in the second, in 1640. And all three were closely associated with a Court in which the King was as much a connoisseur of the arts as he was a perennial innocent in matters of politics and society at large. Their Cavalier commitment may be said to have been total, as it was also for Herrick, though in different ways, as one would expect of an Anglican clergyman— but not so different as all that. Herrick was educated at Cambridge, as Suckling was (Carew and Lovelace were Oxford men); he clearly had his years in London, too, if a lesser day in Court, and he fondly recollects the good old days in apostrophes to Ben Jonson.

Jonson himself has helped a suggestible posterity to see the so-called 'Sons of Ben' as a sort of masonic lodge of classically inclined Court poets. Holding lordly court in such congenial quarters as the Devil Tavern's 'Apollo Room' (which Jonson named), remarking that 'my son Cartwright writes all like a man', and writing 'An Epistle to One That Asked to be Sealed of the Tribe of Ben', with its ringing allusion to Revelation 7: 8 ('Of the tribe of Benjamin were sealed twelve thousand'), Jonson lent lofty countenance and even conviction to those who have sought a tribe or family that is the classical, secular, social, mannerly, and lucid counterpart of the strongly vernacular, divine, private,

self-assertive, and often obscure Metaphysical 'school' of Donne
and others, itself accredited by convenience more than by
credentials. There is something to be said for the Sons of Ben as
a historical grouping of well educated and convivial tavern wits
bowing to Jonson's poetical majority and commanding presence,
but Herrick is almost the only certain as well as No. 1 Son, and
even he found his own way, though he walked in his poetical
father's footsteps to get there. Suckling's dislike of Jonson is
abundantly apparent in 'The Wits', which lampoons him;
Lovelace was too young to have known him well, if at all; and
Carew seems to have been an ambivalent and occasional 'cousin'
in the indeterminate sense. In short, there is no real Tribe of Ben,
so far as these Cavalier poets are concerned. Many poets of the
period have varied orders of poetical expression, and Carew, for
example, can sound very like Jonson in his epitaphs and like
Donne in his great elegy on the Dean of Paul's. This is not
surprising, for an age eminently conscious of decorum as a
principle of total integration—something quite beyond what
'decorous' implies.

What, then, is 'Cavalier poetry'? By tradition it is *precisely* the
corpus of poems by these four 'Cavalier Lyrists',[1] and by that
measure it is a composite of the qualities abstracted from their
collected works. The other way of defining the poetry is by
attending to the senses and applications of the term 'Cavalier',
which derives ultimately from late Latin *caballarius* 'horseman',
and yields in the seventeenth century such pertinent senses as
(*OED*): 'a horseman; esp. a horse-soldier; a knight'; 'a gentleman
trained to arms, "a gay sprightly military man" ', in Dr. Johnson's phrase, or 'a courtly gentleman, a gallant'; and 'a name
given to those who fought on the side of Charles I in the war
between him and Parliament: a 17th c. Royalist'. In attributive
or adjectival use, 'gallant' (citing Suckling: 'The people are
naturally [i.e. by nature] not valiant, and not much cavalier');
'careless in manner, off-hand, free and easy'; and 'Royalist'. The
word was also incorporated in 'Cavalierism' (1642) for 'the
practice or principles of . . . the adherents of Charles I; an
expression characteristic of the Cavalier party.'

It is thus hardly surprising that Charles delighted to be
portrayed by Van Dyck as 'just dismounted from his horse on a
hunting expedition', and it is in fact to Van Dyck 'that we owe

---

[1] The title of ch. i of the *Cavalier and Puritan* volume (vii) of the old *Cambridge
History of English Literature*, ed. Sir A. W. Ward and A. R. Waller (1911).

an artistic record of this society with its defiantly aristocratic bearing and its cult of courtly refinement'; he 'showed the Stuart monarch as he would have wished to live in history: a figure of matchless elegance, of unquestioned authority and high culture, the patron of the arts, and the upholder of the divine right of kings, a man who needs no outward trappings of power to enhance his natural dignity'—in short, a Cavalier King.[2] With reference to such qualities as these, which were inherently aesthetic as well as 'social', it used to be customary to speak of 'the Cavalier spirit', and once, indeed, there seems to have been one, which, lost to history, found its archetypal way readily into the fictions of gallantry of Dumas and Rostand, for example.

In 'The Line of Wit' F. R. Leavis did much to prepare for more recent thinking about the poets of the Caroline period by arguing that, in 'the idiomatic quality of the Caroline lyric, its close relation to the spoken language, we do not find it easy to separate Donne's influence from Jonson's'; the line 'runs from Ben Jonson (and Donne) through Carew and Marvell to Pope'; and the Cavalier manifestation, 'which is sufficiently realized in a considerable body of poems, may be described as consciously urbane, mature, and civilized.'[3] More recently Josephine Miles has studied the poetry of the period in relation to 'a part of literary style more clearly limitable than tone or theme or genre or even manner', namely 'mode: the selective use of the elements and structures of language'.[4] Her studies have led to the conclusion that in some vital respects 'the so-called "sons of Ben" turn out to be even more strongly sons of Donne'.[5] For, in connection with a stylistic factor 'in which Donne's uses are clearly dominant', of thirty poets those with the nearest affinities are Carew, Suckling, Shirley, and Herrick. Another factor places Lovelace as a member of smaller mid-century groups including, in proximate order, Cowley, Marvell, Crashaw, and Quarles. The study reveals for the first group a poetical vocabulary 'remarkably packed with verbs of action, and with a world-time-love-death-reciprocal-action complex which we may recognize as part of what has been called "metaphysical". These terms together bear a very high proportion of the whole burden of metaphysical

[2] E. H. Gombrich, *The Story of Art*, 12th edn. (1972), pp. 316–17.

[3] *Revaluation: Tradition and Development in English Poetry* (1947), pp. 18, 19, 29.

[4] *Eras and Modes in English Poetry*, 2nd edn. (1964), p. viii.

[5] Josephine Miles and Hanan C. Selvin, 'Factor Analysis of Seventeenth Century Poetry', *The Computer and Literary Style*, ed. Jacob Leed (1966), p. 122.

vocabulary'. The practice of the mid-century group, in its 'more domesticated metaphysics', was also a 'carrying on and modifying of the Donne tradition'. Finally, in a strictly grammatical perspective (the ratio of verbs to adjectives, nouns, and verbs together), one finds Milton, Sylvester, and Spenser at one extreme, and at the other Carew, Herrick, Jonson, Donne, and Suckling, in order of increasing difference. In short, the 'idiolects' of the Cavalier poets are manifestly non-Spenserian. Theirs are Strong Lines, by turns more like Jonson's (especially Carew and Herrick), but quite as often like Donne's (Lovelace and Suckling). Ultimately, their poetical ethos is their own.

These Cavalier poets are the most prominent and significant of the royalist poets of the reign of Charles I. It is not so often, nowadays, that one meets with an overgeneralized notion of literary Cavalierism, but such a notion persists, in some quarters: viewed as interchangeable, Carrick and Herew, Sucklace and Loveling, materialize in this presbyopic vision as a four-way poetical Janus that their trochaic surnames seem to suggest. But for all they have in common they clearly had their differences: Herrick died a priest at 83, Carew a debauchee at 45 or 46, Lovelace a bankrupt gentleman at 39, and Suckling a rash royalist conspirator at 32. Juxtaposed in contrast here are Herrick's scholarly squinting, winely smiling, city-country curiosity; Carew's shaded vein of witty but felt-in-the-blood-and-felt-along-the-heart sense of transiency; Suckling's often surprisingly modest and almost always playful but not unreflective *sprezzatura*; and Lovelace's soldier's-courtier's-philosopher's brightly interwoven thought, charm, and keen bravura.

Herrick had the best chance of major poetical achievement, and *Hesperides* and *Noble Numbers* in a measure reflect the fifty-six years that preceded their publication in 1648. Crashaw attained a generally granted poetical majority in fewer years (36 or 37) than Carew or Lovelace lived, and in an earlier generation Marlowe at 29 left a corpus of work far more substantial than Suckling did in his thirty-two years. The achievement of each and all of these poets is not insubstantial, nevertheless, and what Dr. Johnson wrote of the Earl of Rochester (who died at 33) applies in some degree to Carew and Lovelace and in a pronounced degree to Suckling: 'in all his works there is sprightliness and vigour, and everywhere may be found tokens of a mind which study might have carried to excellence. What more can be expected from a life spent in ostentatious contempt of regularity, and ended before the abilities of many other men began to be displayed?' ('Life of Rochester'). A brief descriptive survey will help to convey a sense of the character of the respective canons of these Cavalier poets.

Herrick's first datable poem, 'A Country Life' (32), was probably written *c*. 1610, when the poet was nineteen.[6] He wrote virtually all the rest of his poems before 1648, when the 1,130 poems of *Hesperides* (with the 272 of *Noble Numbers*) were published. Only eight of his poems are known to have been published before *Hesperides*, and only thirty-nine (and one of the *Noble Numbers*) circulated in manuscript, so Herrick evidently shared the time's and gentleman's preference for private to public circulation, at least for most works short of an authorized collection. As Mark L. Reed asserts, in arguing that many of Herrick's poems could have been written before Herrick moved to Dean Prior in 1630, 'if these poems do not grow from and sing of Devonshire', as some of them certainly did, however, 'they do, in a manner unparalleled by any other group of lyrics of the time, grow from and sing of England . . ., more exactly of the beauties and meaning of the countryside, the inhabitants, and popular activity of England itself.' They are, in fact, manifestations of a wholly new consciousness: 'the growing awareness in the English artistic sensibility of natural scenery and folk and rural life other than that of Arcadia or classical verse.'[7]

If one examines and loosely classifies the first and last twenty poems in *Hesperides*, an interesting fact emerges that tends to be true of most of the collection: Herrick's world is prominently one of apostrophic address, in which he enacts the 'social life' of a person who finds much of his companionship in his imagination.[8] The following kinds of poem make up the forty: thirteen epigrams, fifteen apostrophes (including five to his 'mistresses' named or collective, and ten to other persons and things), five soliloquies and epigrammatic meditations, three poems to and on himself, two 'other' dramatic monologues, a narrative witch-poem in lyric stanzas ('The Hag'), and a *carmen figuratum*. As for the longer poems that are customarily taken to measure poetical

---

[6] The poem-numbers given here and below in parentheses are those of the poems in this edition.

[7] 'Herrick Among the Maypoles: Dean Prior and the *Hesperides*', *SEL* v (1965), 133–50 (quotations from pp. 148–50).

[8] The poems are classified for convenience by salient characteristics; there are obviously alternative ways of classifying many poems.

reach, Herrick's fifteen include three wedding poems, three 'fairy' poems, and nine 'miscellaneous' poems: 'Corinna's Going a Maying', two 'Country Life' poems, a 'Farewell' and a 'Welcome to Sack', 'His Age', 'A Panegyric', 'The Parting Verse', and 'The Apparition of His Mistress Calling Him to Elysium'. These range from 54 to 170 lines; twelve of them are included in the present collection. The shorter masterpieces, which are not easily categorized, are such poems as 'Delight in Disorder', 'To the Virgins, to Make Much of Time', and 'Upon Julia's Clothes', and Herrick is no doubt most widely known for these shorter poems, which are indeed among his best.

In a creative life of at least two decades' duration (*c.* 1619–40), Carew wrote *Coelum Brittanicum* (a masque, 1634), 121 poems, and translations of nine Psalms. His first datable poem, 'A Fly That Flew into My Mistress' Eye' (24), was written when he was twenty-five or thereabouts, but it is difficult to imagine that he didn't write similar lyrics before that age. Thirty-five of his poems are more or less 'occasional' in the strict sense, and many of these are datable at least within a year or so. Ten of the poems were printed during his lifetime, and his poems circulated widely in manuscript, as was usual with the members of his circle; at least two manuscript collections contain a substantial number (42 and 65, respectively). Just over half of his poems are conveniently characterized as amatory poems, complaints, and compliments. Of his twelve longer poems (56–166 lines, five in the present collection), his longest and one of his two most famous is the erotic body-topographical poem, 'A Rapture' (28). The categories of the remaining poems do not contain many members, and the social connection looms large, from the two bountiful Country-House Poems (19, 39), the seven elegies and consolatory poems of which the elegy on Donne is generally thought to be his best poem (34), the two poems on sickness, the four celebratory and congratulatory marriage-poems (48), the three New Year's greetings (40), the five epitaphs (29–32), the two miscellaneous occasional-poems (35, 38), to the two verse epistles (one the Country-House Poem, 39). This group of social genres suggests that some claim could be made for Carew as the master of Cavalier greeting-card verse, but virtually all such poems at Carew's hand transcend their genres, and few fall short of considerable accomplishment. Carew also has a poem to a painter, three pastoral and amatory dialogues (26), a dramatic monologue (21), a remonstration to Ben Jonson (33), four choric songs, six commendatory poems (41, 42), and a poem for a picture (36). His magnitude as a poet is established rather less by the canon as a whole, perhaps, than by the brilliance of his performance in a wide variety of individual poems both short and long. In Carew's short and profligate life a real poetic and intellectual gift was largely dissipated.

The scope of Suckling's work is represented in part by a group of religious and Christmas-seasonal poems written in or before 1626, when the poet was seventeen; his four plays, *The Sad One* (*c.* 1632, unfinished), *Aglaura* (1637), *The Goblins* (1638–41), and *Brennoralt* (1639–41); his *Account of Religion by Reason*; several political tracts; and over fifty letters, some of literary character and many of literary quality. Of his seventy-eight poems, written between 1626 and 1641, the two 'major' ones introduced minor genres into English verse, 'The Wits' as a 'trial for the bays' of poetry (26, 1637), and 'A Ballad upon a Wedding' as a burlesque, rusticated epithalamion (27, 1639). Suckling was the arch-Cavalier in prizing 'black eyes, or a lucky hit / At bowls, above all the trophies of wit', as he claimed to do, and it is doubtful whether he would have gone on to truly disciplined and serious work even if he had not died a suicide at thirty-two; but he managed to get rather a lot done for all his apparent insouciance, and he is the most often neglected, underrated, and misrepresented of the Cavalier poets. The canon consists in only 2,010 lines, and only the poems already mentioned are of any length (118 and 132 lines). The rest average about twenty-three lines.

Of the prominently quasi-dramatic poems in the secular-metaphysical manner, there are two dialogues (7, 28); eighteen answers, arguments, and dramatic monologues (10–15, 22, 23); three *carpe diem* poems (13); four compliments and protestations (4, 8); two valedictions (25); eleven exclamations, expostulations, and 'soliloquies' (3, 16–20); and three 'impersonations' (2). A second group is made up of descriptive, narrative, or explicitly 'written' poems: three imprecations (9), five narratives and retrospectives, a 'trial for the bays' (26), a dramatic-narrative burlesque epithalamion (27), two 'songs' (6), four occasional-commendatory poems, a prologue, a verse epistle, four extended conceits and definitions (1, 21, 24), an 'amatory cosmology' poem, and a poem in the 'praise of ugliness' genre. Finally, the eleven (juvenile) religious poems. Suckling's verse is emphatically an art of stance, poise, and the medium, and his single most famous

poem, probably, is a pungent avowal of constant inconstancy
that concludes,

> Had it any been but she,
> And that very very face,
> There had been at least ere this
> A dozen dozen in her place.

If it is taken as 'male-chauvinistic' psycho-sociology, it may
displease (or elate); if it is taken as lyric fiction, it can sing for
itself.

Lucasta's sixty-one poems (1–25 here) were published in 1649,
when Lovelace was thirty-one, and most of the forty-three in
Lucasta. Posthume Poems (1659, 26–47 here) were probably written
1649–57. Like Carew and Suckling, Lovelace turned his hand to
drama, with his comedy *The Scholars*, written during his first year
at Oxford when he was 16–17 (1634–5), and *The Soldier* (1640).
He is best known for his war-connected (1, 2) and prison poems
(9, 10, 17), but well known also for his poems of compliment
and amatory lyrics, of which there are forty-four in all (28 in
Lucasta, 16 in *Posthume Poems*) and fifteen in this collection. What
Lovelace is less well known for (except through 'The Grasshopper'), but which are very characteristic as well as unique for
his time, are his nine meditative 'creature poems' (most included
here), and his 'painting poems' (13, 45). His occasional verse is
scant and most of it is late, except for the prologue and epilogue
to *The Scholars*. The four funeral-elegiac poems were written
1638–49, and the anniversary (44) and wedding poems after 1649.
Lovelace's longest, and in several other ways also 'major', poems
conclude each volume: *Aramantha: A Pastoral* (384 lines) complements but far exceeds 'Amyntor's Grove' in accomplishment
as well as length, in *Lucasta*; and 'On Sanazar's Being Honoured'
(267 lines), in *Posthume Poems*, is his only formal satire. Also
typical of Lovelace are his meditation and advice poems (15, 43),
and a mixed bag of ten ironical meditations and anti-love songs
(e.g. 22, 23). The remaining poems are four mythological
conceits and paradoxes (6, 7), four dialogues (42, which is also a
political satire), a political 'Mock-Song' (39), and a translation
(a number of other translations are appended at the end of
Posthume Poems).

The character and direction of Lovelace's poetical career is
similar to the movement of poetry in general during the mid-
seventeenth century, from the private and personal, through the

social, to the public, or at any rate impersonal, including the detached and philosophical (lyrics continue to be written, but most are depersonalized songs). If, as seems likely, some of the compliments and amatory lyrics in *Posthume Poems* were in fact written before 1649 but not included in *Lucasta*, then the poems written after 1649, the year Charles was beheaded, are characterized by an increasingly meditative strain and a gathering gloom. There is not a simple transformation of gallant courtier into hounded and pessimistic royalist fugitive, but a general movement of the kind seems indicated: from a witty amatory lyrist to a poet personally and poetically *engagé* to one whose main hope of stability and deliverance is found in personal stoicism and friendship. Lovelace's gifts did develop in his known twenty-two years as poet, and interesting and larger accomplishment might have been expected of him had he lived beyond thirty-nine.

It is fair to say that of these four Cavalier poets only Herrick outlived his poetical gifts, but he had the good fortune within his lifetime to bring them to their relative perfection in full in a book of his own making, *Hesperides* well named.

THIS EDITION

This edition of 335 poems is based on the old-spelling Oxford English Texts of Carew, Herrick, Lovelace, and Suckling, but I have drawn on all the textual evidence and variants as well as the texts presented by the OET editors to provide texts for the authority of which I must assume responsibility. I have found few occasions to give substantive readings different from those of the OET texts, and in one such case I differ from my earlier self.

The best and most important poems by the four poets are included, along with peculiarly representative and specially interesting poems, many of which have not been anthologized previously. The result is, I think, a corpus of poems for each poet that allows him to be seen both at his best and as he is. As the major and most prolific poet of the group, Herrick is represented by the most poems, 208 (and an alternative version of one). These constitute only 18 per cent of the canon of his secular poems but a rather higher percentage of his lines of verse: many of the poems in *Hesperides* are epigrammatic distichs and quatrains, but most of his longer poems (with a smaller percentage of his shorter poems) are included here. The three less prolific poets are represented by fewer poems, but also by a higher percentage of their total poems:

Carew, 51 (42 per cent); Lovelace, 47 (45 per cent); and Suckling, 28 (36 per cent). The poems follow the order of the Oxford English Texts, of which the Suckling is chronologically arranged; the others follow the order of the early substantive editions, which, like the early editions of Suckling's poems, are not chronological. Generally speaking, the poems toward the beginning of *Hesperides* seem to be earlier and those toward the end later, but the arrangement is not systematic. *Lucasta* dates the poems in that volume as written in or before 1649, and many if not all of the *Posthume Poems* were written in 1649–57. The datable poems in Carew's *Poems* (1640) are not arranged in chronological order.

The modernizing principles and practices I have followed are these. Capitals are much heavier in early texts than in modern practice, as a rule; those that seem to serve the purposes of emphasis and personification have been retained, but there are degrees of personification, and I have used or refused a capital according to what seemed appropriate in the individual instance. I have retained most italics except those used for proper names, and I have kept much of the seventeenth-century punctuation, which has a distinctly and often significantly rhetorical character, though I have of course departed from it where it seems 'wrong' by any measure and where it might seriously confuse the sense for modern readers. In altering punctuation, I have attended to the apparent designs as well as the imperatives of the context.

Words are given in standard modern spelling except where early-text spellings contribute to the poetic effects (e.g. 'ribband' for the modern 'ribbon'). To clarify the metrics for modern readers, I use an apostrophe to indicate silence and a *grave* accent or diaeresis to indicate sounding; e.g. (1) 'In stone, with a crook'd sickle in her hand' (C–39: 62); (2) 'But to the pure refinèd ore' (C–18: 19); and (3) 'Whilst I the smooth calm oceän invade' (C–28: 82). In the case of rhyme-words, readers will readily recognize variant pronunciations of the kind found in metrically disyllabic *-ion* (e.g. 'so kiss on / million', H–19: 5–6), and I have not marked these with a diaeresis. The supplied apostrophes often but do not always correspond with apostrophes in the early texts.

POEMS

POEMS

ROBERT HERRICK
(1591–1674)

I

The Argument of His Book

I sing of brooks, of blossoms, birds, and bowers;
Of April, May, of June, and July flowers.
I sing of Maypoles, hock-carts, wassails, wakes;
Of bridegrooms, brides, and of their bridal-cakes.
I write of youth, of love, and have access,   5
By these, to sing of cleanly wantonness.
I sing of dews, of rains, and piece by piece
Of balm, of oil, of spice, and ambergris.
I sing of times trans-shifting; and I write
How roses first came red, and lilies white.   10
I write of groves, of twilights, and I sing
The Court of Mab, and of the Fairy-King.
I write of hell; I sing (and ever shall)
Of heaven, and hope to have it after all.

The title of Herrick's secular poems is *Hesperides*, 'daughters of evening'; their
mother was Night (Hesiod), and they dwelt in the far west, near the Atlas
mountains or in the Fortunate Isles, where with the aid of a dragon called
Ladon they guarded a tree bearing golden apples that had been given as a
wedding gift by Gē, or Earth, to Hera when she married Zeus. The name was
applied to the garden as well as to the daughters, and Herrick obviously
intended it to have ranging significance in relation to the poems of the
collection; the west of the garden and of Devonshire is an obvious example.

1. 3 *hock-carts*: carts which carried home the last load of the harvest. *wakes*:
village festivals as well as vigils for the dead.

2

When He Would Have His Verses Read

In sober mornings do not thou rehearse
The holy incantation of a verse;
But when that men have both well drunk, and fed,
Let my enchantments then be sung, or read.
When laurel spirts i' th' fire, and when the hearth   5
Smiles to itself, and gilds the roof with mirth;
When up the thyrse is raised, and when the sound!
Of sacred orgies flies, a round, a round!
When the rose reigns, and locks with ointments shine,
Let rigid Cato read these lines of mine.   10

3

To Perilla

Ah my Perilla! dost thou grieve to see
Me, day by day, to steal away from thee?
Age calls me hence, and my grey hairs bid come,
And haste away to mine eternal home;
'Twill not be long, Perilla, after this   5
That I must give thee the supremest kiss:
Dead when I am, first cast in salt, and bring
Part of the cream from that religious spring,
With which, Perilla, wash my hands and feet;
That done, then wind me in that very sheet   10
Which wrapped thy smooth limbs (when thou didst implore
The gods' protection but the night before).
Follow me weeping to my turf, and there
Let fall a primrose, and with it a tear;

2. 1 *rehearse*: recite. 5 *When laurel spirts i' th' fire.* 'Burning bay leaves was a Christmas observance' (Pollard, who also points out that Herrick has in mind Catullus, *Carm.* lxiv. 256–69). 7 *thyrse*: see G. 8 *orgies*: 'songs of Bacchus' (Herrick). 10 *Cato*: the Roman Censor, notorious for his severity.

3. As in other death-rite poems, 'Herrick is concerned primarily that the proper rite be performed over his remains'; see Robert H. Deming, 'Herrick's Funereal Poems', *SEL* ix (1969), 158–60. 8 *Part of the cream* etc.: tears; strong religious

Then, lastly, let some weekly strewings be   15
Devoted to the memory of me:
Then shall my ghost not walk about, but keep
Still in the cool and silent shades of sleep.

4

To His Mistresses

Help me! Help me! now I call
To my pretty witchcrafts all:
Old I am, and cannot do
That I was accustomed to.
Bring your magics, spells, and charms,   5
To enflesh my thighs and arms:
Is there no way to beget
In my limbs their former heat?
Aeson had (as poets feign)
Baths that made him young again;   10
Find that med'cine (if you can)
For your dry-decrepit man,
Who would fain his strength renew,
Were it but to pleasure you.

5

The Shoe-Tying

Anthea bade me tie her shoe;
I did, and kissed the instep, too;
And would have kissed unto her knee,
Had not her blush rebukèd me.

associations, both Roman and Christian, in the salt; see Robert H. Deming,
'Robert Herrick's Classical Ceremony', *ELH* xxxiv (1967), 327–48.   15 *weekly
strewings*: of flowers on the grave.   17 *Then shall my ghost not walk about*: a Roman
concern, that the *Manes* or spirits of the departed be given rest by special rites
and, sometimes, vengeance (cf. *Hamlet*).

4. 9–10 Medea the sorceress restored Aeson to youth by boiling him in a
cauldron with magic herbs (Ovid, *Met.* vii. 297 ff.).

6

Upon the Loss of His Mistresses

I have lost, and lately, these
Many dainty mistresses:
Stately Julia, prime of all;
Sappho next, a principal;
Smooth Anthea, for a skin   5
White and heaven-like crystalline;
Sweet Electra, and the choice
Myrrha, for the lute and voice;
Next Corinna, for her wit,
And the graceful use of it;   10
With Perilla, all are gone;
Only Herrick's left alone,
For to number sorrow by
Their departures hence and die.

7

The Vine

I dreamed this mortal part of mine
Was metamorphosed to a vine,
Which, crawling one and every way,
Enthralled my dainty Lucia.
Methought her long, small legs and thighs   5
I with my tendrils did surprise;
Her belly, buttocks, and her waist
By my soft nervelets were embraced;

---

7. The tradition of the narrated religious or sensual 'dream' has antecedents in Greek poetry and affinities with such works as Cicero's *Somnium Scipionis* (and Macrobius' commentary on it), the *Roman de la Rose*, and the Old English 'Dream of the Rood'. The most direct source of the sub-genre of the (day)dream of the mistress is probably Ovid, *Amores*, I. v. The fact that the vine is a traditional Christian emblem gives piquancy to the vine of Herrick's fantasy. 8 *nervelet*: 'tendril' (*OED*, citing this use only); 'nerves' was used for the 'ribs' of a leaf.

About her head I writhing hung,
And with rich clusters (hid among   10
The leaves) her temples I behung:
So that my Lucia seemed to me
Young Bacchus ravished by his tree.
My curls about her neck did crawl,
And arms and hands they did enthrall: 15
So that she could not freely stir
(All parts there made one prisoner).
But when I crept with leaves to hide
Those parts which maids keep unespied,
Such fleeting pleasures there I took   20
That with the fancy I awoke;
And found (ah me!) this flesh of mine
More like a stock than like a vine.

8

The Parcae, or Three Dainty Destinies: the Armillet

Three lovely sisters working were
    (As they were closely set)
Of soft and dainty maiden-hair
    A curious armillet.
I, smiling, asked them what they did   5
    (Fair Destinies all three),
Who told me they had drawn a thread
    Of life, and 'twas for me.
They showed me then how fine 'twas spun;
    And I replied thereto,   10
'I care not now how soon 'tis done
    Or cut, if cut by you.'

---

13 *ravished by his tree*: 'enthralled' with grapevines.   23 *stock*: trunk or stem (as distinct from root and branches).

8. *Parcae*: Fates (see G).   *armillet*: small bracelet.

B

9

Discontents in Devon

More discontents I never had
  Since I was born than here,
Where I have been and still am sad,
  In this dull Devonshire;
Yet justly too I must confess   5
  I ne'er invented such
Ennobled numbers for the press
  Than where I loathed so much.

10

Cherry-Ripe

'Cherry-ripe, ripe, ripe', I cry,
  'Full and fair ones; come and buy':
If so be you ask me where
  They do grow, I answer, 'There,
Where my Julia's lips do smile;   5
  There's the land or cherry-isle,
Whose plantations fully show
  All the year where cherries grow.'

11

To His Mistresses

Put on your silks, and piece by piece
  Give them the scent of ambergris;
And for your breaths, too, let them smell
  Ambrosia-like, or nectarel;
While other gums their sweets perspire,   5
  By your own jewels set on fire.

9. 8 *Than*: 'As' in modern usage.

11. 4 *nectarel*: like nectar, fragrant (*OED*, citing this as the only example).
5 *gums*: tree-secretions burned as incense.   *sweets perspire*: the pun turns on the
homonyms, 'sweat/sweet'.

12

Dreams

Here we are all, by day; by night w'are hurled
By dreams, each one, into a several world.

13

Ambition

In man, ambition is the common'st thing;
Each one, by nature, loves to be a king.

14

His Request to Julia

Julia, if I chance to die
Ere I print my poetry,
I most humbly thee desire
To commit it to the fire:
Better 'twere my book were dead   5
Than to live not perfected.

15

Money Gets the Mastery

Fight thou with shafts of silver, and o'ercome,
When no force else can get the masterdom.

---

12. Martin quotes from Joseph Hall, *Meditations* (1616), iii. 20: 'It was a witty
and true speech . . . of Heraclitus, that all men, awaking, are in one world;
but, when we sleep, each man goes into a several world by himself.'

15. Proverbial wisdom; Tilley M 1075, 'Money makes masteries'.

16

Steam in Sacrifice

If meat the gods give, I the steam
High-towering will devote to them,
Whose easy natures like it well,
If we the roast have, they the smell.

17

All Things Decay and Die

All things decay with time : the forest sees
The growth and downfall of her aged trees;
That timber tall, which three-score *lustres* stood
The proud *dictator* of the state-like wood,
I mean (the sovereign of all plants) the oak,   5
Droops, dies, and falls without the cleaver's stroke.

18

Upon His Sister-in-Law, Mistress Elizabeth Herrick

First, for effusions due unto the dead
My solemn vows have here accomplishèd;
Next, how I love thee, that my grief must tell,
Wherein thou liv'st for ever. Dear, farewell.

17. 3 *lustres*: five-year periods.

18. Herrick's brother's widow, Elizabeth, kept house for him at Dean Prior, where she was buried on 11 April 1643.

19

To Anthea

Ah my Anthea! must my heart still break?
(Love makes me write what shame forbids to speak.)
Give me a kiss, and to that kiss a score;
Then to that twenty, add a hundred more;
A thousand to that hundred: so kiss on,   5
To make that thousand up a million.
Treble that million, and when that is done,
Let's kiss afresh, as when we first begun.
But yet, though Love likes well such scenes as these,
There is an act that will more fully please: 10
Kissing and glancing, soothing, all make way
But to the acting of this private play;
Name it I would, but being blushing-red
The rest I'll speak when we meet both in bed.

20

To the King, upon His Coming with His Army into the West

Welcome, most welcome, to our vows and us,
Most great and universal *Genius*!
The drooping West, which hitherto has stood
As one, in long-lamented widowhood,
Looks like a bride now, or a bed of flowers,   5
Newly refreshed both by the sun and showers.
War, which before was horrid, now appears
Lovely in you, brave Prince of Cavaliers!

---

19. 2 Ovid, *Heroides*, iv. 10: 'Dicere quae puduit, scribere iussit amor'.   3–8 A
free translation of Catullus, *Carm.* v. 7–9.

20. *into the West*: on the way to Cornwall; the Parliamentary infantry was
defeated by Charles's army in September 1644.

A deal of courage in each bosom springs
By your access, O you the best of kings! 10
Ride on with all white *omens*, so that where
Your standard's up we fix a conquest there.

21

To the Reverend Shade of His Religious Father

That for seven *lustres* I did never come
To do the rites to thy religious tomb,
That neither hair was cut or true tears shed
By me o'er thee (as *justments* to the dead),
Forgive, forgive me, since I did not know 5
Whether thy bones had here their rest or no.
But now 'tis known: behold, behold, I bring
Unto thy ghost th' effusèd offering;
And look what smallage, nightshade, cypress, yew,
Unto the shades have been or now are due, 10
Here I devote; and something more than so:
I come to pay a debt of birth I owe.
Thou gav'st me life (but mortal); for that one
Favour, I'll make full satisfaction;
For my life mortal, rise from out thy hearse, 15
And take a life immortal from my verse.

11 *Ride on*: cf. Ps. 45: 4: 'And in thy majesty ride prosperously because of truth
and meekness and righteousness...' 12 *white*: auspicious ('candida ... omina'
in Propertius, IV. i. 67–8).

21. Herrick's father died in a fall when the poet was fourteen months old.
Herrick's visit was paid and his poem was written in 1627, if ll. 1–2 are to be
taken literally. On the details of Roman ceremonial in the poem see Patrick,
p. 41, and Deming, 'Herrick's Funereal Poems', *SEL* ix (1969), 160–2.

22

Delight in Disorder

A sweet disorder in the dress
Kindles in clothes a wantonness:
A lawn about the shoulders thrown
Into a fine distraction;
An erring lace, which here and there   5
Enthralls the crimson stomacher;
A cuff neglectful, and thereby
Ribbands to flow confusedly;
A winning wave (deserving note)
In the tempestuous petticoat;   10
A careless shoe-string, in whose tie
I see a wild civility;
Do more bewitch me than when art
Is too precise in every part.

23

To Dean Bourn, a Rude River in Devon,
by Which Sometimes He Lived

Dean Bourn, farewell; I never look to see
Dean, or thy warty incivility.
Thy rocky bottom, that doth tear thy streams
And makes them frantic, ev'n to all extremes,
To my content I never should behold,   5
Were thy streams silver or thy rocks all gold.

22. Herrick elaborates upon the song 'Still to be neat' in Jonson's *Epicoene*, I. i. 91–102. The idea that there can be a special 'order' in disorder must be almost as old as the idea of order itself; the speaker in the poem favours a 'sweet disorder', where 'art / Is [not] *too* precise in every part.' The opposition is between the 'natural' and the affected order. This poem is at once straightforward and subtly artful, and it has stimulated a good deal of commentary, though not as much as the more complex 'Upon Julia's Clothes' (H–172).

23. Pollard quotes from an interesting piece by Barron Field in the *Quarterly Review* of August 1910: 'We found many persons in the village who could repeat

Rocky thou art, and rocky we discover
Thy men; and rocky are thy ways all over.
O men, O manners! Now and ever known
To be a rocky generation!   10
A people currish, churlish as the seas,
And rude (almost) as rudest salvages;
With whom I did and may re-sojourn when
Rocks turn to rivers, rivers turn to men.

24

To Julia

How rich and pleasing thou, my Julia, art
In each thy dainty and peculiar part!
First, for thy queenship, on thy head is set
Of flowers a sweet commingled coronet;
About thy neck a carcanet is bound,   5
Made of the ruby, pearl, and diamond;
A golden ring, that shines upon thy thumb;
About thy wrist, the rich Dardanium.
Between thy breasts (than down of swans more white)
There plays the sapphire with the chrysolite.   10
No part besides must of thyself be known,
But by the topaz, opal, chalcedon.

some of his lines, and none who were not acquainted with his "Farewell to Dean Bourn", which they said he uttered as he crossed the brook upon being ejected by Cromwell from the vicarage, to which he had been presented by Charles the First. But they added with an air of innocent triumph, "he did see it again", as was the fact after the restoration' (i. 264).   10 *a rocky generation*: Jer. 5: 3: 'they have refused to receive correction: they have made their faces harder than a rock'.

24. 5 *carcanet*: necklace.   8 *Dardanium*: 'a bracelet from Dardanus so called' (Herrick).

25

To Laurels

A funeral stone
Or verse I covet none,
But only crave
Of you that I may have
A sacred laurel springing from my grave;   5
Which being seen
Blest with perpetual green,
May grow to be
Not so much called a tree
As the eternal monument of me.   10

26

His Cavalier

Give me that man that dares bestride
The active sea-horse, and with pride
Through that huge field of waters ride;

Who, with his looks, too, can appease
The ruffling winds and raging seas   5
In midst of all their outrages.

This, this a virtuous man can do,
Sail against rocks and split them, too,
Ay, and a world of pikes pass through!

25. 5 *sacred laurel*: as a crown of victory in poetry.
26. 9 *pikes*: (1) pikestaffs; (2) voracious fish.

27

To the Generous Reader

See, and not see; and if thou chance t' espy
Some aberrations in my poetry,
Wink at small faults; the greater ne'ertheless
Hide, and with them their father's nakedness.
Let's do our best our watch and ward to keep: 5
Homer himself, in a long work, may sleep.

28

To Critics

I'll write, because I'll give
You critics means to live:
For should I not supply
The cause, th' effect would die.

29

Barley-Break: or, Last in Hell

We two are last in hell: what may we fear
To be tormented, or kept prisoners here?
Alas, if kissing be of plagues the worst,
We'll wish in hell we had been last and first!

30

The Definition of Beauty

Beauty no other thing is than a beam
Flashed out between the middle and extreme.

---

27. 4 'Shem and Japheth . . . covered the nakedness of their father' (Gen. 9: 23).
6 *Homer*, etc.: after Horace, *Ars Poet.*, ll. 359–60.
29. On 'Barley-Break' see G.

31

To Dianeme

Dear, though to part it be a hell,
Yet Dianeme now farewell:
Thy frown (last night) did bid me go;
But whither, only grief does know.
I do beseech thee, ere we part   5
(If merciful as fair thou art;
Or else desir'st that maids should tell
Thy pity by love's chronicle),
O Dianeme, rather kill
Me than to make me languish still!   10
'Tis cruelty in thee to th' height
Thus, thus to wound, not kill outright.
Yet there's a way found (if thou please)
By sudden death to give me ease;
And thus devised, do thou but this,   15
Bequeath to me one parting kiss;
So sup'rabundant joy shall be
The executioner of me.

32

A Country Life: To His Brother, Master Thomas Herrick

Thrice, and above, blest, my soul's half, art thou,
    In thy both last and better vow:
Couldst leave the city for exchange to see
    The country's sweet simplicity,
And it to know and practise, with intent   5
    To grow the sooner innocent,
By studying to know virtue, and to aim
    More at her nature than her name.
The last is but the least; the first doth tell
    Ways less to live than to live well;   10

32. Thomas (b. 1588) left London in about 1610 to become a farmer. This poem is related to the Country-House Poem (see G).

And both are known to thee, who now canst live
    Led by thy conscience, to give
Justice to soon-pleased Nature, and to show
    Wisdom and she together go
And keep one centre; this with that conspires   15
    To teach man to confine desires,
And know that riches have their proper stint
    In the contented mind, not mint;
And canst instruct that those who have the itch
    Of craving more are never rich.   20
These things thou know'st to th' height, and dost prevent
    That plague, because thou art content
With that Heaven gave thee with a wary hand
    (More blessed in thy brass than land)
To keep cheap nature even and upright,   25
    To cool not cocker appetite.
Thus thou canst tersely live to satisfy
    The belly chiefly, not the eye,
Keeping the barking stomach wisely quiet
    Less with a neat than needful diet.   30
But that which most makes sweet thy country life
    Is the fruition of a wife,
Whom (stars consenting with thy fate) thou hast
    Got not so beautiful as chaste;
By whose warm side thou dost securely sleep   35
    (While Love the sentinel doth keep)
With those deeds done by day, which ne'er affright
    Thy silken slumbers in the night;
Nor has the darkness power to usher in
    Fear to those sheets that know no sin,   40
But still thy wife, by chaste intentions led,
    Gives thee each night a maidenhead.
The damasked meadows and the pebbly streams
    Sweeten and make soft your dreams:
The purling springs, groves, birds, and well-weaved bowers, 45
    With fields enamellèd with flowers,
Present their shapes; while fantasy discloses
    Millions of lilies mixed with roses.

24 *brass*: money. 26 *cocker*: pamper. 30 *neat*: dainty.

Then dream ye hear the lamb by many a bleat
    Wooed to come suck the milky teat,   50
While Faunus in the vision comes to keep
    From rav'ning wolves the fleecy sheep—
With thousand such enchanting dreams, that meet
    To make sleep not so sound as sweet.
Nor can these figures so thy rest endear   55
    As not to rise when Chanticleer
Warns the last watch, but with the dawn dost rise
    To work, but first to sacrifice,
Making thy peace with heaven, for some late fault,
    With holy-meal and spirting-salt;   60
Which done, thy painful thumb this sentence tells us,
    Jove for our labour all things sells us.
Nor are thy daily and devout affairs
    Attended with those desp'rate cares
Th' industrious merchant has, who for to find   65
    Gold runneth to the Western Ind
And back again, tortured with fears; doth fly,
    Untaught, to suffer poverty.
But thou at home, blest with securest ease,
    Sitt'st, and believ'st that there be seas,   70
And watery dangers, while thy whiter hap
    But sees these things within thy map;
And, viewing them with a more safe survey,
    Mak'st easy Fear unto thee say,
'*A heart thrice walled with oak and brass that man* 75
    Had, first durst plow the ocean.'
But thou at home, without or tide or gale,
    Canst in thy map securely sail,
Seeing those painted countries, and so guess,
    By those fine shades, their substances;   80
And, from thy compass taking small advice,
    Buy'st travel at the lowest price.

---

51 *Faunus*: a woodland god of crops and herds identified with Pan; cf. Spenser, *Faerie Queene*, VII. vi. 42–53. 56 *Chanticleer*: proper name applied to a cock, such as the hero of Chaucer's 'Nun's Priest's Tale'. 60 *holy-meal and spirting-salt*: as propitiatory offering; Martin cites Horace, *Odes*, III. xxiii. 19–20: 'Farre pio et saliente mica'. 62 Conventional wisdom, as 'the gods sell us all the goods they give us', in Florio's Montaigne. 71 *whiter hap*: better fortune; cf. Tibullus, III. vi. 50, 'candida fata'. 75–6 Martin cites Horace, *Odes*, I. iii. 9–12.

Nor are thine ears so deaf but thou canst hear
    (Far more with wonder than with fear)
Fame tell of states, of countries, courts, and kings,   85
    And believe there be such things;
When of these truths thy happier knowledge lies
    More in thine ears than in thine eyes.
And when thou hear'st, by that too-true report,
    Vice rules the most, or all, at court,   90
Thy pious wishes are (though thou not there)
    Virtue had and moved her sphere.
But thou liv'st fearless, and thy face ne'er shows
    Fortune when she comes or goes;
But with thy equal thoughts prepared dost stand   95
    To take her by the either hand;
Nor car'st which comes the first, the foul or fair:
    A wise man every way lies square,
And like a surly oak with storms perplexed
    Grows still the stronger, strongly vexed.   100
Be so, bold spirit: stand centre-like, unmoved;
    And be not only thought but proved
To be what I report thee, and inure
    Thyself, if want comes, to endure;
And so thou dost, for thy desires are   105
    Confined to live with private Lar,
Not curious whether appetite be fed
    Or with the first or second bread;
Who keep'st no proud mouth for delicious cates:
    Hunger makes coarse meats delicates.   110
Canst, and unurged, forsake that larded fare
    Which Art, not Nature, makes so rare,
To taste boiled nettles, coleworts, beets, and eat
    These, and sour herbs, as dainty meat?
While soft Opinion makes thy *Genius* say,   115
    Content makes all ambrosia.

---

92 *Virtue had and moved her sphere*: i.e. as angelic Intelligences move their spheres
(see NRC).   95–8 Martin (p. 505) cites Puttenham's *Art of English Poesy*, II. xii:
Aristotle, in *Ethics* x, 'termeth a constant minded man even egal and direct on all
sides, and not easily overthrown by every little adversity, *hominem quadratum*, a
square man.'   99 *surly*: imperious, obstinate.   106 *Lar*: household god (see G).

Nor is it that thou keep'st this stricter size
    So much for want as exercise,
To numb the sense of dearth, which, should sin haste it,
    Thou might'st but only see't, not taste it.   120
Yet can thy humble roof maintain a choir
    Of singing crickets by thy fire,
And the brisk mouse may feast herself with crumbs
    Till that the green-eyed kitling comes,
Then to her cabin blest she can escape   125
    The sudden danger of a rape.
And thus thy little well-kept stock doth prove,
    Wealth cannot make a life, but love.
Nor art thou so close-handed, but canst spend
    (Counsel concurring with the end)   130
As well as spare, still conning o'er this theme,
    To shun the first and last extreme,
Ordaining that thy small stock find no breach,
    Or to exceed thy tether's reach;
But to live round, and close, and wisely true   135
    To thine ownself, and known to few.
Thus let thy rural sanctuary be
    Elysium to thy wife and thee,
There to disport yourselves with golden measure,
    For seldom use commends the pleasure.   140
Live, and live blest, thrice-happy pair; let breath,
    But lost to one, be th'other's death.
And as there is one love, one faith, one troth,
    Be so one death, one grave to both.
Till when, in such assurance live, ye may   145
    Nor fear or wish your dying day.

117 *size*: standard.   124 *kitling*: kitten.   135 *round, and close*: straightforwardly,
yet inconspicuously.

33

Divination by a Daffodil

When a daffodil I see,
Hanging down his head towards me,
Guess I may what I must be:
First, I shall decline my head;
Secondly, I shall be dead;   5
Lastly, safely burièd.

34

A Lyric to Mirth

While the milder Fates consent,
Let's enjoy our merriment:
Drink and dance and pipe and play,
Kiss our dollies night and day;
Crowned with clusters of the vine,   5
Let us sit and quaff our wine;
Call on Bacchus, chant his praise;
Shake the thyrse, and bite the bays;
Rouse Anacreon from the dead,
And return him drunk to bed;   10
Sing o'er Horace, for ere long
Death will come and mar the song;
Then shall Wilson and Gautier
Never sing or play more here.

34. 8 *thyrse*: see G.   *bays*: as wreaths of achievement.   13 *Wilson and Gautier*:
Dr. John Wilson (1594–1674), Professor of Music at Oxford, 1656; James
Gouter, or Gaultier, French lutenist (who set Herrick's 'The Curse' to music).

35

Upon Julia's Ribband

As shows the air when with a rainbow graced,
So smiles that ribband 'bout my Julia's waist;
Or like—nay 'tis that zonulet of love,
Wherein all pleasures of the world are wove.

36

The Frozen Zone: or, Julia Disdainful

Whither? say, whither shall I fly,
To slack these flames wherein I fry?
To the treasures shall I go
Of the rain, frost, hail, and snow?
Shall I search the underground,   5
Where all damps and mists are found?
Shall I seek (for speedy ease)
All the floods and frozen seas?
Or descend into the deep,
Where eternal cold does keep?   10
These may cool, but there's a zone
Colder yet than any one:
That's my Julia's breast, where dwells
Such destructive icicles
As that the congelation will   15
Me sooner starve than those can kill.

35. 3 *zonulet*: zonelet; little 'zone', belt, or girdle; probably some of the cosmic sense, too: the 'belts' or encircling regions into which the earth and heavens are divided by the tropics of Cancer and Capricorn and the polar circles, the torrid, temperate, and frigid zones.

36. *Frozen Zone*: Frigid Zone.

37

An Epitaph upon a Sober Matron

With blameless carriage I lived here
To th' (almost) seven and fortieth year.
Stout sons I had, and those twice three;
One only daughter lent to me,
The which was made a happy bride,   5
But thrice three moons before she died;
My modest wedlock, that was known
Contented with the bed of one.

38

Four Things Make Us Happy Here

Health is the first good lent to men;
A gentle disposition, then;
Next, to be rich by no by-ways;
Lastly, with friends t' enjoy our days.

39

Upon Scobble: Epigram

Scobble for whoredom whips his wife, and cries
He'll slit her nose; but, blubb'ring, she replies,
'Good sir, make no more cuts i' th' outward skin:
One slit's enough to let adultery in.'

37. See Martial, x. lxiii, 'Epitaphium nobilis matronae'.

39. 'The name "Scobell" occurs frequently in the Dean Prior Parish Register'
(Martin).

40

The Hour-Glass

That hoür-glass, which there ye see
With water filled (sirs, credit me),
The humour was (as I have read)
But lovers' tears encrystallèd;
Which, as they drop by drop do pass   5
From th' upper to the under glass,
Do in a trickling manner tell
(By many a wat'ry syllable)
That lovers' tears in lifetime shed
Do restless run when they are dead.   10

41

His Farewell to Sack

Farewell thou thing, time-past so known, so dear
To me, as blood to life and spirit; near,
Nay, thou more near than kindred, friend, man, wife,
Male to the female, soul to body, life
To quick action, or the warm soft side   5
Of the resigning yet resisting bride.
The kiss of virgins, first-fruits of the bed,
Soft speech, smooth touch, the lips, the maidenhead:
These, and a thousand sweets, could never be
So near, or dear, as thou wast once to me.   10
O thou the drink of gods, and angels! Wine
That scatter'st spirit and lust, whose purest shine

---

40. Cf. Jonson, 'The Hour-Glass', based on Girolamo Amaltei's 'Horologium Pulverum' (Martin). 3 *humour*: moisture. *as I have read*: 'sc. in Jonson or in the Latin' (Martin).

41. 'The Welcome to Sack' is H–67. *Sack*: a white wine (see G). 2 *spirit*: vital fluid (see G). 3–6 *more near than* governs the individual words (l. 3) and succeeding phrases (ll. 4–6); so '[more near than] life / To quick [i.e. "living"] action'. 12 *scatter'st*: i.e. through the body.

More radiant than the summer's sunbeams shows
Each way illustrious, brave; and like to those
Comets we see by night, whose shagg'd portents   15
Foretell the coming of some dire events;
Or some full flame, which with a pride aspires,
Throwing about his wild and active fires.
'Tis thou, 'bove nectar, O divinest soul,
(Eternal in thyself) that canst control   20
That which subverts whole nature, grief and care,
Vexation of the mind, and damned despair!
'Tis thou, alone, who with thy mystic fan
Work'st more than Wisdom, Art, or Nature can
To rouse the sacred madness and awake   25
The frost-bound blood and spirits, and to make
Them frantic with thy raptures, flashing through
The soul like lightning, and as active, too.
'Tis not Apollo can, or those thrice three
Castalian sisters, sing, if wanting thee.   30
Horace, Anacreon, both had lost their fame,
Hadst thou not filled them with thy fire and flame.
Phoebean splendour! and thou Thespian spring!
Of which sweet swans must drink before they sing
Their true-paced numbers and their holy lays,   35
Which makes them worthy cedar and the bays.
But why, why longer do I gaze upon
Thee with the eye of admiration?
Since I must leave thee, and enforced must say
To all thy witching beauties, 'Go, away.'   40
But if thy whimpering looks do ask me why,
Then know that Nature bids thee go, not I.

15 *shagg'd*: as though 'bushy-tailed'. 17 *flame . . . aspires*: possibly with a turn on 'pyre' (1658 in English [*OED*]; Latin *pyra*). 23 *mystic fan*: Virgil, *Georgics*, i. 166: 'mystica vannus Iacchi'; i.e. the winnowing fan borne ceremonially in the Bacchic festivals. 30 *Sisters*: the Muses; the Castalian Spring on Mt. Parnassus was sacred to them and to Phoebus (bright) Apollo, god of poetry, music, and the sun. 33 *Thespian*. Thespis, a semi-legendary Greek poet, was viewed as the inventor of tragedy and the patron of drama. 34 *swans*: poets; Shakespeare is the 'sweet Swan of Avon' in Jonson's elegy on him (1623), l. 71. 36 *cedar*: i.e. preservation, with reference 'to the use of cedar-oil as a preservative of papyri' (Martin). *bays*: see G.

'Tis her erroneous self has made a brain
Uncapable of such a sovereign
As is thy powerful self. Prithee not smile;   45
Or smile more inly, lest thy looks beguile
My vows denounced in zeal, which thus much show thee,
That I have sworn but by thy looks to know thee.
Let others drink thee freely, and desire
Thee and their lips espoused, while I admire   50
And love thee, but not taste thee. Let my Muse
Fail of thy former helps, and only use
Her inadulterate strength: what's done by me,
Hereafter, shall smell of the lamp, not thee.

42

Upon Mistress Elizabeth Wheeler under the Name of Amarillis

Sweet Amarillis, by a spring's
Soft and soul-melting murmurings,
Slept; and thus sleeping, thither flew
A Robin-redbreast, who at view,
Not seeing her at all to stir,   5
Brought leaves and moss to cover her;
But while he, perking, there did pry
About the arch of either eye,
The lid began to let out day,
At which poor Robin flew away;   10
And seeing her not dead but all disleaved,
He chirped for joy to see himself deceived.

47 *denounced*: proclaimed.   49–51 In the identification of sack as a *fille de joie*,
there may be a (lightened) reminiscence of Revelation, notably 'the great
whore that sitteth upon many waters' and makes men 'drunk with the wine
of her fornication' (17: 1, 4); see especially ll. 41–54.   54 *smell of the lamp, not
thee*. Tilley (L 44) cites this line as an expression of the proverbial distinction
between the 'grape' and the 'lamp' (cf. 'midnight oil') as sources of poetry.

42. Elizabeth Wheeler was born Martha Herrick, daughter of Herrick's uncle
and godfather, Robert Herrick, of Leicester; she married the London goldsmith, John Wheeler, in 1606 (Martin, p. 507).

43

The Eye

Make me a heaven, and make me there
Many a less and greater sphere.
Make me the straight and oblique lines,
The motions, lations, and the signs.
Make me a chariot and a sun,   5
And let them through a zodiac run;
Next, place me zones and tropics there,
With all the seasons of the year.
Make me a sunset, and a night;
And then present the morning's light   10
Clothed in her chamlets of delight.
To these, make clouds to pour down rain,
With weather foul, then fair again.
And when, wise artist, that thou hast,
With all that can be, this heaven graced—   15
Ah! what is then this curious sky
But only my Corinna's eye?

44

The Curse: A Song

Go, perjured man, and if thou e'er return
To see the small remainders in mine urn,
When thou shalt laugh at my religious dust,
And ask, 'Where's now the colour, form, and trust

---

43. Like 'To the Painter, To Draw Him a Picture' (H–108), this is 'an advice-to-a-painter poem' (Patrick, p. 66). The conceit of identifying 'this curious sky' as 'only my Corinna's eye' (ll. 16–17) etc. is based on conventional correspondencies of '-cosms' (see NRC).   4 *lations*: 'The motion[s] of a [heavenly] body from one place to another' (*SOED*).   7 *zones and tropics*: in the pre-Copernican cosmology, these were not confined to the earth but were projected outward to the limits of the (geocentric) universe.   11 *chamlets*: cloaks made of an Eastern material of silk and camel's hair.

44. 3 *religious*: conscientious, faithful.

Of woman's beauty?', and with hand more rude   5
Rifle the flowers which the virgins strewed,
Know, I have prayed to Fury that some wind
May blow my ashes up and strike thee blind.

45

The Vision

Sitting alone (as one forsook),
Close by a silver-shedding brook,
With hands held up to love I wept;
And after sorrows spent, I slept.
Then in a vision I did see   5
A glorious form appear to me:
A virgin's face she had; her dress
Was like a sprightly Spartaness;
A silver bow, with green silk strung,
Down from her comely shoulders hung;   10
And as she stood, the wanton air
Dandled the ringlets of her hair;
Her legs were such Diana shows,
When tucked up she a hunting goes,
With buskins shortened to descry   15
The happy dawning of her thigh,
Which when I saw I made access
To kiss that tempting nakedness;
But she forbad me with a wand
Of myrtle she had in her hand,   20
And, chiding me, said, 'Hence, remove,
Herrick, thou art too coarse to love.'

---

45. On the genre of this poem see H–7 n.   7–16 *A Virgin's face she had*, etc.: as
Pollard notes, Herrick is imitating Virgil, *Aeneid*, i. 315–20.

46

Love Me Little, Love Me Long

You say to me-wards your affection's strong;
Pray love me little, so you love me long.
Slowly goes far; the mean is best: desire
Grown violent does either die or tire.

47

An Epithalamy to Sir Thomas Southwell and His Lady

Now, now's the time so oft by Truth
Promised should come to crown your youth.
    Then, fair ones, do not wrong
    Your joys by staying long,
    Or let Love's fire go out   5
    By lingering thus in doubt;
    But learn that Time, once lost,
    Is ne'er redeemed by cost.
Then away; come, Hymen, guide
To the bed the bashful bride.   10

46. Martin cites some of the proverbs compressed into this quatrain (Tilley M 793, S 544, S 601, and *Oxford Proverbs* 'Soft pace goes far'), and compares Shakespeare, *Rom.* II. vi. 9–15.

47. Martin says that 'Herrick's poem was doubtless written for Sir Thomas's first marriage in 1618.' On the literary genre of the 'epithalamy' see G. Herrick's 'Epithalamy' draws extensively on classical antecedents and on native English customs (the ceremonies at the groom's rather than the bride's house, for example), and it shows direct reliance on Jonson's *Hymenaei*. Martin (pp. 455–60) and Patrick (pp. 81–6) give in full a variant version of this poem from British Museum MS. Harl. 6918. 1 *Truth*: troth or marriage-plighting. 9 *Hymen*: god of marriage.

Is it, sweet maid, your fault these holy
Bridal-rites go on so slowly?
    Dear, is it this you dread,
    The loss of maidenhead?
    Believe me, you will most   15
    Esteem it when 'tis lost:
    Then it no longer keep,
    Lest issue lie asleep.
Then away; come, Hymen, guide
To the bed the bashful bride.   20

These precious, pearly, purling tears
But spring from ceremonious fears;
    And 'tis but native shame
    That hides the loving flame,
    And may a while control   25
    The soft and am'rous soul;
    But yet, Love's fire will waste
    Such bashfulness at last.
Then away; come, Hymen, guide
To the bed the bashful bride.   30

Night now hath watched herself half blind;
Yet not a maidenhead resigned!
    'Tis strange, ye will not fly
    To love's sweet mystery.
    Might yon full moon the sweets   35
    Have, promised to your sheets,
    She soon would leave her sphere
    To be admitted there.
Then away; come, Hymen, guide
To the bed the bashful bride.   40

On, on, devoutly, make no stay;
While Domiduca leads the way,
    And *Genius,* who attends
    The bed for lucky ends;
    With Juno goes the Hours   45
    And Graces strewing flowers,
    And the boys with sweet tunes sing;
    Hymen, O Hymen, bring
Home the turtles; Hymen, guide
To the bed the bashful bride.   50

Behold! how Hymen's taper-light
Shows you how much is spent of night!
    See, see the bridegroom's torch
    Half wasted in the porch!
    And now those tapers five,   55
    That show the womb shall thrive,
    Their silvery flames advance,
    To tell all prosperous chance
Still shall crown the happy life
Of the goodman and the wife.   60

Move forward then your rosy feet,
And make whate'er they touch turn sweet.
    May all like flowery meads
    Smell where your soft foot treads,
    And everything assume   65
    To it the like perfume
    As Zephyrus when he 'spires
    Through woodbine and sweetbriars.
Then away; come, Hymen, guide
To the bed the bashful bride.   70

---

42 *Domiduca*: one of eight masquers representing distinct functions of Juno
(from *Hymenaei*, l. 293).   43 *Genius*: here, specifically a god of nature or child-
bearing, the male equivalent of Juno (after Jonson's *Hymenaei*, ll. 537–40, and
note: 'Deus Naturae, siue gignendi').   45 *Juno*: consort of Jupiter, queen of
heaven, and representative of the female principle of life.   49 *turtles*: turtle-
doves.   55 *those tapers five*. Jonson (*Hymenaei*, ll. 196–211 and n.) explains five
as being inseparable into equal parts (quintessential, like Sir Thomas Browne's
quincunx in *The Garden of Cyrus*): 'one will ever / Remain as common; so we
see / The binding force of unity.'

And now the yellow veil, at last,
Over her fragrant cheek is cast.
    Now seems she to express
    A bashful willingness,
    Showing a heart consenting,   75
    As with a will repenting.
    Then gently lead her on
    With wise suspicion,
For that, matrons say, a measure
Of that passion sweetens pleasure.   80

You, you that be of her near'st kin,
Now o'er the threshold force her in.
    But to avert the worst,
    Let her her fillets first
    Knit to the posts, this point   85
    Remembering, to anoint
    The sides; for 'tis a charm
    Strong against future harm
And the evil deeds, the which
There was hidden by the witch.   90

O Venus, thou, to whom is known
The best way how to loose the zone
    Of virgins! Tell the maid
    She need not be afraid;
    And bid the youth apply   95
    Close kisses, if she cry;
    And charge he not forbears
    Her, though she woo with tears.
Tell them now they must adventure,
Since that Love and Night bid enter.   100

92 *zone*: belt, girdle.

No fatal owl the bedstead keeps
With direful notes to fright your sleeps;
   No Furies hereabout,
   To put the tapers out,
   Watch, or did make the bed: 105
   'Tis omen full of dread;
   But all fair signs appear
   Within the chamber here.
Juno here, far off, doth stand
Cooling sleep with charming wand.   110

Virgins, weep not; 'twill come, when,
As she, so you'll be ripe for men.
   Then grieve her not with saying
   She must no more a Maying,
   Or by rosebuds divine   115
   Who'll be her valentine,
   Nor name those wanton reaks
   You've had at barley-breaks,
But now kiss her, and thus say,
'Take time, lady, while ye may.'   120

Now bar the doors; the bridegroom puts
The eager boys to gather nuts.
   And now, both Love and Time
   To their full height do climb.
   Oh, give them active heat   125
   And moisture, both complete;
   Fit organs for increase,
   To keep and to release
That which may the honoured stem
Circle with a diadem!   130

---

103 *Furies*. Represented as winged women, sometimes with snakes about them, they were avengers of crime, especially against the ties of kinship. 117 *reaks*: pranks, games. 118 *Barley-break*[s]: a game (see G). 122 gather nuts that were 'thrown to the torchbearers as the bride approaches, in the belief that they conduced to fertility' (Patrick); cf. Catullus, *Carm*. lxi. 127–30. 129–30 *stem . . . diadem*: with reference partly to family trees: crown the stem (source) with sovereignty ('diadem').

And now, behold! the bed or couch
That ne'er knew bride's or bridegroom's touch
    Feels in itself a fire,
    And tickled with desire
    Pants with a downy breast,   135
    As with a heart possessed,
    Shrugging as it did move
    Ev'n with the soul of love.
And, oh! had it but a tongue,
'Doves', 'twould say, 'ye bill too long!'   140

O enter, then! but see ye shun
A sleep until the act be done.
    Let kisses, in their close,
    Breathe as the damask rose,
    Or sweet as is that gum   145
    Doth from Panchaia come.
    Teach Nature now to know
    Lips can make cherries grow
Sooner than she, ever yet,
In her wisdom could beget.   150

On your minutes, hours, days, months, years,
Drop the fat blessing of the spheres,
    That good, which heaven can give
    To make you bravely live,
    Fall like a spangling dew   155
    By day and night on you.
    May Fortune's lily hand
    Open at your command,
With all lucky birds to side
With the bridegroom and the bride.   160

---

146 *Panchaia*: mythical place of origin of various precious gums, spices, and
incense; confused with Arabia Felix and referred to by Jonson after Virgil and
Claudian (Martin, p. 512, and Patrick, p. 81).

Let bounteous Fates your spindles full
Fill, and wind up with whitest wool.
    Let them not cut the thread
    Of life until ye bid.
    May Death yet come at last,   165
    And not with desperate haste,
    But when ye both can say,
    'Come, let us now away',
Be ye, to the barn then borne,
Two, like two ripe shocks of corn.   170

48

Upon a Young Mother of Many Children

Let all chaste matrons, when they chance to see
My numerous issue, praise and pity me:
Praise me, for having such a fruitful womb;
Pity me, too, who found so soon a tomb.

49

To Electra

I'll come to thee in all those shapes
As Jove did when he made his rapes:
Only I'll not appear to thee
As he did once to Semele.
Thunder and lightning I'll lay by,   5
To talk with thee familiarly.
Which done, then quickly we'll undress
To one and th' other's nakedness,
And ravished plunge into the bed
(Bodies and souls comminglèd),   10

---

161 *Fates*: so in the variant version and hence 'them' (l. 163); *H 48* reads
'Fate'. See G.

49. 1–4 as in the rapes of Danaë, Europa, and Leda, not as he appeared to
Semele; at her prayer, Zeus visited her in all his glory, and she was consumed
by lightning.

And kissing so as none may hear
We'll weary all the fables there.

50

The Cruel Maid

Ah, cruel maid, because I see
You scornful of my love and me,
I'll trouble you no more, but go
My way, where you shall never know
What is become of me; there I 5
Will find me out a path to die,
Or learn some way how to forget
You and your name for ever. Yet,
Ere I go hence, know this from me,
What will, in time, your fortune be; 10
This to your coyness I will tell,
And having spoke it once, farewell.
The lily will not long endure,
Nor the snow continue pure;
The rose, the violet, one day 15
See, both these lady-flowers decay:
And you must fade, as well as they.
And it may chance that love may turn,
And (like to mine) make your heart burn
And weep to see't; yet this thing do, 20
That my last vow commends to you:
When you shall see that I am dead,
For pity let a tear be shed;
And (with your mantle o'er me cast)
Give my cold lips a kiss at last; 25
If twice you kiss, you need not fear
That I shall stir, or live more here.
Next, hollow out a tomb to cover
Me; me, the most despisèd lover:
And write thereon, *This, reader, know,* 30
Love killed this man. No more but so.

---

50. 1 *Ah*: at Martin's suggestion (p. 513), on the analogy of 'Ah, cruel Love!'
beginning 'To Pansies' (H–191); *H 48* reads 'And'.

51

To Dianeme

Sweet, be not proud of those two eyes,
Which star-like sparkle in their skies;
Nor be you proud, that you can see
All hearts your captives, yours yet free;
Be you not proud of that rich hair,   5
Which wantons with the lovesick air;
When as that ruby, which you wear,
Sunk from the tip of your soft ear,
Will last to be a precious stone
When all your world of beauty's gone.   10

52

To a Gentlewoman Objecting to Him His Grey Hairs

Am I despised because you say,
And I dare swear, that I am grey?
Know, lady, you have but your day,
And time will come when you shall wear
Such frost and snow upon your hair.   5
And when (though long) it comes to pass
You question with your looking-glass,
And in that sincere crystal seek
But find no rosebud in your cheek,
Nor any bed to give the show   10
Where such a rare Carnation grew,
Ah! then too late, close in your chamber keeping,
        It will be told
        That you are old,
By those true tears y'are weeping.   15

52. Source, *Anacreontea* vii. 6 (*though long*): *H 48*, Martin, and Patrick have
'(though . . . pass)'.

53

*Upon a Black Twist, Rounding the Arm of
the Countess of Carlisle*

I saw about her spotless wrist
Of blackest silk a curious twist,
Which, circumvolving gently, there
Enthralled her arm as prisoner.
Dark was the jail, but as if light   5
Had met t' engender with the night;
Or so as darkness made a stay
To show at once both night and day.
I fancy more! But if there be
Such freedom in captivity,   10
I beg of Love that ever I
May in like chains of darkness lie!

54

On Himself

I fear no earthly powers,
But care for crowns of flowers,
And love to have my beard
With wine and oil besmeared.
This day I'll drown all sorrow;   5
Who knows to live to morrow?

53. On the Countess see G, 'Carlisle'. 9 *more*: *H 48* and Patrick (see n.,
pp. 94–5); Martin reads 'none!' (see n., pp. 513–14); 'more [freedom]'
(Patrick), or perhaps '[To show] more'.

54. Source, *Anacreontea* viii. 1–10; there is a version by Thomas Stanley. Pollard
notes that the poem was 'probably suggested by Anacreon' xxxvi.

C

55

Upon Pagget

Pagget, a schoolboy, got a sword, and then
He vowed destruction both to birch and men:
Who would not think this younker fierce to fight?
Yet coming home, but somewhat late (last night),
'Untruss', his master bade him; and that word   5
Made him take up his shirt, lay down his sword.

56

Upon the Same [Detractor]

I asked thee oft what poets thou hast read
And lik'st the best. Still thou reply'st, 'The dead'.
I shall, ere long, with green turfs covered be;
Then sure thou'lt like, or thou wilt envy me.

57

Julia's Petticoat

Thy azure robe I did behold,
As airy as the leaves of gold;
Which erring here, and wandering there,
Pleased with transgression everywhere:
Sometimes 'twould pant, and sigh, and heave,   5
As if to stir it scarce had leave;

---

55. 3 *younker*: youngster; cf. Shakespeare, *MV* II. vi. 14: 'How like a younker or a prodigal . . .'

56. Adapted from Martial, VIII. lxix.

57. 2 *leaves of gold*: with allusion possibly to gold-foil (*ME*), but not probably to gold leaf (earliest *OED*-recorded use, 1727).

But having got it, thereupon
'Twould make a brave expansion;
And pounced with stars, it showed to me
Like a celestial canopy.   10
Sometimes 'twould blaze, and then abate,
Like to a flame grown moderate;
Sometimes away 'twould wildly fling;
Then to thy thighs so closely cling
That some conceit did melt me down,   15
As lovers fall into a swoon;
And all confused, I there did lie
Drowned in delights, but could not die.
That leading cloud I followed still,
Hoping t' have seen of it my fill;   20
But ah, I could not: should it move
To life eternal, I could love!

58

To Music

Begin to charm, and as thou strok'st mine ears
With thy enchantment, melt me into tears.
Then let thy active hand scud o'er thy lyre,
And make my spirits frantic with the fire.
That done, sink down into a silvery strain,   5
And make me smooth as balm and oil again.

9 *pounced*: pinked, ornamented; *OED* (citing this use), 'sprinkled with powder'.
15 *conceit*: idea, fantasy.   19 *that leading cloud*: 'the Lord went before them by
day in a pillar of cloud' (Exod. 13: 21).

59

Distrust

To safeguard man from wrongs, there nothing must
Be truer to him than a wise distrust.
And to thyself be best this sentence known:
Hear all men speak, but credit few or none.

60

Corinna's Going a Maying

Get up, get up for shame, the blooming morn
Upon her wings presents the god unshorn.
    See how Aurora throws her fair
    Fresh-quilted colours through the air:
    Get up, sweet slug-a-bed, and see   5
    The dew bespangling herb and tree.
Each flower has wept and bowed toward the east
Above an hour since; yet you not dressed,
    Nay! not so much as out of bed?
    When all the birds have matins said   10
    And sung their thankful hymns? 'Tis sin,
    Nay, profanation to keep in,
Whenas a thousand virgins on this day
Spring, sooner than the lark, to fetch in May.

Rise, and put on your foliage, and be seen   15
To come forth, like the spring-time, fresh and green,
    And sweet as Flora. Take no care
    For jewels for your gown or hair;

---

59. 4 Cf. Polonius: 'Give every man thine ear, but few thy voice; /
Take each man's censure, but reserve thy judgement' (*Ham.* i. iii. 68–9); 'to
thine own self be true' (l. 78) is echoed elsewhere (H–32: 135–6).

60. 'Corinna' is the feminine form of 'Corin'; both are type-names for pastoral
figures. 2 *the god unshorn*: i.e. the sun god, whether as Helios or Apollo,
radiating both hair and light in the image. From Horace, *Odes*, i. xxi. 2:
'Intonsum pueri dicite Cynthium'. 3 *Aurora*: 'the blooming morn' (l. 1) and
goddess of the dawn. 17 *Flora*: a goddess of fertility and flowers.

Fear not: the leaves will strew
Gems in abundance upon you;   20
Besides, the childhood of the day has kept,
Against you come, some orient pearls unwept;
    Come, and receive them while the light
    Hangs on the dew-locks of the night,
    And Titan on the eastern hill   25
    Retires himself, or else stands still
Till you come forth. Wash, dress, be brief in praying:
Few beads are best when once we go a Maying.

Come, my Corinna, come; and, coming, mark
How each field turns a street, each street a park   30
    Made green and trimmed with trees; see how
    Devotion gives each house a bough
    Or branch: each porch, each door, ere this,
    An ark, a tabernacle, is,
Made up of whitethorn neatly interwove,   35
As if here were those cooler shades of love.
    Can such delights be in the street
    And open fields and we not see't?
    Come, we'll abroad; and let's obey
    The proclamation made for May,   40
And sin no more, as we have done, by staying;
But my Corinna, come, let's go a Maying.

There's not a budding boy or girl, this day,
But is got up and gone to bring in May.
    A deal of youth, ere this, is come   45
    Back, and with whitethorn laden home.

---

25 *Titan*: the sun (god).   28 *beads*: prayers (ME 'bedes'), as said with rosary
beads, perhaps.   32–5 *Devotion gives*, etc.: Martin cites Lev. 23: 40–3, and Ovid,
Fasti, iii. 528.   35 *whitethorn*: 'symbolizing joy and pain' (Patrick); Martin
compares Jonson's *Hymenaei*, ll. 53–4: 'a youth . . . bearing another light, of
whitethorn', and ll. 172–3.   40 *Proclamation made for May*: perhaps only in
allusion to the traditional rites of spring, but perhaps also with allusion to some
such proclamation as 'The King's Majesty's Declaration to His Subjects
Concerning Lawful Sports To Be Used' (1618), in which the festive-minded
were not to be hindered by Puritans and like-minded others from 'any lawful
recreation; such as dancing . . . , archery . . . , leaping, vaulting, or any such
harmless recreation, nor from having of May-games, Whitsun ales, and Morris
Dances, and the setting up of May-Poles and other sports therewith used.'

Some have dispatched their cakes and cream
Before that we have left to dream;
And some have wept, and wooed, and plighted troth,
And chose their priest, ere we can cast off sloth.   50
    Many a green-gown has been given,
    Many a kiss, both odd and even;
    Many a glance too has been sent
    From out the eye, love's firmament;
Many a jest told of the keys betraying   55
This night, and locks picked, yet we're not a Maying.

Come, let us go, while we are in our prime,
And take the harmless folly of the time.
    We shall grow old apace, and die
    Before we know our liberty.   60
    Our life is short, and our days run
    As fast away as does the sun;
And as a vapour, or a drop of rain,
Once lost, can ne'er be found again,
    So when or you or I are made   65
    A fable, song, or fleeting shade,
    All love, all liking, all delight
    Lies drowned with us in endless night.
Then while time serves, and we are but decaying,
Come, my Corinna, come, let's go a Maying.   70

51 *green gown*: both literal and a metaphor for one of the consequences of being rolled over in the clover. 57–70 Martin comments on the universality of the sentiment (*carpe diem*) and lists a number of significant antecedents, noting that 'some major elements' in Herrick's 'amalgam . . . were collected also by Burton into a single passage, 3. 4. 2. 1 (p. 684), with which Herrick's lines probably have some direct connection'. 67–8 *All love, all liking, all delight* etc.: a paraphrase of Catullus, *Carm.* v. 5–6.

61

The Captived Bee; or, the Little Filcher

As Julia once a slumbering lay,
It chanced a bee did fly that way
(After a dew, or dew-like shower)
To tipple freely in a flower.
For some rich flower he took the lip   5
Of Julia, and began to sip;
But when he felt he sucked from thence
Honey, and in the quintessence,
He drank so much he scarce could stir,
So Julia took the pilferer.   10
And thus surprised (as filchers use)
He thus began himself t' excuse:
'Sweet lady-flower, I never brought
Hither the least one thieving thought,
But taking those rare lips of yours   15
For some fresh, fragrant, luscious flowers,
I thought I might there take a taste,
Where so much syrup ran at waste.
Besides, know this, I never sting
The flower that gives me nourishing,   20
But with a kiss, or thanks, do pay
For honey that I bear away.'
This said, he laid his little scrip
Of honey 'fore her ladyship,
And told her (as some tears did fall)   25
That that he took and that was all.
At which she smiled, and bade him go
And take his bag; but thus much know,
When next he came a pilfering so,
He should from her full lips derive   30
Honey enough to fill his hive.

61. 23 *scrip*: bag.

62

An Ode to Master Endymion Porter, upon His Brother's Death

Not all thy flushing suns are set,
      Herrick, as yet;
Nor doth this far-drawn hemisphere
Frown and look sullen everywhere.
Days may conclude in nights, and suns may rest,   5
      As dead, within the west,
Yet the next morn regild the fragrant east.

Alas for me, that I have lost
      E'en all almost!
Sunk is my sight, set is my sun,   10
And all the loom of life undone;
The staff, the elm, the prop, the sheltering wall
      Whereon my vine did crawl
Now, now, blown down; needs must the old stock fall.

Yet, Porter, while thou keep'st alive,   15
      In death I thrive,
And like a phoenix re-aspire
From out my nard and funeral fire;
And as I prune my feathered youth, so I
      Do mar'l how I could die,   20
When I had thee, my chief preserver, by.

I'm up, I'm up, and bless that hand
      Which makes me stand
Now as I do; and but for thee,
I must confess, I could not be.   25
The debt is paid, for he who doth resign
      Thanks to the generous vine
Invites fresh grapes to fill his press with wine.

---

62. Endymion Porter (1587–1649) was a courtier, ambassador, writer of verses, and patron of poets, including Herrick, Jonson, Dekker, Davenant, and others. 'His Brother' is William Herrick, a younger brother who is addressed in the following poem and who died before June 1632.

63

To His Dying Brother, Master William Herrick

Life of my life, take not so soon thy flight,
But stay the time till we have bade good night.
Thou hast both wind and tide with thee; thy way
As soon dispatched is by the night as day.
Let us not then so rudely henceforth go   5
Till we have wept, kissed, sighed, shook hands or so.
There's pain in parting, and a kind of hell,
When once true lovers take their last farewell.
What, shall we two our endless leaves take here
Without a sad look, or a solemn tear?   10
He knows not love that hath not this truth proved,
Love is most loth to leave the thing beloved.
Pay we our vows, and go; yet when we part,
Then, even then, I will bequeath my heart
Into thy loving hands; for I'll keep none   15
To warm my breast when thou my pulse art gone.
No, here I'll last, and walk (a harmless shade)
About this urn wherein thy dust is laid,
To guard it so as nothing here shall be
Heavy, to hurt those sacred seeds of thee.   20

64

How Lilies Came White

White though ye be, yet, lilies, know,
From the first ye were not so;
    But I'll tell ye
    What befell ye:
Cupid and his mother lay   5
In a cloud; while both did play,

63. William Herrick, 1593–1632.

He with his pretty finger pressed
The ruby niplet of her breast;
Out of which, the cream of light,
   Like to a dew,   10
   Fell down on you,
And made ye white.

65

Upon Some Women

Thou who wilt not love, do this;
Learn of me what woman is:
Something made of thread and thrum,
A mere botch of all and some;
Pieces, patches, ropes of hair,   5
Inlaid garbage everywhere;
Outside silk and outside lawn,
Scenes to cheat us neatly drawn;
False in legs and false in thighs,
False in breast, teeth, hair, and eyes;   10
False in head, and false enough:
Only true in shreds and stuff.

66

Supreme Fortune Falls Soonest

While leanest beasts in pastures feed,
The fattest ox the first must bleed.

65. 3 *thrum*: any loose thread or tuft. 8 *Scene*[s]: curtain, veil, decorative hanging.

67

The Welcome to Sack

So soft streams meet, so springs with gladder smiles
Meet after long divorcement by the isles,
When Love (the child of likeness) urgeth on
Their crystal natures to an union;
So meet stol'n kisses when the moony nights   5
Call forth fierce lovers to their wished delights;
So kings and queens meet when desire convinces
All thoughts but such as aim at getting princes,
As I meet thee. Soul of my life and fame!
Eternal lamp of love! whose radiant flame   10
Out-glares the heavens' Osiris, and thy gleams
Out-shine the splendour of his midday beams.
Welcome, O welcome, my illustrious spouse,
Welcome as are the ends unto my vows:
Ay, far more welcome than the happy soil   15
The sea-scourged merchant, after all his toil,
Salutes with tears of joy, when fires betray
The smoky chimneys of his Ithaca!
Where hast thou been so long from my embraces,
Poor pitied exile? Tell me, did thy Graces   20
Fly discontented hence, and for a time
Did rather choose to bless another clime?
Or went'st thou to this end, the more to move me,
By thy short absence, to desire and love thee?
Why frowns my sweet? Why won't my saint confer   25
Favours on me, her fierce idolater?
Why are those looks, those looks the which have been
Time-past so fragrant, sickly now drawn in
Like a dull twilight? Tell me, and the fault
I'll expiate with sulphur, hair, and salt,   30
And with the crystal humour of the spring
Purge hence the guilt and kill this quarrelling.

---

67. 'His Farewell to Sack' is H–41. On 'Sack' see G.   7 *convinces*: overpowers.
11 *Osiris*: 'the Sun' (Herrick).   18 *Ithaca*: the home and island kingdom of
Odysseus (see G), to whom sack is compared as 'exile' (l. 20).   30 *sulphur, hair,
and salt*: as expiatory offerings.   31 *crystal humour*: clear water.

Woo't thou not smile, or tell me what's amiss?
Have I been cold to hug thee, too remiss,
Too temperate in embracing? Tell me, has desire   35
To thee-ward died i' th' embers, and no fire
Left in this raked-up ash-heap as a mark
To testify the glowing of a spark?
Have I divorced thee only to combine
In hot adultery with another wine?   40
True, I confess I left thee, and appeal
'Twas done by me more to confirm my zeal
And double my affection on thee, as do those
Whose love grows more enflamed by being foes.
But to forsake thee ever, could there be   45
A thought of suchlike possibility,
When thou thyself dar'st say thy isles shall lack
Grapes before Herrick leaves Canary Sack?
Thou mak'st me airy, active to be borne,
Like Iphyclus upon the tops of corn.   50
Thou mak'st me nimble as the wingèd hours,
To dance and caper on the heads of flowers
And ride the sunbeams. Can there be a thing
Under the heavenly Isis that can bring
More love unto my life, or can present   55
My *Genius* with a fuller blandishment?
Illustrious idol! could th' Egyptians seek
Help from the garlic, onion, and the leek,
And pay no vows to thee who wast their best
God, and far more transcendent than the rest?   60
Had Cassius, that weak water-drinker, known
Thee in thy vine, or had but tasted one
Small chalice of thy frantic liquor, he
As the wise Cato had approved of thee.
Had not Jove's son, that brave Tyrinthian swain   65
(Invited to the Thespian banquet), ta'en

---

38 *testify*. The context suggests a sly pun on 'testes'. 50 *Iphiclus*: a legendary Argonaut whose fleetness of foot was said to be as it is characterized here. 54 *Isis*: 'the Moon' (Herrick). 61 *Cassius*: Brutus's abstemious fellow conspirator with the 'lean and hungry look', who 'loves no plays' and 'hears no music' (*JC* I. ii. 192 ff.). 64 *Cato*: called the Censor for his famed severity. 65 *Jove's son*: 'Hercules' (Herrick).

Full goblets of thy generous blood, his sprite
Ne'er had kept heat for fifty maids that night.
Come, come and kiss me; Love and lust commends
Thee, and thy beauties; kiss, we will be friends   70
Too strong for Fate to break us: look upon
Me, with that full pride of complexion
As queens meet queens; or come thou unto me
As Cleopatra came to Anthony,
When her high carriage did at once present,   75
To the triumvir, love and wonderment.
Swell up my nerves with spirit; let my blood
Run through my veins like to a hasty flood.
Fill each part full of fire, active to do
What thy commanding soul shall put it to.   80
And till I turn apostate to thy love,
Which here I vow to serve, do not remove
Thy fires from me; but Apollo's curse
Blast these-like actions, or a thing that's worse,
When these circùmstants shall but live to see   85
The time that I prevaricate from thee,
Call me the son of beer, and then confine
Me to the tap, the toast, the turf; let wine
Ne'er shine upon me; may my numbers all
Run to a sudden death and funeral.   90
And last, when thee, dear spouse, I disavow,
Ne'er may prophetic Daphne crown my brow.

68 *fifty maids*: the daughters of Thespius (see Rose, *Mythology*, p. 208). 85 *circum-stants*: bystanders. 86 *Thee*: *H 48*, Martin, and Patrick have a full stop. 88 *the tap, the toast, the turf*: i.e. the beer-barrel tap, the sops of toasted bread, and perhaps 'the earth because beer lacks the power to exalt him' (Patrick, p. 112, who contrasts ll. 49 ff.). 89 *numbers*: verses. 92 *Daphne*: pursued by Apollo, she was changed to a bay or laurel tree, which provided the crowns for victory in poetry.

68

To Live Merrily, and To Trust to Good Verses

Now is the time for mirth,
   Nor cheek or tongue be dumb;
For with the flowery earth
   The golden pomp is come.

The golden pomp is come;   5
   For now each tree does wear
(Made of her pap and gum)
   Rich beads of Amber here.

Now reigns the Rose, and now
   Th' Arabian dew besmears   10
My uncontrollèd brow
   And my retorted hairs.

Homer, this health to thee,
   In sack of such a kind
That it would make thee see,   15
   Though thou wert ne'er so blind.

Next, Virgil I'll call forth
   To pledge this second health
In wine, whose each cup's worth
   An Indian commonwealth.   20

A goblet next I'll drink
   To Ovid, and suppose,
Made he the pledge, he'd think
   The world had all one Nose.

68. This poem seems to me to contain a number of turns, beginning with the 'Verses' of the title. Patrick (p. 115) has noted the sense of 'rains' in 'reigns' (l. 9); other possible and likely turns of various kinds are 'time[thyme]' (1), 'pomp[pump]' (4–5), etc.   10 *Arabian dew*: Ovid, *Her.* xv. 76: 'Arabo . . . rore'. 24 *Nose*: punning on the surname of Ovidius Naso and alluding to the fabulous perfume of Catullus, *Carm.* xiii. 11–14: Catullus' friend would ask the gods that he should be made all nose.

Then this immensive cup 25
  Of aromatic wine,
Catullus, I quaff up
  To that terse muse of thine.

Wild I am now with heat;
  O Bacchus, cool thy rays! 30
Or frantic I shall eat
  Thy thyrse and bite the bays.

Round, round, the roof does run;
  And, being ravished thus,
Come, I will drink a tun 35
  To my Propertius.

Now, to Tibullus, next
  This flood I drink to thee;
But stay, I see a text
  That this presents to me. 40

Behold, Tibullus lies
  Here burnt, whose small return
Of ashes scarce suffice
  To fill a little urn.

Trust to good verses, then; 45
  They only will aspire,
When pyramids, as men,
  Are lost i' th' funeral fire.

And when all bodies meet
  In Lethe to be drowned,
Then only numbers sweet 50
  With endless life are crowned.

---

32 *thyrse*: see G.   39 *a text*: translated in ll. 41–4 from Ovid, *Am.* iii. ix. 39–40.
46 *aspire*: breathe, rise up like incense; be ambitious of.   51 *numbers*: verses.

69

Fair Days; or, Dawns Deceitful

Fair was the dawn, and but e'en now the skies
Showed like to cream inspired with strawberries;
But on a sudden all was changed and gone
That smiled in that first-sweet complexion.
Then thunder-claps and lightning did conspire   5
To tear the world, or set it all on fire.
What trust to things below, whenas we see,
As men, the heavens have their hypocrisy?

70

Lips Tongueless

For my part, I never care
For those lips that tongue-tied are:
Telltales I would have them be
Of my mistress and of me.
Let them prattle how that I   5
Sometimes freeze and sometimes fry;
Let them tell how she doth move
For- or backward in her love;
Let them speak by gentle tones
One and th' other's passions: 10
How we watch and seldom sleep,
How by willows we do weep,
How by stealth we meet and then
Kiss and sigh, so part again.
This the lips we will permit   15
For to tell, not publish it.

71

To Violets

Welcome, Maids of Honour,
         You do bring
         In the Spring
And wait upon her.

She has virgins many,   5
         Fresh and fair;
         Yet you are
More sweet than any.

You're the maiden posies,
         And so graced   10
         To be placed
'Fore damask roses.

Yet, though thus respected,
         By and by
         Ye do lie,   15
Poor girls, neglected.

72

Upon Bunce: Epigram

Money thou ow'st me; prithee fix a day
For payment promised, though thou never pay:
Let it be Doomsday; nay, take longer scope:
Pay when th'art honest; let me have some hope.

73

To the Virgins, To Make Much of Time

Gather ye rosebuds while ye may,
  Old time is still a flying;
And this same flower that smiles today
  Tomorrow will be dying.

The glorious lamp of heaven, the sun,   5
  The higher he's a getting;
The sooner will his race be run,
  And nearer he's to setting.

That age is best which is the first,
  When youth and blood are warmer;   10
But being spent, the worse and worst
  Times still succeed the former.

Then be not coy, but use your time;
  And while ye may, go marry:
For, having lost but once your prime,   15
  You may for ever tarry.

73. One of Herrick's most famous poems, and the analogue of Marvell's 'To His Coy Mistress'. Both Martin (pp. 517–18) and Patrick (p. 118) have detailed notes on Herrick's classical and English antecedents. An additional important source, the parable of the wise and foolish virgins, 'which took their lamps and went forth to meet the bridegroom' (Matt. 25: 1–13), helps to provide much of the peculiar sense and force of this very Christian *carpe diem* poem; in another context, Martin rightly points out that Herrick 'is clearly indebted not only to Latin poetry but to the Bible (where the thought of "carpe diem" is introduced in order to be deprecated)' (p. 514, note on 'Corinna's Going a Maying', ll. 57–70). The parable also makes clear why they are '*the* virgins'; the poem is not, after all, addressed 'To Virgins'. There is a musical setting by William Lawes.   1 *may*: intentional syllepsis; 'may' as (1) auxiliary of predication (can), and (2) in the sense of 'Corinna's Going a Maying'.   2 *time*: also 'thyme'?

74

To His Friend, on the Untunable Times

Play I could once; but, gentle friend, you see
My harp hung up, here on the willow tree.
Sing I could once; and bravely too inspire
(With luscious numbers) my melodious lyre.
Draw I could once (although not stocks or stones,   5
Amphion-like) men made of flesh and bones
Whither I would; but ah! I know not how,
I feel in me this transmutation now.
Grief, my dear friend, has first my harp unstrung,
Withered my hand, and palsy-struck my tongue.   10

75

His Poetry His Pillar

Only a little more
    I have to write,
        Then I'll give o'er,
And bid the world good night.

'Tis but a flying minute,   5
    That I must stay,
        Or linger in it;
And then I must away.

O Time that cutt'st down all,
    And scarce leav'st here   10
        Memorial
Of any men that were!

74. The bridge between tenor and vehicle is 'discord': inharmonious historical times make song impossible. Cf. Ps. 137: 4.   6 *Amphion*: see G.

75. Martin cites Horace, *Odes*, III. xxx. 1–2, and Burton ('Of so many myriads of poets . . . scarce one of a thousand's work remains').

How many lie forgot
   In vaults beneath,
   And piecemeal rot   15
Without a fame in death?

Behold this living stone
   I rear for me,
   Ne'er to be thrown
Down, envious Time, by thee.   20

Pillars let some set up
   (If so they please);
   Here is my hope,
And my pyramides.

76

The Bubble: A Song

To my revenge and to her desperate fears,
Fly, thou mad bubble of my sighs and tears.
In the wild air, when thou hast rolled about
And (like a blasting planet) found her out,
Stoop, mount, pass by to take her eye, then glare   5
Like to a dreadful comet in the air;
Next, when thou dost perceive her fixèd sight,
For thy revenge to be most opposite,
Then like a globe, or ball of wildfire, fly,
And break thyself in shivers on her eye.   10

---

76. The bubble turned 'dreadful comet' seems to take some of its character from
falconry: to 'stoop' (l. 5) is to descend upon the prey.   9 *wildfire*: a combustible
substance easily ignited and difficult to extinguish; called 'Greek fire' after the
use of it by Greeks at Constantinople to set ships afire.

77

A Meditation for His Mistress

You are a tulip seen today,
But, dearest, of so short a stay
That where you grew scarce man can say.

You are a lovely July-flower,
Yet one rude wind, or ruffling shower,   5
Will force you hence (and in an hour).

You are a sparkling rose i' th' bud,
Yet lost ere that chaste flesh and blood
Can show where you or grew or stood.

You are a full-spread, fair-set vine,   10
And can with tendrils love entwine,
Yet dried ere you distil your wine.

You are like balm enclosèd (well)
In amber, or some crystal shell,
Yet lost ere you transfuse your smell.   15

You are a dainty violet,
Yet withered ere you can be set
Within the virgin's coronet.

You are the queen all flowers among,
But die you must, fair maid, ere long,   20
As he, the maker of this song.

78

The Fairy Temple; or, Oberon's Chapel
Dedicated to Master John Merrifield,
Counsellor at Law

Rare temples thou hast seen, I know,
And rich for in- and outward show:
Survey this chapel, built, alone,
Without or lime, or wood, or stone;
Then say if one thou'st seen more fine   5
Than this, the Fairies' once, now thine.

The Temple

A way enchased with glass and beads
There is that to the chapel leads,
Whose structure (for his holy rest)
Is here the halcyon's curious nest,
Into the which who looks shall see   5
His temple of idolatry,
Where he of godheads has such store
As Rome's Panthèon had not more.
His house of Rimmon this he calls,
Girt with small bones instead of walls.   10
First, in a niche more black than jet
His idol-cricket there is set;
Then in a polished oval by
There stands his idol-beetle-fly;
Next in an arch akin to this   15
His idol-canker seated is;
Then in a round is placed by these
His golden god, Cantharides.

78. 'Fairy Poems' were most in fashion in 1626–7: Sir Simeon Steward's
Description of the King of Faeries Clothes was printed in 1626, and Michael
Drayton's *Nymphidia* in 1627. Herrick's four contributions to the genre are this
poem and H–100, 129, and 160. Martin suggests the probable identity of
Merrifield (p. 520). 4 *halcyon*: see G. 9 *Rimmon*: a pagan deity whose place
of worship is referred to in 2 Kgs. 5: 18. 16 *canker*[-worm]. 18 *Cantharides*:
Spanish fly, an aphrodisiac.

So that, where'er ye look, ye see
No capital, no cornice free, 20
Or frieze, from this fine frippery.
Now this the Fairies would have known:
Theirs is a mixed religion;
And some have heard the Elves it call
Part pagan, part papistical. 25
If unto me all tongues were granted,
I could not speak the saints here painted:
Saint Tit, Saint Nit, Saint Is, Saint Itis,
Who 'gainst Mab's state placed here right is.
Saint Will-o'-th'-Wisp (of no great bigness) 30
But alias called here *Fatuus Ignis*;
Saint Frip, Saint Trip, Saint Fill, Saint Fillie,
Neither those other saintships will I
Here go about for to recite
Their number almost infinite, 35
Which one by one here set down are
In this most curious calendar.
First, at the entrance of the gate
A little puppet-priest doth wait,
Who squeaks to all the comers there, 40
'Favour your tongues, who enter here.
Pure hands bring hither, without stain.'
A second pules, *'Hence, hence, profane.'*
Hard by, i' th' shell of half a nut,
The holy water there is put; 45
A little brush of squirrels' hairs
(Composed of odd, not even pairs)
Stands in the platter, or close by,
To purge the Fairy family.
Near to the altar stands the priest, 50
There offering up the holy grist;
Ducking in mood, and perfect tense,
With (much-good-do-'t him) reverence.

---

28 *Saint Tit*, etc.: type-diminutives; Tit, for example, is 'apparently of ono-
matopoeic origin, as a term for a small animal or object' (*SOED*). 37 *calendar*:
register of saints. 41–3 *Favour your tongues*, etc.: *Favete linguis*, etc.; Latin tags
quoted from 'Saint Ben' Jonson's *Sejanus*, v. 171–7. 46 *brush*: aspergillum, or
holy-water 'sprinkler'. 51 *grist*: ground corn, meal.

The altar is not here four-square,
Nor in a form triangular;   55
Nor made of glass, or wood, or stone,
But of a little transverse bone,
Which boys and bruckled children call
(Playing for points and pins) 'cockal';
Whose linen drapery is a thin   60
Subtile and ductile codlin's skin,
Which o'er the board is smoothly spread,
With little seal-work damaskèd.
The fringe that circumbinds it, too,
Is spangle-work of trembling dew,   65
Which, gently gleaming, makes a show,
Like frost-work glittering on the snow.
Upon this fetuous board doth stand
Something for showbread, and at hand
(Just in the middle of the altar)   70
Upon an end, the Fairy-Psalter,
Graced with the trout-fly's curious wings,
Which serve for watchet ribbonings.
Now, we must know, the Elves are led
Right by the rubric which they read;   75
And if report of them be true,
They have their text for what they do;
Ay, and their Book of Canons, too.
And as Sir Thomas Parson tells,
They have their Book of Articles;   80
And if that Fairy Knight not lies,
They have their Book of Homilies,

54–7 *The altar is not here*, etc.: ecclesiastical pleasantry based on disputes over
the proper materials and shape; generally speaking, the stone altar associated
with the Roman Catholic sacrifice of the mass became the wood 'communion
table' ('God's board', 1549 *Prayer Book*) of protestant Anglicanism.   58 *bruckled*:
begrimed.   59 *cockal*: knuckle-bone used in the game 'cockal', or 'dibs'.
68 *fetuous*: featous, elegant.   69 *showbread*: see G.   73 *watchet*: sky-blue
78, 80, 82 *Book[s] of Canons, Articles, Homilies*: Canons (passed 1604–6) were the
principal body of canonical legislation since the Reformation; *Articles*, finally
in 1563 the Thirty-Nine Articles, were the set of doctrinal formulas accepted
as defining essential Church of England dogma; *Homilies*, two books of sermons
originally designed to be read by disaffected and unlearned clergy, ranked
along with the *Book of Common Prayer* and the Thirty-Nine Articles as a
repository of Anglican doctrine.

And other scriptures that design
A short but righteous discipline.
The basin stands the board upon   85
To take the free oblation,
A little pin-dust, which they hold
More precious than we prize our gold;
Which charity they give to many
Poor of the parish (if there's any).   90
Upon the ends of these neat rails
(Hatched with the silver-light of snails)
The Elves, in formal manner, fix
Two pure and holy candlesticks,
In either which a small tall bent   95
Burns for the altar's ornament.
For sanctity, they have, to these,
Their curious copes and surplices
Of cleanest cobweb hanging by
In their religious vestery.   100
They have their ash-pans and their brooms
To purge the chapel and the rooms;
Their many mumbling mass-priests here,
And many a dapper chorister;
Their ushering vergers here, likewise,   105
Their canons and their chanteries;
Of cloister-monks they have enow,
Ay, and their abbey-lubbers, too:
And if their legend do not lie,
They much affect the papacy;   110
And since the last is dead, there's hope
Elve Boniface shall next be pope.
They have their cups and chalices,
Their pardons and indulgences;
Their beads of nits, bells, books, and wax   115
Candles (forsooth) and other knacks;
Their holy oil, their fasting-spittle;
Their sacred salt, here (not a little);

92 *hatched*: inlaid.   95 *bent*: stiff grass.   109 *legend*: strictly, collection of saints'
lives.   115 *beads of nits*: rosaries of insect-eggs (or as some say 'nuts', which
seem large, however, for the users).   117 *fasting-spittle*: saliva of a fasting person.

Dry chips, old shoes, rags, grease, and bones,
Beside their fumigations   120
To drive the Devil from the codpiece
Of the friar (of work an odd piece);
Many a trifle, too, and trinket,
And for what use, scarce man would think it.
Next, then, upon the chanter's side   125
An apple's core is hung up dried,
With rattling kernels, which is rung
To call to morn- and evensong.
The saint to which the most he prays,
And offers incense nights and days,   130
The Lady of the Lobster is,
Whose foot-pace he doth stroke and kiss,
And, humbly, chives of saffron brings
For his most cheerful offerings.
When, after these, h'as paid his vows,   135
He lowly to the altar bows;
And then he dons the silkworm's shed
(Like a Turk's turban on his head)
And reverently departeth thence,
Hid in a cloud of frankincense;   140
And, by the glow-worm's light well guided,
Goes to the feast that's now provided.

---

125 *chanter's side* (*cantoris*) opposite the dean's side (*decani*) of
the choir.   131 *Lady of the Lobster*: part of a lobster's stomach 'fancifully
supposed to resemble the outline of a seated female figure' (Martin, p. 521).
132 *foot-pace*: a step, carpet, or mat; prie-dieu.   137 *shed*: cocoon (corresponding
to a priest's biretta).   142 *the feast*, etc.: 'Oberon's Feast' (H–100), presumably.

79

To Mistress Katherine Bradshaw, the Lovely,
That Crowned Him with Laurel

My muse in meads has spent her many hours,
Sitting, and sorting several sorts of flowers,
To make for others garlands, and to set
On many a head, here, many a coronet;
But, amongst all encircled here, not one   5
Gave her a day of coronation,
Till you, sweet mistress, came and interwove
A laurel for her, ever young as love;
You first of all crowned her: she must, of due,
Render for that a crown of life to you.   10

80

The Plaudite, *or End of Life*

If after rude and boisterous seas
My wearied pinnace here finds ease,
If so it be I've gained the shore
With safety of a faithful oar;
If having run my bark on ground   5
Ye see the aged vessel crowned,
What's to be done, but on the sands
Ye dance, and sing, and now clap hands?
The first act's doubtful, but (we say)
It is the last commends the play.   10

79. Martin gives details about her (p. 521). 10 *crown of life*: from Rev. 2: 10.

80. *Plaudite*: 'Applaud', Latin imperative plural addressed to Roman theatre audiences at the end of a performance.

81

To the Most Virtuous Mistress Pot,
Who Many Times Entertained Him

When I through all my many poems look,
And see yourself to beautify my book,
Methinks that only lustre doth appear
A light fulfilling all the region here.
Gild still with flames this firmament, and be   5
A lamp eternal to my poetry,
Which, if it now or shall hereafter shine,
'Twas by your splendour, lady, not by mine.
The oil was yours; and that I owe for yet:
He pays the half who does confess the debt.   10

82

To Music, To Becalm His Fever

Charm me asleep, and melt me so
    With thy delicious numbers
That, being ravished, hence I go
    Away in easy slumbers.
        Ease my sick head,   5
        And make my bed,
    Thou power that canst sever
        From me this ill,
        And quickly still,
        Though thou not kill,   10
            My fever.

Thou sweetly canst convert the same
    From a consuming fire
Into a gentle-licking flame,
    And make it thus expire.   15
        Then make me weep
        My pains asleep,

---

81. *Pot*: a drinking vessel.   **10** *He pays*, etc.: proverbial (Tilley C 589).

And give me such reposes
  That I, poor I,
  May think thereby   20
  I live and die
    'Mongst roses.

Fall on me like a silent dew,
  Or like those maiden showers
Which by the peep of day do strew   25
  A baptism o'er the flowers.
    Melt, melt my pains
    With thy soft strains,
That, having ease me given,
    With full delight,   30
    I leave this light,
    And take my flight
      For heaven.

83

Upon Julia's Breasts

Display thy breasts, my Julia; there let me
Behold that circummortal purity,
Between whose glories there my lips I'll lay,
Ravished in that fair *Via Lactea*.

84

No Lock against Lechery

Bar close as you can, and bolt fast too your door,
To keep out the lecher, and keep in the whore;
Yet, quickly you'll see by the turn of a pin
The whore to come out, or the lecher come in.

83. 2 *circummortal*: probably of Herrick's coinage to mean 'beyond or above mortal', as Martin notes (p. 521); the root-meaning of *circum*, 'around', is apt. 4 *Via Lactea*: Milky Way.

85

To Music, To Becalm a Sweet-Sick Youth

Charms that call down the moon from out her sphere,
On this sick youth work your enchantments here:
Bind up his senses with your numbers so
As to entrance his pain, or cure his woe.
Fall gently, gently, and a while him keep   5
Lost in the civil wilderness of sleep;
That done, then let him, dispossessed of pain,
Like to a slumbering bride, awake again.

86

The Hock-Cart, or Harvest Home: to the Right Honourable Mildmay, Earl of Westmorland

Come, sons of summer, by whose toil
We are the lords of wine and oil,
By whose tough labours and rough hands
We rip up first, then reap our lands.
Crowned with the ears of corn now come,   5
And, to the pipe, sing harvest home.
Come forth, my lord, and see the cart
Dressed up with all the country art.
See here a malkin, there a sheet,
As spotless pure as it is sweet;   10
The horses, mares, and frisking fillies
(Clad all in linen, white as lilies);
The harvest swains and wenches bound
For joy to see the hock-cart crowned.
About the cart, hear how the rout   15
Or rural younglings raise the shout,

85. *Sweet-Sick*: sick of an excess of confections or affection.

86. *Harvest Home*: the festival to celebrate the successful 'homing' of the harvest. Mildmay Fane (d. 1666), second Earl of Westmorland (1628), was the author of *Otia Sacra* (1648). 9 *malkin*: mop; scarecrow.

Pressing before, some coming after,
Those with a shout, and these with laughter.
Some bless the cart, some kiss the sheaves,
Some prank them up with oaken leaves,   20
Some cross the fill-horse, some with great
Devotion stroke the home-borne wheat;
While other rustics, less attent
To prayers than to merriment,
Run after with their breeches rent.   25
Well, on, brave boys, to your lord's hearth,
Glittering with fire, where for your mirth
Ye shall see first the large and chief
Foundation of your feast, fat beef;
With upper stories, mutton, veal,   30
And bacon (which makes full the meal);
With several dishes standing by,
As here a custard, there a pie,
And here all tempting frumenty.
And for to make the merry cheer,   35
If smirking wine be wanting here,
There's that which drowns all care, stout beer;
Which freely drink to your lord's health,
Then to the plough (the commonwealth),
Next to your flails, your fans, your fats;   40
Then to the maids with wheaten hats,
To the rough sickle, and crook'd scythe,
Drink, frolic boys, till all be blithe.
Feed, and grow fat; and as ye eat
Be mindful that the lab'ring neat,   45
As you, may have their fill of meat.
And know, besides, ye must revoke
The patient ox unto the yoke,
And all go back unto the plough
And harrow, though they're hanged up now.   50
And, you must know, your lord's word's true,
Feed him ye must, whose food fills you,

---

21 *cross the fill-horse*: make the sign of the cross over the shaft-horse.   34 *frumenty*: from Latin *frumentum* 'corn, grain'; hulled wheat boiled in milk and seasoned with cinnamon, sugar, etc. (the 'furmity' of Hardy's *Mayor of Casterbridge* that, spiked with rum, led to Michael Henchard's undoing).   40 *fans*: winnowing-fans ('fanes', *H 48*). *fats*: vats.

And that this pleasure is like rain,
Not sent ye for to drown your pain,
But for to make it spring again.   55

87

The Perfume

Tomorrow, Julia, I betimes must rise,
For some small fault, to offer sacrifice:
The altar's ready, fire to consume
The fat; breathe thou, and there's the rich perfume.

88

Upon Her Voice

Let but thy voice engender with the string,
And angels will be born while thou dost sing.

89

Not to Love

He that will not love must be
My scholar, and learn this of me:
There be in love as many fears
As the summer's corn has ears;
Sighs, and sobs, and sorrows more   5
Than the sand that makes the shore;
Freezing cold, and fiery heats,
Fainting swoons, and deadly sweats;
Now an ague, then a fever,
Both tormenting lovers ever.   10

---

55 *spring*: (1) rise, in general and as a stream of water rises (cf. 'drown', l. 54); (2) spring, the season; (3) grow.

Wouldst thou know, besides all these,
How hard a woman 'tis to please?
How cross, how sullen, and how soon
She shifts and changes like the moon?
How false, how hollow she's in heart?   15
And how she is her own least part?
How high she's prized, and worth but small?
Little thou'lt love, or not at all.

90a

To Music: A Song

Music, thou queen of heaven, care-charming spell,
        That strik'st a stillness into hell:
Thou that tam'st tigers and fierce storms (that rise)
        With thy soul-melting lullabies:
Fall down, down, down, from those thy chiming spheres,   5
To charm our souls, as thou enchant'st our ears.

90b

Music

Music, thou Soul of Heaven, care-charming spell,
        Who strikes a stillness into hell;
Thou whose accents and conspiring tones
        Gives life and motion unto stones;

90a. 3 *tigers*: *H 48* has a comma, which for some confuses the sense and may have led to an editorial 'correction' (see H–90b: 5–6 n.).

90b. This poem, of which a version of ll. 1–2 and 5–8 makes up the *Hesperides* text of H–90a, was first printed from a seventeenth-century manuscript (Bodleian MS. Eng. Poet. c. 50) by Margaret Crum in 'An Unpublished Fragment of Verse by Herrick', *RES* xi (1960), 186–9. She writes that the MS. 'includes copies for whose variants the most natural explanation is that they represent a stage before the last correction'. This is an edited and modernized text of the diplomatic transcription printed in *RES*. 4 *gives*: third-person plural in -s was common (Abbott, sec. 333).

D

Thou that tam'st tigers, and fierce storms doth raise   5
    With thy soul-melting lullabies;
Fall down from those thy chiming spheres
And charm our souls, as thou enchants our ears.

If the sweet Thracian could with his soft numbers
    Lull the mad Furies into slumbers,   10
If that Arion could allure to swim
    The blue-backed Dolphin after him,
Or if Amphion stones to kiss could bring
    With his delicioüs singíng,
Thy circumfusèd rapture much more then   15
Must move to love us softer-moulded men.

91

To the Western Wind

Sweet Western Wind, whose luck it is
    (Made rival with the air)
To give Perenna's lip a kiss
    And fan her wanton hair,

Bring me but one, I'll promise thee,   5
    Instead of common showers,
Thy wings shall be embalmed by me,
    And all beset with flowers.

---

5 *Thou that tam'st tigers*: taming wild beasts by his lyric powers was Orpheus' speciality.   5–6 *doth raise*: possibly a scribal sophistication, because both the sense and the rhyme are imperfect by seventeenth-century as well as modern measures; 'rise' (as in 'To Music') rhymes with 'lullabies', but 'raise' does not; 'rase' (sweep away, destroy completely) gives a plausible sense, but Herrick nowhere (else) uses it.   9 *the sweet Thracian*: Orpheus (see G).   11 *Arion*: a semi-mythical poet who was carried to land by a dolphin charmed by the song he had been allowed to sing before being thrown overboard by pirates.   13 *Amphion*: a legendary musician (see G).

92

How Roses Came Red

Roses at first were white,
　Till they could not agree,
Whether my Sappho's breast
　Or they more white should be.

But being vanquished quite,　　　　　　5
　A blush their cheeks bespread;
Since which (believe the rest)
　The roses first came red.

93

How Violets Came Blue

Love on a day (wise poets tell)
　Some time in wrangling spent,
Whether the violets should excel,
　Or she, in sweetest scent.

But Venus having lost the day,　　　　5
　Poor girls, she fell on you;
And beat ye so (as some dare say),
　Her blows did make ye blue.

94

Upon Groins: Epigram

Groins, for his fleshly burglary of late,
Stood in the holy-forum candidate:
The word is Roman, but in English known;
Penance, and standing so, are both but one.

95

To the Willow Tree

Thou art to all lost love the best,
    The only true plant found,
Wherewith young men and maids distressed
    And left of love are crowned.

When once the lover's rose is dead   5
    Or laid aside forlorn,
Then willow garlands 'bout the head,
    Bedewed with tears, are worn.

When with neglect (the lover's bane)
    Poor maids rewarded be   10
For their love lost, their only gain
    Is but a wreath from thee.

And underneath thy cooling shade
    (When weary of the light),
The love-spent youth, and love-sick maid,   15
    Come to weep out the night.

---

94. 2 *holy-forum*: 'Herrick puns on *holey* and *fore-room*' (Patrick, p. 146).
2–4 *Stood . . . candidate*, etc.: a Roman *candidatus* was so called because he wore
a glittering white (*candida*) toga.   3–4 *the word . . . penance*: *paenitentia*; allusion
is made to the English punishment for fornication, by which the 'penitent'
stood in a sheet before his parish church's congregation on three successive
Sundays. Thus penitent and candidate are the same.

96

To Anthea, Who May Command Him Anything

Bid me to live, and I will live
   Thy protestant to be;
Or bid me love, and I will give
   A loving heart to thee.

A heart as soft, a heart as kind,   5
   A heart as sound and free,
As in the whole world thou canst find,
   That heart I'll give to thee.

Bid that heart stay, and it will stay,
   To honour thy decree;   10
Or bid it languish quite away,
   And 't shall do so for thee.

Bid me to weep, and I will weep,
   While I have eyes to see;
And having none, yet I will keep   15
   A heart to weep for thee.

Bid me despair, and I'll despair,
   Under that cypress tree;
Or bid me die, and I will dare
   E'en death to die for thee.   20

Thou art my life, my love, my heart,
   The very eyes of me;
And hast command of every part,
   To live and die for thee.

---

96. 2 *protestant*: one who protests devotion, a suitor (possibly with a turn on the
religious-sectarian sense).

97

To Meadows

Ye have been fresh and green,
　　Ye have been filled with flowers;
And ye the walks have been
　　Where maids have spent their hours.

You have beheld how they   5
　　With wicker arks did come
To kiss, and bear away
　　The richer cowslips home.

Y'ave heard them sweetly sing,
　　And seen them in a round,   10
Each virgin, like a spring,
　　With honeysuckles crowned.

But now we see none here,
　　Whose silvery feet did tread,
And with dishevelled hair   15
　　Adorned this smoother mead.

Like unthrifts, having spent
　　Your stock and needy grown,
Y'are left here to lament
　　Your poor estates, alone.   20

98

Crosses

Though good things answer many good intents,
Crosses do still bring forth the best events.

99

A Nuptial Song, or Epithalamy, on Sir Clipsby Crew and His Lady

What's that we see from far? the spring of day
Bloomed from the east, or fair enjewelled May
    Blown out of April, or some new
    Star filled with glory to our view,
          Reaching at heaven, 5
To add a nobler planet to the seven?
    Say, or do we not descry
Some goddess in a cloud of tiffany
    To move, or rather the
    Emergent Venus from the sea? 10

'Tis she! 'Tis she! or else some more divine
Enlightened substance; mark how from the shrine
    Of holy saints she paces on,
    Treading upon vermilion
          And amber, spice- 15
ing the chafed air with fumes of Paradise.
    Then come on, come on, and yield
A savour like unto a blessed field,
    When the bedabbled morn
    Washes the golden ears of corn. 20

See where she comes, and smell how all the street
Breathes vineyards and pomegranates: oh, how sweet!
    As a fired altar is each stone,
    Perspiring pounded cinnamon.
          The phoenix-nest, 25
Built up of odours, burneth in her breast.
    Who therein would not consume
His soul to ash-heaps in that rich perfume,

99. *Sir Clipsby Crew*: lived 1599–1648; matriculated at St. John's College, Cambridge, 1616; admitted to Lincoln's Inn, 1619; knighted 1620; at St. Margaret's Westminster, married Jane (1609–39), second daughter of Sir John Pulteney, of Misterton, Leicester, 1625. 8 *tiffany*: transparent silk (from *theophany* 'god-showing'). 18 *a savour*, etc.: Gen. 27: 27 speaks of 'the smell of a field which the Lord hath blessed'. 25 *phoenix*: a mythical bird (see G); it reappears by allusion in ll. 137-40.

Bestroking Fate the while
He burns to embers on the pile?   30

Hymen, O Hymen! Tread the sacred ground;
Show thy white feet, and head with marjoram crowned;
     Mount up thy flames, and let thy torch
     Display the bridegroom in the porch,
          In his desires   35
More towering, more disparkling than thy fires;
     Show her how his eyes do turn
And roll about, and in their motions burn
          Their balls to cinders; haste,
          Or else to ashes he will waste.   40

Glide by the banks of virgins, then, and pass
The showers of roses, lucky four-leaved grass,
     The while the cloud of younglings sing,
     And drown ye with a flowery spring;
          While some repeat   45
Your praise, and bless you, sprinkling you with wheat;
     While that others do divine,
Blest is the bride on whom the sun doth shine;
          And thousands gladly wish
          You multiply, as doth a fish.   50

And beauteous bride we do confess y'are wise
In dealing forth these bashful jealousies:
     In Love's name do so, and a price
     Set on yourself by being nice;
          But yet take heed: 55
What now you seem, be not the same indeed,
     And turn apostate; Love will
Part of the way be met or sit stone-still.
          On, then, and though you slow-
          ly go, yet, howsoever, go.   60

31 *Hymen*: god of marriage, represented as a youth carrying a torch. 36
disparkling: a resonant (sometimes corrupt) form of 'disparpling': scattering
abroad, dispersing, 'wide-spreading'. 47 *divine*: practise divination. 50 *You
multiply, as doth a fish*: an odd expression that has close parallels in 'The Entertainment' (H–105), 'Fishlike, increase then [in bed] to a million' (l. 12), and in the
last line of 'The May-Pole', 'Then multiply all, like to fishes.' Cf. Gen. 1 : 21–2.

And now y'are entered; see, the coddled cook
Runs from his torrid zone to pry, and look,
    And bless his dainty mistress; see,
    The aged point out, 'This is she,
        Who now must sway   65
The house (Love shield her) with her yea and nay';
    And the smirk butler thinks it
Sin, in's nap'ry, not to express his wit:
        Each striving to devise
    Some gin wherewith to catch your eyes.   70

To bed, to bed, kind turtles, now, and write
This the short'st day, and this the longest night,
    But yet too short for you; 'tis we
    Who count this night as long as three,
        Lying alone,   75
Telling the clock strike ten, eleven, twelve, one.
    Quickly, quickly then prepare,
And let the young men and the bridemaids share
        Your garters, and their joints
    Encircle with the bridegroom's points.   80

By the bride's eyes, and by the teeming life
Of her green hopes, we charge ye, that no strife
    (Farther than gentleness tends) gets place
    Among ye, striving for her lace:
        O do not fall   85
Foul in these noble pastimes, lest ye call
    Discord in, and so divide
The youthful bridegroom and the fragrant bride,
        Which Love forfend! but spoken
    Be't to your praise, no peace was broken.   90

---

61 *coddled*: boiled gently, stewed.   67 *smirk*: neat, trim.   68 *nap'ry*: the making-
up of household and table linen.   70 *gin*: snare, trap.   71 *turtles*: turtle-doves.
80 *points*: tagged laces for attaching hose to doublet.   87 *discord*: semi-
personification: Eris, goddess of discord.

Strip her of springtime, tender-whimpering maids,
Now autumn's come, when all these flowery aids
    Of her delays must end; dispose
    That lady-smock, that pansy, and that rose
        Neatly apart;   95
But for prick-madam and for gentle-heart,
    And soft maiden's-blush, the bride
Makes holy these; all others lay aside:
        Then strip her, or unto her
    Let him come who dares undo her.   100

And to enchant ye more, see everywhere
About the roof a siren in a sphere
    (As we think), singing to the din
    Of many a warbling cherubin:
        O mark ye how   105
The soul of nature melts in numbers; now
    See, a thousand Cupids fly,
To light their tapers at the bride's bright eye.
        To bed, or her they'll tire,
    Were she an element of fire.   110

And to your more bewitching, see the proud,
Plump bed bear up, and swelling like a cloud,
    Tempting the two too modest; can
    Ye see it brustle like a swan,
        And you be cold   115
To meet it when it woos and seems to fold
    The arms to hug you? Throw, throw
Yourselves into the mighty overflow
        Of that white pride, and drown
    The night with you in floods of down.   120

102-6 *siren in a sphere*, etc.: a Renaissance-classicized version of heavenly harmony in the Christian-Platonized Ptolemaic cosmology: Intelligences and spheres make music akin to that of heaven itself. See G and Sir John Davies's 'Orchestra' (1594). 114 *brustle*: bristle, raise the feathers. 117 *you*. H 48 reads 'it', but all MSS. (and Martin) read 'you'. 119 *that white pride*: allusion to the myth of Leda and the swan (Zeus).

The bed is ready, and the maze of love
Looks for the treaders; everywhere is wove
   Wit and new mystery; read, and
   Put in practice, to understand
      And know each wile,   125
Each hieroglyphic of a kiss or smile;
   And do it to the full; reach
High in your own conceit, and some way teach
     Nature and art one more
     Play than they ever knew before.   130

If needs we must, for ceremony's sake,
Bless a sack posset, luck go with it; take
   The night-charm quickly; you have spells,
   And magics for to end, and hells
      To pass; but such   135
And of such torture as no one would grutch
   To live therein for ever: fry
And consume, and grow again to die,
     And live, and in that case
     Love the confusion of the place.   140

But since It must be done, dispatch, and sew
Up in a sheet your bride, and what if so
   It be with rock, or walls of brass,
   Ye tower her up, as Danae was;
      Think you that this   145
Or hell itself a powerful bulwark is?
   I tell ye no; but like a
Bold bolt of thunder he will make his way,
     And rend the cloud, and throw
     The sheet about like flakes of snow.   150

---

122 *treaders*: (1) pacers, (2) lovers (*tread* 'of birds: to copulate', *SOED*). 123
mystery: also in the obsolete sense of art, craft. 128 *conceit*: conception. 132 *sack
posset*: hot milk curdled with sack (see G), sugar, and spices. 136 *grutch*: grudge.
140 *confusion*: destruction, death; a strong word in earlier usage, here with
allusion to the death (and rebirth) of the phoenix (q.v. in G). 141 *It*: capital-
ized in *H 48*, hardly by accident. 141–50 *sew | Up in a sheet*, etc.: the ancient
bride-bedding ceremonies also included casting off the bride's left stocking.
144 *Danae*: see G.

All now is hushed in silence; Midwife-Moon,
With all her owl-eyed issue; begs a boon
　　　Which you must grant, that's entrance; with
　　　Which extract all we can call pith
　　　　　And quintessence   155
Of planetary bodies; so commence
　　　All fair constellations
Looking upon ye, that two nations
　　　　　Springing from two such fires
May blaze the virtue of their sires.   160

100

Oberon's Feast

Shapcott! to thee the Fairy State
I with discretion dedicate,
Because thou prizest things that are
Curious and unfamiliar.
Take first the feast; these dishes gone,   5
We'll see the Fairy Court anon.

A little mushroom table spread,
After short prayers they set on bread:
A moon-parched grain of purest wheat,
With some small glittering grit to eat   10
His choice bits with; then in a trice
They make a feast less great than nice.
But all this while his eye is served,
We must not think his ear was sterved,

158 *two nations*: 'And the Lord said unto her [Rebekah], two nations are in thy womb' (Gen. 25: 23).

100. This, one of Herrick's four 'Fairy' or 'Oberon Poems', seems to follow directly after 'The Fairy Temple' (H–78), which ends, '[He,] by the glow-worm's light well guided, / Goes to the feast that's now provided' (ll. 141–2). 1 *Shapcott*: Herrick's 'peculiar [i.e. particular] Friend, Master Thomas Shapcott, Lawyer' (in another title), 1587–1670. 6 *anon*: that is, in 'Oberon's Palace' (H–129).

But that there was in place to stir   15
His spleen the chirring grasshopper,
The merry cricket, puling fly,
The piping gnat for minstrelsy.
And now we must imagine, first,
The Elves present to quench his thirst   20
A pure seed-pearl of infant dew,
Brought and besweetened in a blue
And pregnant violet; which done,
His kitling eyes begin to run
Quite through the table, where he spies   25
The horns of papery butterflies,
Of which he eats, and tastes a little
Of that we call the cuckoo's spittle.
A little fuzz-ball pudding stands
By, yet not blessèd by his hands;   30
That was too coarse; but then forthwith
He ventures boldly on the pith
Of sugared rush, and eats the sag
And well bestrutted bee's sweet bag,
Gladding his palate with some store   35
Of emmet's eggs; what would he more?
But beards of mice, a newt's stewed thigh,
A bloated earwig, and a fly;
With the red-capped worm that's shut
Within the concave of a nut   40
Brown as his tooth; a little moth,
Late fattened in a piece of cloth;
With withered cherries, mandrake's ears,
Mole's eyes; to these, the slain-stag's tears,
The unctuous dewlaps of a snail,   45
The broke-heart of a nightingale

16 *spleen*: 'an abdominal organ consisting of a ductless gland . . . regarded as the seat of melancholy or morose feelings' and also as 'the seat of laughter or mirth' (*SOED*). 24 *kitling*: kitten. 28 *cuckoo's spittle*: a frothy secretion exuded by frog-hoppers to envelop the larvae. 29 *fuzz-ball*: puffball mushroom, probably *Lycoperdon perlatum*. 33-4 *sag and well bestrutted*: sagging and swollen. 36 *emmet's*: ant's. 46-7 *a nightingale | O'ercome in music*: as in a contest between a nightingale and a lute-player, of which literary accounts were common before and after Herrick; one of the most impressive is Crashaw's 'Music's Duel', an enlarged version of that in Famianus Strada's Latin *Prolusiones* (1617).

O'ercome in music; with a wine
Ne'er ravished from the flattering vine
But gently pressed from the soft side
Of the most sweet and dainty bride,   50
Brought in a dainty daisy, which
He fully quaffs up to bewitch
His blood to height; this done, commended
Grace by his priest; *the feast is ended.*

101

To Virgins

Hear, ye virgins, and I'll teach
What the times of old did preach.
Rosamond was in a bower
Kept, as Danae in a tower;
But yet Love (who subtle is)   5
Crept to that, and came to this.
Be ye locked up like to these,
Or the rich Hesperides;
Or those babies in your eyes,
In their crystal nunneries;   10
Notwithstanding, Love will win,
Or else force a passage in:
And as coy be as you can,
Gifts will get ye, or the man.

50 *bride*: possibly 'rose' (Broadbent, i. 177), but more likely bridewort, or
meadowsweet (Patrick, p. 163), of which 'it is reported that the flowers boiled in
wine and drunk do make the heart merry' (*Gerard's Herbal*, 1636, p. 245).

101. 3 *Rosamond*: Fair Rosamond Clifford, a mistress of Henry II, for whom the
King 'had made . . . a house of wonderful working, so that no man or woman
might come to her but he that was instructed by the King' (according to John
Stow); in this sequestering she resembled Danaë (l. 4; see G). The 'bower' is
explained by 'this house after some was named Labyrinthus, or Dedalus work,
wrought like unto a knot in a garden, called a maze'; thought by some to have
been poisoned by Henry's Queen, she was 'buried at Godstow in an house of
nuns, beside Oxford'. The legend is given literary from by Thomas Deloney,
Samuel Daniel, and Joseph Addison. 4 *Danae*: see G. 5–6 *Love (who subtle
is) | Crept*, etc.: proverbial, as 'Love will find a way' (Tilley L 531) and 'Love
will creep where it cannot go [i.e. walk]' (K 49). 8 See H–1 n. 9 *babies in
your eyes*: (1) *pupillae*, 'wards, minors', and the eyes' pupils; (2) the images of
others reflected in the eyes.

102

The Bellman

From noise of scare-fires rest ye free,
From murders *Benedicite*.
From all mischances that may fright
Your pleasing slumbers in the night,
Mercy secure ye all, and keep   5
The goblin from ye, while ye sleep.
Past one o'clock, and almost two,
My masters all, Good day to you.

103

On Himself

Here down my wearied limbs I'll lay,
My pilgrim's staff, my weed of gray,
My palmer's hat, my scallop's-shell,
My cross, my cord, and all, farewell.
For having now my journey done   5
(Just at the setting of the sun),
Here I have found a chamber fit
(God and good friends be thanked for it),
Where if I can a lodger be
A little while from tramplers free,   10
At my up-rising next, I shall,
If not requite, yet thank ye all.
Meanwhile, the Holy Rood hence fright
The fouler fiend and evil sprite
From scaring you or yours this night.   15

---

102. *The Bellman*: a town-crier, who also acted as night-watchman and gave the hours; the fictional speaker of the poem. 1 *scare-fires*: sudden fires that frighten.

103. 2 *weed*: garment. 3 *scallop's-shell*: a pilgrim's badge.

104

Upon a Child That Died

Here she lies, a pretty bud,
Lately made of flesh and blood;
Who as soon fell fast asleep,
As her little eyes did peep.
Give her strewings, but not stir   5
The earth that lightly covers her.

105

*The Entertainment, or Porch-Verse, at the Marriage of Master
Henry Northleigh and the Most Witty Mistress Lettice Yard*

Welcome! but yet no entrance, till we bless
First you, then you, and both for white success.
Profane no porch, young man and maid, for fear
Ye wrong the threshold-god that keeps peace here:
Please him, and then all good-luck will betide   5
You, the brisk bridegroom, you the dainty bride.
Do all things sweetly, and in comely wise;
Put on your garlands first, then sacrifice;
That done, when both of you have seemly fed,
We'll call on Night, to bring ye both to bed;   10
Where being laid, all fair signs looking on,
Fish-like, increase then to a million:
And milliöns of springtimes may ye have,
Which spent, one death bring to ye both one grave.

105. Henry Northleigh, of Alphington, Devon, and Lettice Yard were married
in 1639 at Walborough, Devon. *Porch-Verse*: 'the "Porch" seems to be that of
the bridegroom's house, . . . not that of the church' (Martin, p. 526). 2 *white*:
a tacit Latinism: *candidus*, 'white, fortunate'. 12 *Fish-like, increase*: see H–99:
50 and n.

106

The Good-Night, or Blessing

Blessings in abundance come
To the bride and to her groom;
May the bed, and this short night,
Know the fullness of delight!
Pleasures many here attend ye,   5
And ere long a boy Love send ye,
Curled and comely, and so trim,
Maids (in time) may ravish him.
Thus a dew of graces fall
On ye both; good night to all.   10

107

To Daffodils

Fair daffodils, we weep to see
    You haste away so soon:
As yet the early-rising sun
    Has not attained his noon.
            Stay, stay,   5
        Until the hasting day
            Has run
        But to the evensong;
And, having prayed together, we
        Will go with you along.   10

We have short time to stay, as you,
    We have as short a spring;
As quick a growth to meet decay,
    As you, or anything.
            We die,   15
        As your hours do, and dry
            Away,
        Like to the summer's rain;
Or as the pearls of morning's dew,
        Ne'er to be found again.   20

108

A New-Year's Gift Sent to Sir Simeon Steward

No news of navies burnt at seas;
No noise of late-spawned *Tityries*:
No closet plot, or open vent,
That frights men with a Parliament;
No new device, or late-found trick,   5
To read by th' stars the kingdom's sick;
No gin to catch the state, or wring
The free-born nostrils of the king,
We send to you; but here a jolly
Verse crowned with ivy, and with holly,   10
That tells of winter's-tales and mirth
That milkmaids make about the hearth,
Of Christmas sports, the wassail-bowl
That's tossed up after fox-i'-th'-hole,
Of blind-man-buff, and of the care   15
That young men have to shoe the mare;
Of Twelfth-tide cakes, of pease, and beans
Wherewith ye make those merry scenes,
Whenas ye choose your king and queen,
And cry out, 'Hey, for our town green';   20
Of ash-heaps, in the which ye use
Husbands and wives by streaks to choose;

108. Steward and Herrick were probably acquainted at Trinity Hall, Cambridge; both contributed to the corpus of 'Fairy Poems' written in the mid 1620s. 2 *Tityries*: H 48, 'Tittyries'; a secret social and political brotherhood made up of upper-class tavern roisterers who took their name, *Tityre Tues*, from the first line of Virgil's *Eclogues* ('Tityre tu', 'thou, Tityrus'). Contemporary references to their activities in 1623 prompt Martin to date this poem 1624. 4 *Parliament*: summoned in January to meet on 12 February 1624. 7 *gin*: snare, trap. 10 *crowned with ivy, and with holly*: appropriately, as the ancient Christmas carol 'The Holly and the Ivy' suggests. Both were probably adapted from pagan-Roman rites and customs: the holly was used in the Saturnalia, and the ivy was originally dedicated to Bacchus (as a supposed preventative of drunkenness). 14 *fox-i'-th'-hole*: a hopping game. 16 *shoe the mare*: a game, possibly of the 'pin the tail on the donkey' type. 19 *king and queen*: traditionally, the Bean King (*Rey de Habas*) of Twelfth Night, the Bean-King's festival, was the child who found the bean hidden in the Twelfth Night cake. 21 *ash-heaps*: hoppers for dissolving alkaline salts from ashes, here apparently as a kind of marital lottery.

Of crackling laurel, which fore-sounds
A plenteous harvest to your grounds;
Of these and suchlike things for shift   25
We send instead of New-Year's gift.
Read, then, and when your faces shine
With buxom meat and capering wine,
Remember us in cups full crowned,
And let our city-health go round,   30
Quite through the young maids and the men,
To the ninth number, if not ten;
Until the fired chestnuts leap
For joy to see the fruits ye reap
From the plump chalice, and the cup,   35
That tempts till it be tossèd up;
Then, as ye sit about your embers,
Call not to mind those fled Decembers;
But think on these, that are t' appear,
As daughters to the instant year;   40
Sit crowned with rosebuds, and carouse,
Till Liber Pater twirls the house
About your ears; and lay upon
The year your cares that's fled and gone.
And let the russet swains the plough   45
And harrow hang up resting now;
And to the bagpipe all address,
Till sleep takes place of weariness.
And thus, throughout, with Christmas plays
Frolic the full twelve holy-days.   50

42 *Liber Pater*: Bacchus.   43-4 That is, lay your cares upon the year, etc.
50 *holy-days*: holidays, but with an emphasis that the modern spelling lacks for
modern eyes; Herrick seems to differentiate, since he spells 'holiday' in H–336,
l. 16.

109

Matins, or Morning Prayer

When with the virgin morning thou dost rise,
Crossing thyself, come thus to sacrifice:
First wash thy heart in innocence, then bring
Pure hands, pure habits, pure, pure everything.
Next to the altar humbly kneel, and thence   5
Give up thy soul in clouds of frankincense.
Thy golden censers filled with odours sweet
Shall make thy actions with their ends to meet.

110

To Lar

No more shall I, since I am driven hence,
Devote to thee my grains of frankincense;
No more shall I from mantel-trees hang down,
To honour thee, my little parsley crown;
No more shall I (I fear me) to thee bring   5
My chives of garlic for an offering;
No more shall I, from henceforth, hear a choir
Of merry crickets by my country fire.
Go where I will, thou lucky Lar stay here,
Warm by a glittering chimney all the year.   10

110. Written, it would appear, in 1647, when Herrick was ejected from Dean
Prior by the Parliamentarians. On 'Lar(es)' see G.   3 *mantel-trees*: beams (later
stones or arches) across the opening of a fireplace, supporting the masonry
above.

III

His Age, Dedicated to His Peculiar Friend, Master John Wickes,
under the Name of Posthumus

Ah Posthumus! our years hence fly,
And leave no sound; nor piety,
    Or prayers, or vow
Can keep the wrinkle from the brow:
    But we must on,   5
As Fate does lead or draw us; none,
None, Posthumus, could ere decline
The doom of cruel Proserpine.

The pleasing wife, the house, the ground
Must all be left, no one plant found   10
    To follow thee,
Save only the curst cypress tree:
    A merry mind
Looks forward, scorns what's left behind;
Let's live, my Wickes, then, while we may,   15
And here enjoy our holiday.

W'ave seen the past-best times, and these
Will ne'er return; we see the seas
    And moons to wane,
But they fill up their ebbs again;   20
    But vanished man,
Like to a lily lost, ne'er can,
Ne'er can repullulate, or bring
His days to see a second spring.

---

111. Herrick's close friend, John Wickes (or Weeks), was at Cambridge with him,
and the two were ordained together at Peterborough in April 1623. Wickes was
rector of Shirwall, Devon, from 1627 at least until 1634; he eventually became
chaplain to Archbishop Laud, an association that suggests not only his but
Herrick's High Churchmanship. Wickes and Herrick were associated with
Endymion Porter, the friend and patron of many poets of the time. All MSS. of
the poem have two additional stanzas after l. 48.   1–4 A fairly close translation
of Horace, *Odes*, II. xiv. 1–4.   7–8 *None . . . Proserpine*: Horace, *Odes*, I. xxviii.
20. Proserpine, queen of the lower world and wife of Pluto, was sometimes
identified with Hecate; her Greek name, Persephone, was usually said to derive
from a phrase meaning 'bringer of fear'.   23 *repullulate*: bud or sprout again.

But on we must, and thither tend,   25
Where Anchus and rich Tullus blend
            Their sacred seed;
Thus has infernal Jove decreed;
            We must be made,
Ere long, a song, ere long, a shade.   30
Why, then, since life to us is short,
Let's make it full up by our sport.

Crown we our heads with roses, then,
And 'noint with Tyrian balm; for when
            We two are dead,   35
The world with us is burièd.
            Then live we free,
As is the air, and let us be
Our own fair wind, and mark each one
Day with the white and lucky stone.   40

We are not poor, although we have
No roofs of cedar, nor our brave
            Baiae, nor keep
Account of such a flock of sheep,
            Nor bullocks fed   45
To lard the shambles, barbels bred
To kiss our hands; nor do we wish
For Pollio's lampreys in our dish.

---

26 *Anchus and rich Tullus*: Horace adds 'pius Aeneas' to 'Tullus dives
et Ancus' (*Odes*, IV. vii. 14).   33 Cf. Wisd. 2: 8: 'Let us crown ourselves with
rosebuds, before they be withered.'   34 *Tyrian balm*: Patrick says 'purple
balm-wine'; 'Tyrian' is often virtually synonymous with 'purple', but 'balm' is
everywhere else used in the sense 'ointment', which also fits the ' 'noint' here.
43 *Baiae*: a fashionable Roman resort on an inlet of the Bay of Naples.
46 *shambles*: butchers' slaughter-house. *barbels*: large freshwater fish.   48
Pollio's lampreys: they were fed on a servant thrown into a pond by Vedius
Apollo.

If we can meet, and so confer,
Both by a shining salt-cellar;   50
      And have our roof,
Although not arched, yet weather-proof,
      And ceiling free
From that cheap-candle bawdery;
We'll eat our bean with that full mirth   55
As we were lords of all the earth.

Well, then, on what seas we are tossed,
Our comfort is, we can't be lost.
      Let the winds drive
Our bark; yet she will keep alive   60
      Amidst the deeps;
'Tis constancy, my Wickes, which keeps
The pinnace up, which, though she errs
I' th' seas, she saves her passengers.

Say we must part (sweet mercy bless   65
Us both i' th' sea, camp, wilderness),
      Can we so far
Stray, to become less circular
      Than we are now?
No, no, that selfsame heart, that vow   70
Which made us one, shall ne'er undo,
Or ravel so, to make us two.

Live in thy peace; as for myself,
When I am bruisèd on the shelf
      Of time, and show   75
My locks behung with frost and snow;
      When with the rheum,
The cough, the phthisic, I consume
Unto an almost-nothing; then,
The ages fled, I'll call again;   80

---

54 *cheap-candle bawdery*: the debate continues whether 'bawdery' means
'dirt' in the physical sense only or in both the physical and the figurative
('obscenity') senses.   68 *circular*: the circle was viewed as the perfect form: can
our friendship diminish through separation? The compasses of Donne's
'Valediction: Forbidding Mourning' make this notion strikingly concrete.
78 *phthisic*: pulmonary pneumonia, or consumption.

And with a tear compare these last
Lame and bad times with those are past,
     While Baucis by,
My old, lean wife, shall kiss it dry;
     And so we'll sit   85
By th' fire, foretelling snow and slit,
And weather by our aches grown
Now old enough to be our own

True calendars, as puss's ear
Washed o'er 's to tell what change is near;   90
     Then to assuage
The gripings of the chine by age,
     I'll call my young
Iülus to sing such a song
I made upon my Julia's breast,   95
And of her blush at such a feast.

Then shall he read that flower of mine
Enclosed within a crystal shrine;
     A primrose next;
A piece, then, of a higher text,   100
     For to beget
In me a more transcendent heat
Than that insinuating fire
Which crept into each aged sire

---

83 *Baucis*: Baucis and Philemon received the disguised Zeus and Hermes hospitably after they had been repulsed by the rich; for reward, at their request the house was turned into a temple with the couple as priest and priestess, who, years after, were simultaneously changed into trees. 86 *slit*: sleet. 87 *aches*: pronounced 'aitches'. 90 *Washed o'er 's*, etc.: as puss's ear is washed over to make the resulting static electricity barometric. *H 48* text reads 'or 's', which is 'corrected' in the Errata to 'o're,'. 92 *chine*: backbone. 94 *Iülus*: or Ascanius, Aeneas' (and the speaker's) son, claimed to be the ancestor of the Roman *gens* Julia, of which Julius Caesar was a member. 94–5 *such a song*, etc.: 'Upon the Nipples of Julia's Breast' (H–127). 97–8 *that flower*, etc.: 'The Lily in a Crystal'. 99 *primrose*: 'The Primrose'. 100 *a higher text*: one of the *Noble Numbers*? Responding to Phoebus' dismissing of the attractions of worldly fame, Lycidas says 'that strain I heard was of a higher mood' (l. 87).

When the fair Helen from her eyes   105
Shot forth her loving sorceries;
       At which I'll rear
Mine aged limbs above my chair,
         And, hearing it,
Flutter and crow, as in a fit   110
Of fresh concupiscence, and cry,
'No lust there's like to poetry!'

Thus frantic-crazy man (God wot),
I'll call to mind things half forgot,
       And oft between   115
Repeat the times that I have seen!
        Thus ripe with tears,
And twisting my Iülus' hairs,
Doting, I'll weep and say (in truth),
'Baucis, these were my sins of youth.'   120

Then next I'll cause my hopeful lad
(If a wild apple can be had)
       To crown the hearth
(Lar thus conspiring with our mirth);
        Then to infuse   125
Our browner ale into the cruse,
Which, sweetly spiced, we'll first carouse
Unto the *Genius* of the house.

Then the next health to friends of mine
(Loving the brave Burgundian wine),   130
       High sons of pith,
Whose fortunes I have frolicked with,
        Such as could well
Bear up the magic bough and spell,
And dancing 'bout the mystic thyrse   135
Give up the just applause to verse.

---

122 *wild apple*: that is, to provide logs. 124 *Lar*: household god (see G).
126 *cruse*: earthenware pot or jar. 128 *Genius*: tutelary spirit (see G). 131–6 In
the version of this poem shared by the MSS. (see Martin, p. 484), four friends
are named; these are identified certainly or tentatively by Martin (p. 529) and
Patrick (p. 184). 135 *thyrse*: see G.

To those, and then again to thee,
We'll drink, my Wickes, until we be
        Plump as the cherry,
Though not so fresh, yet full as merry   140
        As the cricket,
The untamed heifer, or the pricket,
Until our tongues shall tell our ears
We're younger by a score of years.

Thus, till we see the fire less shine   145
From th' embers than the kitling's eyne,
        We'll still sit up,
Sphering about the wassail cup
        To all those times
Which gave me honour for my rhymes;   150
The coal once spent, we'll then to bed,
Far more than night bewearièd.

112

To My Ill Reader

Thou saist my lines are hard,
    And I the truth will tell:
They are both hard and marred,
    If thou not read'st them well.

113

The Power in the People

Let kings command, and do the best they may,
The saucy subjects still will bear the sway.

142 *pricket*: a second-year buck.   146 *kitling*: kitten.   148 *sphering*: circling (cf. 'circular', l. 68).

112. A version of Martial I. xxxviii.

114

Nothing New

Nothing is new: we walk where others went.
There's no vice now but has his president.

115

*To the Most Fair and Lovely Mistress Anne Soame,
Now Lady Abdy*

So smell those odours that do rise
From out the wealthy spiceries;
So smells the flower of blooming clove,
Or roses smothered in the stove;
So smells the air of spicèd wine,   5
Or essences of jessamine;
So smells the breath about the hives,
When well the work of honey thrives,
And all the busy factors come
Laden with wax and honey home;   10
So smell those neat and woven bowers,
All over-arched with orange-flowers,
And almond blossoms, that do mix
To make rich these aromatics;
So smell those bracelets and those bands   15
Of amber chafed between the hands,
When thus enkindled they transpire
A noble perfume from the fire.

114. 'There is no new thing under the sun' (Eccles. 1: 9), and 'the sun also
ariseth' (1: 5). Herrick's 'president' loses some pertinent significance in the
usual modern spelling of the intended sense, 'precedent'.

115. Anne, daughter of Herrick's mother's sister Anne and Sir Thomas Soame
(1622–79); she was the second wife of Sir Thomas Abdy, who was created a
baronet on 3 December 1641; as Martin suggests (p. 531), '*now* Lady Abdy'
could have been added after the poem was written, and the title would seem
odd if that were not the case. As Pollard notes, the poem is modelled on
Martial, III. lxv. 4 *stove*: drying chamber or box. 6 *jessamine*: jasmine.
9 *factors*: workers. 16 *amber*[gris].

The wine of cherries, and to these
The cooling breath of raspises;   20
The smell of morning's milk and cream,
Butter of cowslips mixed with them,
Of roasted warden or baked pear,
These are not to be reckoned here;
Whenas the meanest part of her   25
Smells like the maiden-pomander.
Thus sweet she smells, or what can be
More liked by her, or loved by me.

116

A Panegyric to Sir Lewis Pemberton

Till I shall come again, let this suffice,
 I send my salt, my sacrifice,
To thee, thy lady, younglings, and as far
 As to thy *Genius* and thy Lar;
To the worn threshold, porch, hall, parlour, kitchen,   5
 The fat-fed smoking temple which in
The wholesome savour of thy mighty chines
 Invites to supper him who dines;
Where laden spits, warped with large ribs of beef,
 Not represent but give relief   10
To the lank stranger and the sour swain;
 Where both may feed, and come again,
For no black-bearded vigil from thy door
 Beats with a buttoned-staff the poor;
But from thy warm love-hatching gates each may   15
 Take friendly morsels, and there stay
To sun his thin-clad members, if he likes,
 For thou no porter keep'st who strikes.

---

20 *raspises*: raspberries.   23 *warden*: an old variety of baking pear.

116. Sir Lewis Pemberton matriculated at Christ's College, Cambridge, in 1609, was Sheriff of Nottinghamshire in 1621, and died in 1640. This poem belongs to the genre of the Country-House Poem (see G). As Patrick notes, the poem also shows the influence of Joseph Hall's *Virgidemiarum*, v. 2.   4 *Genius*: tutelary spirit (see G).   *Lar*: household god (see G).   7 *chines*: backbone cuts of meat.   13 *vigil*: a guard or watch (unusual, as is Milton's 'vigilance', for one who keeps a watch or vigil).   14 *buttoned-staff*: knobbed staff.

No comer to thy roof his guest-rite wants,
  Or, staying there, is scourged with taunts 20
Of some rough groom, who (yerked with corns) says, 'Sir,
  Y'ave dipped too long i' th' vinegar;
And, with our broth and bread, and bits, sir friend,
  Y'ave farcèd well, pray make an end;
Two days y'ave larded here; a third, ye know, 25
  Makes guests and fish smell strong; pray go
You to some other chimney, and there take
  Essay of other giblets; make
Merry at another's hearth; y'are here
  Welcome as thunder to our beer: 30
Manners knows distance, and a man unrude
  Would soon recoil, and not intrude
His stomach to a second meal.' No, no,
  Thy house, well fed and taught, can show
No such crabbed vizard: thou hast learnt thy train 35
  With heart and hand to entertain,
And by the arms-full (with a breast unhid),
  As the old race of mankind did,
When either's heart and either's hand did strive
  To be the nearer relative; 40
Thou dost redeem those times, and what was lost
  Of ancient honesty may boast
It keeps a growth in thee, and so will run
  A course in thy fame's-pledge, thy son.
Thus, like a Roman tribune, thou thy gate 45
  Early sets ope to feast, and late,
Keeping no currish waiter to affright,
  With blasting eye, the appetite,
Which fain would waste upon thy cates, but that
  The trencher-creature marketh what 50
Best and more suppling piece he cuts, and by
  Some private pinch tells danger's nigh,
A hand too desp'rate, or a knife that bites
  Skin deep into the pork, or lights
Upon some part of kid, as if mistook, 55
  When checkèd by the butler's look.

---

21 *yerked*: pinched. 24 *farced*: stuffed. 31 *knows*: third-person plural in -s
(Abbott, sec. 333). 50 *trencher-creature*: depreciative for a servant who carves.

No, no, thy bread, thy wine, thy jocund beer
    Is not reserved for Trebius here,
But all who at thy table seated are
    Find equal freedom, equal fare;   60
And thou, like to that hospitable god,
    Jove, joy'st when guests make their abode
To eat thy bullocks' thighs, thy veals, thy fat
    Wethers, and never grudgèd at.
The *pheasant, partridge, godwit, reeve, ruff, rail,*   65
    The *cock,* the *curlew,* and the *quail*;
These, and thy choicest viands, do extend
    Their taste unto the lower end
Of thy glad table: not a dish more known
    To thee than unto any one.   70
But as thy meat, so thy *immortal wine*
    Makes the smirk face of each to shine
And spring fresh rosebuds, while the salt, the wit,
    Flows from the wine, and graces it;
While reverence, waiting at the bashful board,   75
    Honours my lady and my lord.
No scurrile jest, no open scene is laid
    Here, for to make the face afraid;
But temperate mirth dealt forth, and so discreet-
    ly that it makes the meat more sweet,   80
And adds perfumes unto the wine, which thou
    Dost rather pour forth than allow
By cruse and measure; thus devoting wine
    As the Canary Isles were thine;
But with that wisdom, and that method, as   85
    No one that's there his guilty glass
Drinks of distemper, or has cause to cry
    Repentance to his liberty.
No, thou know'st order, ethics, and hast read
    All economics, know'st to lead   90
A house-dance neatly, and canst truly show
    How far a figure ought to go

---

58 *Trebius*: friend of the epicure Lucullus (Juvenal, v. 19).   72 *smirk*: smiling,
cheerful.   83 *cruse*: earthenware pot or jar.   87 *of distemper*: to excess.   89 *hast*:
H 48, 'ha's' (explained as a northern second-person-singular inflection).   92
figure: movement, or set of movements, in dancing.

Forward or backward, sideward, and what pace
    Can give and what retract a grace;
What gesture, courtship, comeliness agrees,   95
    With those thy primitive decrees,
To give subsistence to thy house, and proof
    What *Genii* support thy roof,
Goodness and greatness, not the oaken piles;
    For these and marbles have their whiles   100
To last, but not their ever: virtue's hand
    It is which builds 'gainst Fate to stand.
Such is thy house, whose firm foundation's trust
    Is more in thee than in her dust
Or depth; these last may yield and yearly shrink,   105
    When what is strongly built no chink
Or yawning rupture can the same devour,
    But fixed it stands, by her own power
And well-laid bottom, on the iron and rock,
    Which tries and counter-stands the shock   110
And ram of time, and by vexation grows
    The stronger; *Virtue dies when foes*
Are wanting to her exercise, but great
    And large she spreads by dust and sweat.
Safe stand thy walls and thee, and so both will,   115
    Since neither's height was raised by th' ill
Of others; since no stud, no stone, no piece,
    Was reared up by the poor man's fleece;
No widow's tenement was racked to gild
    Or fret thy ceiling, or to build   120
A sweating-closet to anoint the silk-
    soft skin, or bathe in ass's milk;
No orphan's pittance, left him, served to set
    The pillars up of lasting jet,
For which their cries might beat against thine ears,   125
    Or in the damp jet read their tears.
No plank from hallowed altar does appeal
    To yond Star Chamber, or does seal

---

128 *Star Chamber*: the court chiefly of criminal jurisdiction that developed from sittings of the King's Council in the Star Chamber at Westminster; the reference here is to the heavens and a higher court.

A curse to thee or thine; but all things even
    Make for thy peace, and pace to heaven.   130
Go on directly so, as just men may
    A thousand times more swear than say,
'This is that princely Pemberton, who can
    Teach man to keep a god in man';
And when wise poets shall search out to see   135
    Good men, they find them all in thee.

117

Upon Master Ben Jonson: Epigram

After the rare arch-poet Jonson died,
The sock grew loathsome, and the buskin's pride
Together with the stage's glory stood
Each like a poor and pitied widowhood.
The cirque profaned was, and all postures racked;   5
For men did strut, and stride, and stare, not act.
Then temper flew from words, and men did squeak,
Look red, and blow, and bluster, but not speak;
No holy-rage or frantic-fires did stir
Or flash about the spacious theatre.   10
No clap of hands, or shout, or praise's proof
Did crack the playhouse sides, or cleave her roof.
Artless the scene was, and that monstrous sin
Of deep and arrant ignorance came in;
Such ignorance as theirs was who once hissed   15
At thy unequalled play, *The Alchemist:*
Oh fie upon 'em! Lastly, too, all wit
In utter darkness did, and still will, sit
Sleeping the luckless age out, till that she
Her resurrection has again with thee.   20

117. 2 *sock . . . buskin*: sock (*soccus*) for comedy and buskin, or boot (*cothurnus*), for tragedy, from Roman theatrical costuming. 5 *cirque*: circus, or theatre.

118

A Canticle to Apollo

Play, Phoebus, on thy lute,
And we will all sit mute,
By listening to thy lyre
That sets all ears on fire.

Hark, hark, the god does play!   5
And as he leads the way
Through heaven, the very spheres,
As men, turn all to ears.

119

Clothes Do But Cheat and Cozen Us

Away with silks, away with lawn,
I'll have no scenes, or curtains drawn:
Give me my mistress as she is,
Dressed in her nak'd simplicities;
For as my heart, e'en so mine eye   5
Is won with flesh, not drapery.

---

118. *Canticle*: *canticulum*, diminutive of *canticum*, 'song'; ordinarily a song or prayer—other than one of the Psalms—taken from the Bible for Christian liturgical use. This poem is a good example of Herrick's fusion of Christianity and Greco-Roman classicism—in David/Apollo, for example.   7–8 *spheres, | As men, turn all to ears*: cf. Catullus, *Carm.* xiii, with its perfume that when smelled would make Fabullus wish to be all nose.

119. 2 *scenes*: painted hangings.

E

120

To Dianeme

Show me thy feet; show me thy legs, thy thighs;
Show me those fleshy principalities;
Show me that hill (where smiling Love doth sit)
Having a living fountain under it;
Show me thy waist; then let me therewithal,   5
By the ascension of thy lawn, see all.

121

To His Book

Have I not blessed thee? Then go forth; nor fear
Or spice, or fish, or fire, or close-stools here.
But with thy fair Fates leading thee, go on
With thy most white predestination.
Nor think these ages—that do hoarsely sing   5
'The Farting Tanner and Familiar King';
'The Dancing Friar', tattered in the bush;
Those monstrous lies of little Robin Rush,
Tom Chipperfield, and pretty-lisping Ned,
That doted on a maid of gingerbread;   10
'The Flying Pilcher', and 'The Frisking Dace',
With all the rabble of Tim-Trundle's race,
Bred from the dunghills, and adulterous rhymes—
Shall live, and thou not superlast all times.

---

120. *hill*: the *mons Veneris*.

121. 1 *nor fear*, etc.: Pollard: 'Herrick is remembering Persius, i. 43. To form
the paper jacket or *tunica* which wrapt the mackerel in Roman cookery seems
to have been the ultimate employment for many poems' (i. 309). 2 *close-stools*:
enclosed chamber-pots. 4 *white*: fortunate (after a poetical figurative usage of
candidus in Propertius and Tibullus). 6–11 '*The Farting Tanner*', etc.: the
references are to known or probable popular ballads. 12 *Tim-Trundle*: a
publisher, John Trundle, had registered 'The Farting Tanner' for printing in
December 1615.

No, no, thy stars have destined thee to see   15
The whole world die, and turn to dust with thee.
He's greedy of his life who will not fall,
Whenas a public ruin bears down all.

122

The Mad Maid's Song

Good morrow to the day so fair,
　Good morning, sir, to you;
Good morrow to mine own torn hair
　Bedabbled with the dew.

Good morning to this primrose, too;   5
　Good morrow to each maid,
That will with flowers the tomb bestrew
　Wherein my love is laid.

Ah woe is me, woe, woe is me,
　Alack and welladay!   10
For pity, sir, find out that bee
　Which bore my love away.

I'll seek him in your bonnet brave,
　I'll seek him in your eyes;
Nay, now I think th'ave made his grave   15
　I' th' bed of strawberries.

I'll seek him there; I know, ere this,
　The cold, cold earth doth shake him;
But I will go, or send a kiss
　By you, sir, to awake him.   20

Pray hurt him not; though he be dead,
　He knows well who do love him,
And who with green-turfs rear his head,
　And who do rudely move him.

He's soft and tender (pray take heed):   25
   With bands of cowslips bind him,
And bring him home; but 'tis decreed
   That I shall never find him.

123

To Sycamores

I'm sick of love; O let me lie
Under your shades, to sleep or die!
Either is welcome, so I have
Or here my bed or here my grave.
Why do you sigh, and sob, and keep   5
Time with the tears that I do weep?
Say, have ye sense, or do you prove
What crucifixions are in love?
I know ye do; and that's the why
You sigh for love as well as I.   10

124

The Poet Loves a Mistress, but Not To Marry

I do not love to wed,
   Though I do like to woo;
And for a maidenhead
   I'll bed and buy it, too.

I'll praise and I'll approve   5
   Those maids that never vary;
And fervently I'll love,
   But yet I would not marry.

I'll hug, I'll kiss, I'll play,
   And cock-like hens I'll tread,   10
And sport it any way
   But in the bridal bed.

For why? That man is poor
Who hath but one of many;
But crowned he is with store   15
That single may have any.

Why then, say, what is he
(To freedom so unknown)
Who, having two or three,
Will be content with one?   20

125

Upon Showbread: Epigram

Last night thou didst invite me home to eat,
And show'dst me there much plate, but little meat.
Prithee, when next thou dost invite, bar state
And give me meat, or give me else thy plate.

126

Upon Rook: Epigram

Rook he sells feathers, yet he still doth cry
'Fie on this pride, this female vanity'.
Thus, though the rook does rail against the sin,
He loves the gain that vanity brings in.

---

125. This poem is based on an epigram attributed to Martial (Loeb Library, ii. 520, No. II). *Showbread*: see G. 3 *bar state*: spare ceremony.

126. *Rook*: fig., a cheat, swindler, or sharper. 3 *rook . . . rail*: Herrick may intend ornithological wordplay, the rail being a name for the corn-crake.

127

Upon the Nipples of Julia's Breast

Have ye beheld (with much delight)
A red rose peeping through a white?
Or else a cherry (double graced)
Within a lily's centre placed?
Or ever marked the pretty beam   5
A strawberry shows half-drowned in cream?
Or seen rich rubies blushing through
A pure smooth pearl, and orient, too?
So like to this, nay, all the rest,
Is each neat niplet of her breast.   10

128

To Daisies, Not To Shut So Soon

Shut not so soon; the dull-eyed night
    Has not as yet begun
To make a seizure on the light,
    Or to seal up the sun.

No marigolds yet closèd are,   5
    No shadows great appear;
Nor doth the early shepherd's star
    Shine like a spangle here.

Stay but till my Julia close
    Her life-begetting eye;   10
And let the whole world then dispose
    Itself to live or die.

127. 4 *lily's* [Martin]: *H 48* has 'Lillie?'

129

Oberon's Palace

After the feast, my Shapcott, see,
The Fairy Court I give to thee;
Where we'll present our Oberon led
Half tipsy to the Fairy bed,
Where Mab he finds, who there doth lie   5
Not without mickle majesty;
Which done, and thence removed the light,
We'll wish both them and thee good night.

Full as a bee with thyme, and red
As cherry harvest, now high-fed   10
For lust and action, on he'll go,
To lie with Mab though all say no.
Lust has no ears; he's sharp as thorn,
And fretful, carries hay in's horn
And lightning in his eyes, and flings   15
Among the Elves (if moved) the stings
Of peltish wasps; well know his guard
Kings, though they're hated, will be feared.
Wine led him on. Thus to a grove
(Sometimes devoted unto Love)   20
Tinselled with twilight, he and they,
Led by the shine of snails, a way
Beat with their num'rous feet, which by
Many a neat perplexity,
Many a turn, and man' a cross-   25
Track they redeem a bank of moss,
Spongy and swelling, and far more
Soft than the finest Lemster ore,

129. One of Herrick's four 'Fairy Poems'; the first in *Hesperides* is 'The Fairy Temple' (H–78; see text and note).   1 *Shapcott*: Thomas Shapcott (1587–1670), a close friend.   6 *mickle*: great.   14 *hay in's horn*: Horace, *Sat.* i. iv. 34; from the custom of binding the horns as a warning of an ox supposed dangerous; the 'lightning' (l. 15) suggests 'horn' as a powder-flask.   17 *peltish*: angry.   *well* [MSS.]: 'we'l', *H 48.*   26 *redeem*: arrive at.   28 *Lemster ore*: presumably the wool for which Leominster was famous; if so, 'ore' is virtually unique in this figurative application.

Mildly disparkling, like those fires
Which break from the enjewelled tires   30
Of curious brides, or like those mites
Of candied dew in moony nights.
Upon this convex, all the flowers
(Nature begets by th' sun, and showers)
Are to a wild digestion brought,   35
As if Love's sampler here was wrought;
Or Cytherea's *ceston*, which
All with temptation doth bewitch.
Sweet airs move here, and more divine
Made by the breath of great-eyed kine,   40
Who as they low empearl with milk
The four-leaved grass, or moss like silk.
The breath of monkeys met to mix
With musk-flies are th' aromatics
Which cense this arch; and here and there,   45
And farther off, and everywhere,
Throughout that brave mosaic yard
Those picks or diamonds in the card,
With peeps of hearts, of club and spade,
Are here most neatly inter-laid.   50
Many a counter, many a die,
Half rotten, and without an eye,
Lies hereabouts; and, for to pave
The excellency of this cave,
Squirrels' and children's teeth late shed   55
Are neatly here enchequerèd
With brownest toadstones, and the gum
That shines upon the bluer plum;
The nails fall'n off by whitflaws: Art's
Wise hand enchasing here those warts   60

---

29 *disparkling*: ordinarily = *disparpling*, 'scattering abroad, dispersing', but Herrick clearly intends the sense of 'sparkle', too.   30 *tires*: head-dresses.
31 *curious*: elaborately dressed.   37 *Cytherea's ceston*: Venus's belt or girdle (*cestus*).   43 *monkeys*: 'monkey-flowers or figworts?' (Patrick, p. 223).   48 *picks*: playing-card diamonds, from their points.   48–54 MSS. give a twenty-nine-line version; see Martin, p. 486.   49 *peeps*: pips, spots.   51 *counter*: (1) imitation coin, token, or chip; (2) piece used in chess and draughts.   57 *toad-stones*: jewels supposed to be found in the heads of toads; cf. *AYL* II. i. 13–14.
59 *whitflaws*: whitlows; paronychia: finger-nail inflammation.

Which we to others (from ourselves)
Sell, and brought hither by the Elves.
The tempting mole, stol'n from the neck
Of the shy virgin, seems to deck
The holy entrance, where, within,   65
The room is hung with the blue skin
Of shifted snake: enfriezed throughout
With eyes of peacocks' trains, and trout-
Flies' curious wings; and these, among
Those silver-pence that cut the tongue   70
Of the red infant, neatly hung.
The glow-worm's eyes, the shining scales
Of silvery fish, wheat-straws, the snail's
Soft candle-light, the kitling's eyne,
Corrupted wood, serve here for shine.   75
No glaring light of bold-faced day
Or other over-radiant ray
Ransacks this room, but what weak beams
Can make, reflected from these gems,
And multiply; such is the light,   80
But ever doubtful day or night.
By this quaint taper-light he winds
His errors up; and now he finds
His moon-tanned Mab, as somewhat sick,
And (Love knows) tender as a chick.   85
Upon six plump dandillions, high-
Reared, lies her Elvish-majesty,
Whose woolly-bubbles seemed to drown
Her Mabship in obedient down;
For either sheet was spread the caul   90
That doth the infant's face enthrall
When it is born (by some enstyled
The lucky omen of the child),
And next to these, two blankets o'er-
Cast of the finest gossamore;   95
And then a rug of carded wool,
Which, sponge-like drinking in the dull

70–1 *those silver pence*, etc.: worn, sharp-edged coins used to cut the ligament of a
tongue-tied infant 'red' from frustration (Martin, p. 535, after *N & Q*, 1902,
p. 178).   83 *errors*: wanderings.   86 *dandillions*: dandelions.

Light of the moon, seemed to comply,
Cloud-like, the dainty deity.
Thus soft she lies; and overhead   100
A spinner's circle is bespread
With cobweb-curtains, from the roof
So neatly sunk as that no proof
Of any tackling can declare
What gives it hanging in the air;   105
The fringe about this are those threads
Broke at the loss of maidenheads;
And all behung with these pure pearls
Dropped from the eyes of ravished girls
Or writhing brides, when (panting) they   110
Give unto love the straiter way.
For music now, he has the cries
Of feignèd-lost virginities,
The which the Elves make to excite
A more unconquered appetite.   115
The king's undressed; and now upon
The gnat's watchword the Elves are gone,
And now the bed and Mab possessed
Of this great-little kingly guest.
We'll nobly think, what's to be done   120
He'll do, no doubt. *This flax is spun.*

130

Fame Makes Us Forward

To print our poems the propulsive cause
Is fame (the breath of popular applause).

98 *comply*: enfold.

131

To Groves

Ye silent shades, whose each tree here
Some relic of a saint doth wear,
Who, for some sweetheart's sake, did prove
The fire and martyrdom of love:
Here is the legend of those saints   5
That died for love; and their complaints,
Their wounded hearts, and names we find
Encarved upon the leaves and rind.
Give way, give way to me, who come
Scorched with the selfsame martyrdom;   10
And have deserved as much (Love knows)
As to be canonized 'mongst those
Whose deeds and deaths here written are
Within your greeny kalendar.
By all those virgins' fillets hung   15
Upon your boughs, and requiems sung
For saints and souls departed hence
(Here honoured still with frankincense);
By all those tears that have been shed,
As a drink-offering to the dead;   20
By all those true-love knots that be
With mottos carved on every tree;
By sweet Saint Phyllis pity me.
By dear Saint Iphis, and the rest
Of all those other saints now blest,   25
Me, me, forsaken, here admit
Among your myrtles to be writ:
That my poor name may have the glory
To live remembered in your story.

131. This poem is Herrick's counterpart of Donne's 'Canonization'.   14 *calendar*: register of saints.   23 *St. Phyllis*: during her lover Demophoön's prolonged absence she thought herself abandoned, hanged herself, and was turned into a tree that periodically leaved in mourning (Hyginus, *Fabulae*, lix).   24 *Iphis*: when Anaxarete failed to return his love, Iphis hanged himself; at his funeral Anaxarete turned to stone when she looked upon his body (Ovid, *Met.* xiv. 698–764).

132

An Epitaph upon a Virgin

Here a solemn fast we keep,
While all beauty lies asleep;
Hushed be all things; no noise here
But the toning of a tear,
Or a sigh of such as bring   5
Cowslips for her covering.

133

To Blossoms

Fair pledges of a fruitful tree,
      Why do ye fall so fast?
      Your date is not so past;
But you may stay yet here a while,
      To blush and gently smile;   5
            And go at last.

What, were ye born to be
      An hour or half's delight,
      And so to bid goodnight?
'Twas pity Nature brought ye forth   10
      Merely to show your worth,
            And lose you quite.

But you are lovely leaves, where we
      May read how soon things have
      Their end, though ne'er so brave: 15
And after they have shown their pride
      Like you a while, they glide
            Into the grave.

134

Man's Dying-Place Uncertain

Man knows where first he ships himself, but he
Never can tell where shall his landing be.

135

To a Bed of Tulips

Bright tulips, we do know
You had your coming hither;
And fading-time does show
That ye must quickly wither.

Your sister-hood may stay,   5
And smile here for your hour;
But die ye must away,
Ev'n as the meanest flower.

Come, virgins, then, and see
Your frailties, and bemoan ye;   10
For lost like these, 'twill be
As Time had never known ye.

136

To the Water Nymphs, Drinking at the Fountain

Reach, with your whiter hands, to me
Some crystal of the spring,
And I about the cup shall see
Fresh lilies flourishing.

Or else, sweet nymphs, do you but this: 5
    To th' glass your lips incline,
And I shall see by that one kiss
    The water turned to wine.

137

Upon Jack and Jill: Epigram

When Jill complains to Jack for want of meat,
Jack kisses Jill, and bids her freely eat.
Jill says, 'Of what?' Says Jack, 'On that sweet kiss,
Which full of nectar and ambrosia is,
The food of poets.' 'So I thought', says Jill.   5
'That makes them look so lank, so ghost-like still.
Let poets feed on air, or what they will;
Let me feed full, till that I fart', says Jill.

138

To Julia

Julia, when thy Herrick dies,
Close thou up thy poet's eyes;
And his last breath, let it be
Taken in by none but thee.

139

To His Kinswoman, Mistress Penelope Wheeler

Next is your lot, fair, to be numbered one,
    Here, in my book's canonization:
Late you come in; but you a saint shall be,
    In chief, in this poetic liturgy.

139. She was 'perhaps a daughter or sister-in-law of Elizabeth Wheeler'
(Martin, p. 539), who was Martha Herrick, daughter of Robert Herrick of
Leicester, the poet's uncle and godfather.

140

His Winding-Sheet

Come thou, who art the wine and wit
        Of all I've writ,
The grace, the glory, and the best
        Piece of the rest.
Thou art of what I did intend   5
        The all, and end.
And what was made, was made to meet
        Thee, thee my sheet.
Come, then, and be to my chaste side
        Both bed and bride.   10
We two (as relics left) will have
        One rest, one grave.
And, hugging close, we will not fear
        Lust entering here,
Where all desires are dead, or cold   15
        As is the mould;
And all affections are forgot,
        Or trouble not.
Here, here, the slaves and prisoners be
        From shackles free,   20
And weeping widows long oppressed
        Do here find rest.
The wrongèd client ends his laws
        Here, and his cause.
Here those long suits of Chancery lie   25
        Quiet, or die;
And all Star Chamber bills do cease,
        Or hold their peace.
Here needs no Court for our Request,
        Where all are best,   30

---

140. 25 *Chancery*: the Lord Chancellor's court, in Herrick's day the highest
court of judicature next to the House of Lords.   27 *Star Chamber*: a court of
jurisdiction primarily affecting the interests of the crown and noted for
arbitrary procedure; abolished in 1641.   29 *Court for our Request*: the Court of
Requests was held by the Lord Privy Seal and the Master of Requests for the
relief of persons petitioning the king; also abolished in 1641.

All wise, all equal, and all just
    Alike i' th' dust.
Nor need we here to fear the frown
    Of Court or Crown.
Where Fortune bears no sway o'er things,   35
    There all are kings.
In this securer place we'll keep,
    As lulled asleep;
Or for a little time we'll lie
    As robes laid by,   40
To be another day re-worn,
    Turned, but not torn;
Or, like old testaments engrossed,
    Locked up, not lost:
And for a while lie here concealed,   45
    To be revealed
Next at that great Platonic year;
    And then meet here.

141

To Phyllis, To Love and Live with Him

Live, live with me, and thou shalt see
The pleasures I'll prepare for thee:
What sweets the country can afford
Shall bless thy bed, and bless thy board.
The soft sweet moss shall be thy bed,   5
With crawling woodbine over-spread;
By which the silver-shedding streams
Shall gently melt thee into dreams.
Thy clothing, next, shall be a gown
Made of the fleece's purest down.   10
The tongues of kids shall be thy meat,
Their milk thy drink; and thou shalt eat

---

43 *old testaments engrossed*: wills written in large letters and in legal form.   47 *Platonic year*: a period of 30,000 years, at the end of which the heavenly bodies were supposed to have completed their revolutions and to return to their original positions.

The paste of filberts for thy bread
With cream of cowslips butterèd:
Thy feasting-tables shall be hills   15
With daisies spread, and daffodils,
Where thou shalt sit, and redbreast by,
For meat, shall give thee melody.
I'll give thee chains and carcanets
Of primroses and violets.   20
A bag and bottle thou shalt have:
That richly wrought, and this as brave;
So that as either shall express
The wearer's no mean shepherdess.
At shearing-times, and yearly wakes,   25
When Themilis his pastime makes,
There thou shalt be, and be the wit,
Nay more, the feast, and grace of it.
On holidays, when virgins meet
To dance the hays with nimble feet,   30
Thou shalt come forth and then appear
The queen of roses for that year,
And having danced 'bove all the best
Carry the garland from the rest.
In wicker-baskets maids shall bring   35
To thee, my dearest shepherling,
The blushing apple, bashful pear,
And shame-faced plum, all simpering there.
Walk in the groves, and thou shalt find
The name of Phyllis in the rind   40
Of every straight and smooth-skin tree,
Where, kissing that, I'll twice kiss thee.
To thee a sheep-hook I will send,
Be-pranked with ribbands, to this end,
This, this alluring hook might be   45
Less for to catch a sheep than me.
Thou shalt have possets, wassails fine,
Not made of ale, but spicèd wine,

141. 19 *carcanets*: necklaces. 25 *wakes*: village church-dedication feasts.
30 *hays*: winding country dances. 33 *'bove all the best*: *H 48* has in parentheses.
36 *shepher*[d]*ling*: a young or little shepherd.

To make thy maids and self free mirth,
All sitting near the glittering hearth. 50
Thou shalt have ribbands, roses, rings,
Gloves, garters, stockings, shoes, and strings
Of winning colours, that shall move
Others to lust, but me to love.
These, nay, and more, thine own shall be, 55
If thou wilt love, and live with me.

142

Upon Her Feet

Her pretty feet
Like snails did creep
A little out, and then,
As if they playèd at bo-peep,
Did soon draw in again. 5

143

To Dianeme

Give me one kiss,
And no more;
If so be this
Makes you poor,
To enrich you 5
I'll restore,
For that one, two
Thousand score.

142. Cf. Suckling on 'her feet . . . Like little mice' in 'A Ballad upon a Wedding' (S–27), ll. 43–5. 'Her' is the same as 'Upon Mistress Susanna Southwell: Her Cheeks'.

144

To Julia, the Flaminica Dialis, *or Queen-Priest*

Thou know'st, my Julia, that it is thy turn
This morning's incense to prepare, and burn.
The chaplet and *inarculum* here be,
With the white vestures, all attending thee.
This day, the queen-priest thou art made t' appease   5
Love for our very-many trespasses.
One chief transgression is, among the rest,
Because with flowers her temple was not dressed;
The next, because her altars did not shine
With daily fires; the last, neglect of wine;   10
For which her wrath is gone forth to consume
Us all, unless preserved by thy perfume.
Take then thy censer; put in fire, and thus,
O pious priestress, make a peace for us!
For our neglect, Love did our death decree;   15
That we escape, *Redemption comes by thee.*

145

Anacreontic

Born I was to be old,
  And for to die here;
After that, in the mould
  Long for to lie here.
But before that day comes,   5
  Still I be bousing;
For I know, in the tombs
  There's no carousing.

---

144. *Flaminica Dialis*: wife of a priest of Jove, who assisted at the sacrifices.
3 *inarculum*: 'a twig of pomegranate which the queen-priest did use to wear on her head at sacrificing' (Herrick). 14 *priestress*: an early form.

145. 6 *bousing*: boozing.

146

His Content in the Country

Here, here I live with what my board
Can with the smallest cost afford.
Though ne'er so mean the viands be,
They well content my Prew and me.
Or pea, or bean, or wort, or beet,   5
Whatever comes, content makes sweet;
Here we rejoice, because no rent
We pay for our poor tenement,
Wherein we rest, and never fear
The landlord, or the usurer.   10
The quarter-day does ne'er affright
Our peaceful slumbers in the night.
We eat our own, and batten more
Because we feed on no man's score;
But pity those whose flanks grow great,   15
Swelled with the lard of others' meat.
We bless our fortunes when we see
Our own beloved privacy;
And like our living, where we're known
To very few, or else to none.   20

147

Upon Sybilla

With paste of almonds Syb her hands doth scour,
Then gives it to the children to devour.
In cream she bathes her thighs (more soft than silk),
Then to the poor she freely gives the milk.

146. 4 *Prew*: Prudence Baldwin, his housekeeper. 5 *wort*: in general, a vegetable or herb, often a kind of cabbage. 14 *score*: credit account.

147. Herrick spells 'Sibilla' in the title and 'Syb' in l. 1; some resonance of 'sybarite', a luxurious voluptuary (originally of Sybaris), is inevitable and may have been intended.

148

Upon Umber: Epigram

Umber was painting of a lion fierce,
And, working it, by chance from Umber's erse
Flew out a crack so mighty that the fart
(As Umber swears) did make his lion start.

149

The Apparition of His Mistress Calling Him to Elysium

Desunt Nonnulla ――

Come, then, and like two doves with silvery wings
Let our souls fly to th' shades, where, ever, springs
Sit smiling in the meads; where balm and oil,
Roses and cassia, crown the untilled soil;
Where no disease reigns, or infection comes   5
To blast the air but ambergris and gums.
This, that, and every thicket doth transpire
More sweet than storax from the hallowed fire,
Where every tree a wealthy issue bears
Of fragrant apples, blushing plums, or pears;   10
And all the shrubs, with sparkling spangles, show
Like morning-sunshine tinselling the dew.
Here in green meadows sits eternal May,
Purfling the margents, while perpetual day
So double-gilds the air as that no night   15
Can ever rust th' enamel of the light.
Here naked younglings, handsome striplings, run
Their goals for virgins' kisses; which when done,

---

148. This poem finds some of its wit in the friendly sibling rivalry of the
Renaissance between 'the sister arts': 'painting is mute poetry, and poetry a
speaking picture' (Simonides).

149. *Desunt Nonnulla*: some things are missing.   1–20 are adapted from Tibullus,
I. iii. 57–66.   1 *Doves with silvery wings*: cf. Ps. 68: 13.   8 *storax*: a vanilla-
scented balsam used in medicine and perfumes.   14 *purfling*: embroidering (the
edge of a garment).   *margents*: edges.

Then unto dancing forth the learned round
Commixed they meet, with endless roses crowned.   20
And here we'll sit on primrose-banks, and see
Love's chorus led by Cupid; and we'll be
Two loving followers too unto the grove
Where poets sing the stories of our love.
There thou shalt hear divine Musaeus sing   25
Of Hero and Leander; then I'll bring
Thee to the stand where honoured Homer reads
His *Odysseys* and his high *Iliads*,
About whose throne the crowd of poets throng
To hear the incantation of his tongue;   30
To Linus; then to Pindar; and, that done,
I'll bring thee, Herrick, to Anacreon,
Quaffing his full-crowned bowls of burning wine,
And in his raptures speaking lines of thine
Like to his subject; and, as his frantic   35
Looks show him truly Bacchanalian-like,
Besmeared with grapes, welcome he shall thee thither,
Where both may rage, both drink and dance together.
Then stately Virgil, witty Ovid, by
Whom fair Corinna sits, and doth comply   40
With ivory wrists his laureate head, and steeps
His eye in dew of kisses, while he sleeps.
Then soft Catullus, sharp-fanged Martial,
And towering Lucan, Horace, Juvenal,
And snaky Persius, these, and those, whom rage   45
(Dropped for the jars of heaven) filled t' engage
All times unto their frenzies—thou shalt there
Behold them in a spacious theatre.
Among which glories, crowned with sacred bays
And flattering ivy, two recite their plays,   50
Beaumont and Fletcher, swans to whom all ears
Listen, while they, like sirens in their spheres,

25–6 *Musaeus*: (1) legendary pre-Homeric Greek poet; (2) Greek poet of the
fourth or fifth century A.D. who wrote a poem on Hero and Leander that
Marlowe imitated (*Hero and Leander*, i. 52: 'Whose tragedy divine Musaeus
sung'). 31 *Linus*: in this context, the mythic music-master of Hercules. 40
comply: enfold.

Sing their Evadne; and still more for thee
There yet remains to know than thou canst see
By glimmering of a fancy: do but come,   55
And there I'll show thee that capacious room
In which thy father Jonson now is placed,
As in a globe of radiant fire, and graced
To be in that orb crowned (that doth include
Those prophets of the former magnitude)   60
And he one chief. But hark, I hear the cock
(The bellman of the night) proclaim the clock
Of late struck one; and now I see the prime
Of day break from the pregnant east; 'tis time
I vanish; more I had to say;   65
But night determines here, away!

150

The Tithe: to the Bride

If nine times you your bridegroom kiss,
The tenth, you know, the parson's is.
Pay then your tithe; and doing thus
Prove in your bride-bed numerous.
If children you have ten, Sir John   5
Won't for his tenth part ask you one.

53 *Evadne*: in *The Maid's Tragedy.*   57 *now is placed*: the reading 'shall be' in a
text printed in 1640 'suggests that the poem as then published was written
before Jonson's death in 1637' (Martin, p. 542).   61 *he one*: *H 48* and most
editors read 'he one'; Martin emends to 'be our' (see note, p. 542).

150. *Tithe*: a levy, tax, or tribute of one tenth, the amount annually due the
church from parishioners.   5 *Sir John*: the parson.

151

In the Dark None Dainty

Night hides our thefts; all faults then pardoned be:
All are alike fair, when no spots we see.
Lais and Lucrece in the night-time are
Pleasing alike, alike both singular;
Joan and my lady have at that time one,   5
One and the selfsame prized complexion.
Then please alike the pewter and the plate,
The chosen ruby and the reprobate.

152

Upon the Troublesome Times

O times most bad,
Without the scope
Of hope
Of better to be had!

Where shall I go,   5
Or whither run
To shun
This public overthrow?

No places are
(This I am sure)   10
Secure
In this our wasting war.

Some storms w'ave past;
Yet we must all
Down fall,   15
And perish at the last.

151. 3 *Lais and Lucrece*: complementary types of promiscuity and chastity, respectively; from Martial (see H-164, ll. 15-16 n.).

153

His Prayer to Ben Jonson

When I a verse shall make,
Know I have prayed thee,
For old-religion's sake,
Saint Ben, to aid me.

Make the way smooth for me,   5
When I, thy Herrick,
Honouring thee, on my knee
Offer my lyric.

Candles I'll give to thee,
And a new altar;   10
And thou, Saint Ben, shalt be
Writ in my Psalter.

154

The Bad Season Makes the Poet Sad

Dull to myself, and almost dead to these
My many fresh and fragrant mistresses;
Lost to all music now, since every thing
Puts on the semblance here of sorrowing.
Sick is th' land to th' heart, and doth endure   5
More dangerous faintings by her desperate cure.
But if that Golden Age would come again,
And Charles here rule as he before did reign;
If smooth and unperplexed the seasons were
As when the sweet Maria livèd here,   10

---

153. 3 *old-religion* (hyphen editorial): Pollard says 'certainly not Roman Catholicism, though Jonson was a Catholic' (ii. 277); but this probably has reference both to the 'old faith' of pre-Anglican Roman Catholicism and to the poets' faith of the grape that flourished when Jonson was alive.

154. 10 *Maria*: Henrietta Maria, Charles I's Queen.

I should delight to have my curls half drowned
In Tyrian dews, and head with roses crowned;
And once more yet, ere I am laid out dead,
Knock at a star with my exalted head.

155

To Vulcan

Thy sooty godhead I desire
Still to be ready with thy fire;
That should my book despisèd be,
Acceptance it might find of thee.

156

His Own Epitaph

As wearied pilgrims, once possessed
Of longed-for lodging, go to rest,
So I, now having rid my way,
Fix here my buttoned staff and stay.
Youth (I confess) hath me misled;   5
But age hath brought me right to bed.

12 *Tyrian dews*: lit. purple dyes, for which ancient Tyre was famous.   14 *Knock at a star*, etc.: from Horace, *Odes*, i. i. 36.

156. 4 *buttoned staff*: as in the 'cockle hat and staff' (*Hamlet* iv. v. 25) of the pilgrim to the shrine of St. James the Less of Compostela.

157

The Night-Piece, to Julia

Her eyes the glow-worm lend thee,
The shooting stars attend thee;
    And the elves also,
    Whose little eyes glow
Like the sparks of fire, befriend thee.   5

No Will-o'-th'-wisp mislight thee,
Nor snake or slow-worm bite thee;
    But on, on thy way,
    Not making a stay,
Since ghost there's none t' affright thee.   10

Let not the dark thee cumber;
What though the moon does slumber?
    The stars of the night
    Will lend thee their light,
Like tapers clear without number.   15

Then, Julia, let me woo thee,
Thus, thus, to come unto me;
    And when I shall meet
    Thy silvery feet,
My soul I'll pour into thee.   20

158

A Kiss

What is a kiss? Why this, as some approve:
The sure sweet-cement, glue, and lime of love.

---

157. 7 *slow-worm*: blindworm, or in early use adder.   **10** *t'*: *H 48* reads 'to'.

158. Martin cites Donne: 'and the son receives none but by love, and this cement and glue of a zealous and reverential love, a holy kiss' (p. 545; *LXXX Sermons*, 1640, Serm. xli, p. 403c).

159

To His Lovely Mistresses

One night i' th' year, my dearest beauties, come
And bring those dew-drink offerings to my tomb.
When thence ye see my reverend ghost to rise
And there to lick th' effusèd sacrifice,
Though paleness be the livery that I wear,   5
Look ye not wan or colourless for fear.
Trust me, I will not hurt ye, or once show
The least grim look, or cast a frown on you;
Nor shall the tapers when I'm there burn blue.
This I may do, perhaps, as I glide by: 10
Cast on my girls a glance, and loving eye;
Or fold mine arms, and sigh, because I've lost
The world so soon, and in it you the most.
Than these, no fears more on your fancies fall,
Though then I smile and speak no words at all.   15

160

The Beggar to Mab, the Fairy Queen

Please your grace, from out your store
Give an alms to one that's poor,
That your mickle may have more.
Black I'm grown for want of meat:
Give me then an ant to eat;   5
Or the cleft ear of a mouse
Over-soured in drink of souse;
Or, sweet lady, reach to me
The abdomen of a bee;

159. 2 *dew-drink offerings*: with reference to the *libamen(tum)*, a drink-offering often associated with the dead, and perhaps also *libatio* as the Mosaic drink-offering (Vulgate). Patrick (pp. 294–5) cites the 1559 *Book of Common Prayer*: 'The continual dew of thy blessing'.   4 *th' effused sacrifice*: allusion to *Odyssey* xi, where Odysseus propitiates the shades with a blood-offering.   9 *tapers . . . burn blue*, indicating the presence of an evil spirit.

160. 7 *souse*: pickling liquid.

Or commend a cricket's hip,   10
Or his huckson, to my scrip.
Give, for bread, a little bit
Of a pease that 'gins to chit,
And my full thanks take for it.
Flour of fuzz-balls, that's too good   15
For a man in needy-hood;
But the meal of mill-dust can
Well content a craving man;
Any orts the Elves refuse
Well will serve the beggar's use.   20
But if this may seem too much
For an alms, then give me such
Little bits that nestle there
In the prisoner's panier.
So a blessing light upon   25
You and mighty Oberon,
That your plenty last till when
I return your alms again.

161

Farewell Frost, or Welcome the Spring

Fled are the frosts, and now the fields appear
Re-clothed in fresh and verdant diaper.
Thawed are the snows, and now the lusty Spring
Gives to each mead a neat enamelling.
The palms put forth their gems, and every tree   5
Now swaggers in her leafy gallantry.
The while the Daulian minstrel sweetly sings,
With warbling notes, her Terean sufferings.
What gentle winds perspire! As if here
Never had been the Northern Plunderer   10
To strip the trees, and fields, to their distress,
Leaving them to a pitied nakedness.

11 *huckson*: hockshin, the underside of the thigh. *scrip*: beggar's wallet or satchel.
13 *pease*: pea (arch.).   15 *flour of fuzz-balls*: the powdery brown spores of puff-
ball mushrooms, probably *Lycoperdon perlatum*.   19 *orts*: scraps.

And look how, when a frantic storm doth tear
A stubborn oak, or holm (long growing there),
But lulled to calmness then succeeds a breeze   15
That scarcely stirs the nodding leaves of trees;
So when this war (which tempest-like doth spoil
Our salt, our corn, our honey, wine, and oil)
Falls to a temper, and doth mildly cast
His inconsiderate frenzy off at last,   20
The gentle dove may, when these turmoils cease,
Bring in her bill, once more, *the Branch of Peace*.

162

The Hag

The hag is astride
This night for to ride,
The devil and she together;
Through thick and through thin,
Now out and then in,   5
Though ne'er so foul be the weather.

A thorn or a burr
She takes for a spur,
With a lash of a bramble she rides now;
Through brakes and through briars,   10
O'er ditches and mires,
She follows the spirit that guides now.

No beast for his food
Dares now range the wood,
But hushed in his lair he lies lurking;   15
While mischiefs by these,
On land and on seas,
At noon of night are a working.

162. In an age when witches were for many people more than Hallowe'en
masquers, Herrick's 'Hag' poems (also H–200) have a special piquancy, in
which the verse-form, unusual for Herrick, plays its own part. Herrick's hags
probably occupy the same place in his 'beliefs' as his fairies.

The storm will arise
And trouble the skies   20
This night, and more for the wonder
The ghost from the tomb
Affrighted shall come,
Called out by the clap of the thunder.

163

To Electra

I dare not ask a kiss,
    I dare not beg a smile,
Lest having that or this
    I might grow proud the while.

No, no, the utmost share   5
    Of my desire shall be
Only to kiss that air
    That lately kissèd thee.

164

What Kind of Mistress He Would Have

Be the mistress of my choice
Clean in manners, clear in voice;
Be she witty more than wise,
Pure enough, though not precise;
Be she showing in her dress   5
Like a civil wilderness,
That the curious may detect
Order in a sweet neglect;
Be she rolling in her eye,
Tempting all the passers-by,   10
And each ringlet of her hair
An enchantment, or a snare,

164. 4 *precise*: fastidious.

For to catch the lookers-on,
But herself held fast by none.
Let her Lucrece all day be,   15
Thais in the night, to me.
Be she such as neither will
Famish me, nor over-fill.

165

The Funeral Rites of the Rose

The rose was sick, and smiling died;
And (being to be sanctified)
About the bed there sighing stood
The sweet and flowery sisterhood.
Some hung the head, while some did bring   5
(To wash her) water from the spring.
Some laid her forth, while others wept,
But all a solemn fast there kept.
The holy sisters some among
The sacred dirge and trental sung.   10
But ah, what sweets smelt everywhere,
As heaven had spent all perfumes there!
At last, when prayers for the dead
And rites were all accomplishèd,
They, weeping, spread a lawny loom,   15
And closed her up, as in a tomb.

15–16 *Lucrece . . . Thais*: the Roman type of chastity who resisted Tarquin and
the Athenian courtesan who inflamed Alexander the Great, respectively.
Martial, XI. civ. 20–1. Cf. 'Lais and Lucrece' in H–151, l. 20.

165. 10 *trental*: strictly, a set of thirty requiem masses; here, loosely, as lament.

166

His Return to London

From the dull confines of the drooping West,
To see the day spring from the pregnant East,
Ravished in spirit I come, nay, more, I fly
To thee, blest place of my nativity!
Thus, thus, with hallowed foot I touch the ground,   5
With thousand blessings by thy fortune crowned.
O fruitful *Genius*, that bestowest here
An everlasting plenty, year by year!
O place! O people! manners! framed to please
All nations, customs, kindreds, languages!   10
I am a free-born Roman; suffer, then,
That I amongst you live a citizen.
London my home is, though by hard fate sent
Into a long and irksome banishment;
Yet since called back; henceforward let me be,   15
O native country, repossessed by thee!
For, rather than I'll to the West return,
I'll beg of thee first here to have mine urn.
Weak I am grown, and must in short time fall;
Give thou my sacred relics burial.   20

167

His Grange, or Private Wealth

Though clock,
To tell how night draws hence, I've none,
A cock
I have, to sing how day draws on.

166. 7 *Genius*: tutelary spirit (see G).

167. *Grange*: an outlying farm-house, like Marina's 'moated grange' in *Measure for Measure*; specifically, Herrick's vicarage at Dean Prior.

F

I have   5
A maid (my Prew) by good luck sent
To save
That little Fates me gave or lent.
A hen
I keep, which, creeking day by day,   10
Tells when
She goes her long white egg to lay.
A goose
I have, which with a jealous ear
Lets loose   15
Her tongue, to tell that danger's near.
A lamb
I keep (tame) with my morsels fed,
Whose dam
An orphan left him (lately dead).   20
A cat
I keep, that plays about my house,
Grown fat
With eating many a miching mouse.
To these   25
A Tracy I do keep, whereby
I please
The more my rural privacy;
Which are
But toys to give my heart some ease: 30
Where care
None is, slight things do lightly please.

168

Money Makes the Mirth

When all birds else do of their music fail,
Money's the still-sweet-singing nightingale.

6 *Prew*: Prudence Baldwin. 24 *miching*: thieving. 26 *Tracy*: 'His spaniel'
(Herrick).

169

The Apron of Flowers

To gather flowers Sappha went,
   And homeward she did bring
Within her lawny continent
   The treasure of the spring.

She smiling blushed, and blushing smiled,   5
   And sweetly blushing thus,
She looked as she'd been got with child
   By young Favonius.

Her apron gave as she did pass
   An odour more divine,   10
More pleasing, too, than ever was
   The lap of Proserpine.

170

The Peter-Penny

Fresh strewings allow
To my sepulchre now,
To make my lodging the sweeter;
   A staff or a wand
   Put then in my hand,
With a penny to pay St. Peter.   5

169. 3 *continent*: container generally; here, the apron.   8 *Favonius*: the zephyr
or west wind, favourable to vegetation.   12 *Proserpine*: Patrick quotes *Paradise
Lost*, iv. 268–71.

170. *Peter-Penny*: Peter's pence; an annual tax of a penny paid before the
Reformation by owners of land of a certain value to the papal see at Rome.
6 *a penny to pay St. Peter*: Herrick typically fuses Christian and classical through
the traditional offices of St. Peter, the keeper of heaven's gates, and Charon,
the ferryman of Hades, to whom 'Charon's toll' was paid; this was a coin placed
in the mouth of the dead as the ferrying fee for the river Styx.

Who has not a cross
Must sit with the loss,
And no whit further must venture;
    Since the porter he   10
    Will paid have his fee,
Or else not one there must enter.

Who, at a dead lift
Can't send for a gift
A pig to the priest for a roaster,   15
    Shall hear his clerk say,
    'By yea and by nay,
No penny, no Pater Noster.'

171

The Spell

Holy water come and bring,
Cast in salt for seasoning,
Set the brush for sprinkling;
Sacred spittle bring ye hither,
Meal and it now mix together,   5
And a little oil to either;
Give the tapers here their light,
Ring the saints'-bell to affright
Far from hence the evil sprite.

7 *cross*: a coin with a cross on it.   13 *dead lift*: extremity.   17 *By yea and by nay*:
in common usage, from Matt. 5: 34–7.   18 *No penny*, etc.: proverbial (Tilley
P 199) and related to 'Empty hands deserve no prayer' (H 110).

171. Herrick's fondness for ritual is evident here and elsewhere in 'this poetic
liturgy' (H–139: 4), his book.   3 *brush*: aspergillum, or holy-water 'sprinkler'.
8 *saints'-bell*: sanctus or sacring bell.

172

Upon Julia's Clothes

Whenas in silks my Julia goes,
Then, then (methinks) how sweetly flows
That liquefaction of her clothes.

Next, when I cast mine eyes and see
That brave vibration each way free,   5
Oh how that glittering taketh me!

173

Upon Prew, His Maid

In this little urn is laid
Prudence Baldwin, once my maid,
From whose happy spark here let
Spring the purple violet.

172. Probably Herrick's most famous poem, and characteristically short. It is a witty expression of the paradox of the 'angler angled'. The conceit is realized especially through the angling references of ll. 4–6: 'cast', 'that brave vibration' of a hooked fish breaking the water, and 'that glittering taketh *me*'.   6 *taketh*: Herrick's use is especially interesting in relation to the etymology of 'take'. The earliest known use, in Germanic languages, meant 'to put the hand on'; eventually 'to catch' an animal or fish (*OED* B.2b); and in due course non-material senses. Thus this 'fish', the fancied naked Julia, 'taketh' Herrick.

174

The Invitation

To sup with thee thou didst me home invite,
And mad'st a promise that mine appetite
Should meet and tire on such lautitious meat
The like not Heliogabalus did eat,
And richer wine wouldst give to me, thy guest,   5
Than Roman Sulla poured out at his feast.
I came, 'tis true; and looked for fowl of price,
The bastard phoenix, bird of paradise;
And for no less than aromatic wine
Of maiden's-blush, commixed with jessamine.   10
Clean was the hearth, the mantel larded jet,
Which, wanting Lar, and smoke, hung weeping wet;
At last, i' th' noon of winter did appear
A ragg'd soused neat's-foot with sick vinegar;
And, in a burnished flagonet stood by,   15
Beer small as comfort, dead as charity.
At which amazed, and pondering on the food,
How cold it was and how it chilled my blood,
I cursed the master, and I damned the souse,
And swore I'd got the ague of the house.   20
Well, when to eat thou dost me next desire,
I'll bring a fever, since thou keep'st no fire.

---

174. 3 *tire*: feed; strictly, to tear flesh in feeding, like a bird of prey.   *lautitious*: 'sumptuous' (*SOED*, citing this instance only).   4 *Heliogabalus*: Elagabulus, who took his name from the sun-god of Emesa, Elah-Gabal, of whom he was a hereditary priest; he was Emperor of Rome in A.D. 218–22.   6 *Sulla*: Faustus Cornelius Sulla spent most of his inherited wealth in short order, especially on memorial games in 60 B.C.   8 *bastard phoenix, bird of paradise*: Elagabulus coveted the unique phoenix (see G) for his table.   10 *maiden's blush*: pink rose.   12 *Lar*: household god (see G).   14 *soused*: pickled.   *sick*: spoiled.

175

Power and Peace

'Tis never or but seldom known,
Power and Peace to keep one throne.

176

Orpheus

Orpheus he went (as poets tell)
To fetch Eurydice from hell;
And had her; but it was upon
This short but strict condition:
Backward he should not look while he   5
Led her through hell's obscurity.
But ah! it happened, as he made
His passage through that dreadful shade,
Revolve he did his loving eye,
For gentle fear or jealousy;   10
And, looking back, that look did sever
Him and Eurydice for ever.

177

The Amber Bead

I saw a fly within a bead
Of amber cleanly burièd:
The urn was little, but the room
More rich than Cleopatra's tomb.

---

176. Herrick's telling of the traditional story. See G and cf. Lovelace's 'Orpheus
to Beasts' and 'Orpheus to Woods' (L–6, L–7).

178

The Transfiguration

Immortal clothing I put on
So soon as, Julia, I am gone
To mine eternal mansion.

Thou, thou art here, to human sight,
Clothed all with incorrupted light;   5
But yet how more admir'dly bright

Wilt thou appear, when thou art set
In thy refulgent thronèlet,
That shin'st thus in thy counterfeit!

179

To Oenone

Thou saist Love's dart
Hath pricked thy heart,
And thou dost languish, too:
    If one poor prick
    Can make thee sick,   5
Say, what would many do?

180

Upon a Maid

Here she lies (in bed of spice)
Fair as Eve in Paradise;
For her beauty, it was such
Poets could not praise too much.

178. As the title might lead one to expect, this poem alludes extensively to the
Bible, especially 2 Esd. 2: 45 (l. 1), Jn. 14: 2 (l. 2), and Wisd. 18: 4, Ps. 132: 9,
and Isa. 61: 10 (l. 5).

Virgins, come, and in a ring 5
Her supremest requiem sing;
Then depart, but see ye tread
Lightly, lightly, o'er the dead.

181

Upon a Maid

Gone she is a long, long way,
But she has decreed a day
Back to come, and make no stay.
So we keep till her return,
Here, her ashes, or her urn. 5

182

To Master Henry Lawes, the Excellent Composer of Lyrics

Touch but thy lyre, my Harry, and I hear
From thee some raptures of the rare Gautier.
Then if thy voice commingle with the string
I hear in thee rare Laniër to sing;
Or curious Wilson. Tell me, canst thou be 5
Less than Apollo, that usurp'st such Three?
Three, unto whom the whole world give applause;
Yet their Three praises praise but One; that's Lawes.

182. On Lawes see G.   2 *Gautier*: James Gouter or Gaultier ('Gotire', *H 48*; 'Gualtier', Martin and Patrick), *fl.* 1646, French lutanist.   4 *Lanier*: Nicholas Lanier (1588–1666), a musician in the royal household who composed music for Campion and Jonson.   5 *Wilson*: John Wilson (1595–1674), lutanist, musician to Charles I and II, and Professor of Music at Oxford (1656). He is probably the 'Jack Wilson' referred to in a stage direction in the 1623 Folio text of *Much Ado About Nothing*, and he seems to have been active as a performer as well as composer.

183

No Difference in the Dark

Night makes no difference 'twixt the priest and clerk;
Joan as my lady is as good i' th' dark.

184

The Body

The body is the soul's poor house, or home,
Whose ribs the laths are, and whose flesh the loam.

185

Kisses Loathesome

I abhor the slimy kiss
(Which to me most loathsome is).
Those lips please me which are placed
Close, but not too strictly laced;
Yielding I would have them, yet   5
Not a wimbling tongue admit.
What should poking-sticks make there,
When the ruff is set elsewhere?

186

Upon Lulls

Lulls swears he is all heart, but you'll suppose
By his proboscis that he is all nose.

---

185. 6 *wimbling*: hole-boring (a wimble was a type of augur).   7 *poking-sticks*:
for stiffening the plaits of ruffs.   8 *ruff*: lit. a collar of starched linen arranged
in flutings and standing out all round the neck.

186. Adapted from Martial, XII. lxxxviii.

187

Ceremonies for Candlemas Eve

Down with the rosemary and bays,
    Down with the mistletoe;
Instead of holly, now up-raise
    The greener box for show.

The holly hitherto did sway;   5
    Let box now domineer;
Until the dancing Easter-day
    Or Easter's eve appear.

Then youthful box which now hath grace
    Your houses to renew,   10
Grown old, surrender must his place
    Unto the crispèd yew.

When yew is out, then birch comes in,
    And many flowers beside,
Both of a fresh and fragrant kin   15
    To honour Whitsuntide.

Green rushes, then, and sweetest bents,
    With cooler oaken boughs,
Come in for comely ornaments
    To re-adorn the house.   20
Thus times do shift; each thing his turn does hold:
New things succeed, as former things grow old.

187. *Candlemas*: The feast of the 'Purification of Saint Mary the Virgin'
(*Prayer-Books* of 1549 and 1552), later the 'Presentation of Christ in the Temple,
Commonly Called the Purification', etc.: February 2nd, and the end of the
Christmas season. 7 *dancing Easter-day*: the superstition that the sun danced on
this day to celebrate the Resurrection was still alive in the nineteenth century.
17 *bents*: grasses. 21–2 Herrick sees the changes in the church's and nature's
year equally and similarly in cyclical, calendarial, and ceremonial terms.

188

Upon Ben Jonson

Here lies Jonson with the rest
Of the poets, but the best.
Reader, wouldst thou more have known?
Ask his story, not this stone.
That will speak what this can't tell   5
Of his glory. So farewell.

189

An Ode for Him

Ah Ben!
  Say how or when
  Shall we thy guests
Meet at those lyric feasts
  Made at the Sun,   5
  The Dog, the Triple Tun?
Where we such clusters had
As made us nobly wild, not mad;
  And yet each verse of thine
Outdid the meat, outdid the frolic wine.   10

My Ben,
  Or come again
  Or send to us
Thy wit's great over-plus;
  But teach us yet   15
  Wisely to husband it,
Lest we that talent spend,
And, having once brought to an end
  That precious stock, the store
Of such a wit the world should have no more. 20

189. 5–6 *the Sun,* etc.: inns once frequented by Ben and his 'Sons'.

190

Upon Julia Washing Herself in the River

How fierce was I when I did see
My Julia wash herself in thee!
So lilies thorough crystal look,
So purest pebbles in the brook,
As in the river Julia did,   5
Half with a lawn of water hid.
Into thy streams myself I threw,
And struggling there I kissed thee, too,
And more had done (it is confessed),
Had not thy waves forbade the rest.   10

191

To His Honoured and Most Ingenious Friend,
Master Charles Cotton

For brave comportment, wit without offence,
Words fully flowing, yet of influence,
Thou art that man of men, the man alone,
Worthy the public admiration;
Who with thine own eyes read'st what we do write,   5
And giv'st our numbers euphony and weight;
Tell'st when a verse springs high, how understood
To be, or not born of the royal-blood.
What state above, what symmetry below,
Lines have, or should have, thou the best canst show.   10
For which, my Charles, it is my pride to be
Not so much known as to be loved of thee.
Long may I live so, and my wreath of bays
Be less another's laurel than thy praise.

191. Charles Cotton the father (d. 1658), not his more famous son, the poet
(1630–87). The father is praised for his congeniality by Clarendon, and is
addressed by Lovelace in 'The Grasshopper' (L-8). The son contributed, with
Herrick, to *Lachrymae Musarum* (1649), a volume lamenting the death of the
beheaded Charles I.

192

Crutches

Thou seest me, Lucia, this year droop;
Three zodiacs filled more I shall stoop;
Let crutches then provided be
To shore up my debility.
Then while thou laugh'st, I'll, sighing, cry,   5
'A ruin underpropped am I.'
Don will I then my beadsman's gown,
And when so feeble I am grown
As my weak shoulders cannot bear
The burden of a grasshopper,   10
Yet with the bench of aged sires,
When I and they keep termly fires,
With my weak voice I'll sing or say
Some odes I made of Lucia;
Then will I heave my withered hand   15
To Jove the mighty for to stand
Thy faithful friend, and to pour down
Upon thee many a benison.

193

To His Kinsman, Master Thomas Herrick,
Who Desired To Be in His Book

Welcome to this my college, and though late
Th'ast got a place here, standing candidate,
It matters not, since thou art chosen one
Here of my great and good foundation.

---

192. 7 *beadsman*: a pensioner bound to pray for the souls of his benefactors.
10 *grasshopper*: Eccles. 12: 5: 'And the grasshopper shall be a burden', etc.
11 *the bench of aged sires*: as though they were members of a body sitting in a
court of justice.   12 *termly*: fires lighted in term, perhaps with allusion to
quarter-sessions.

193. Thomas was probably the eldest son of the poet's brother Nicholas
(Martin, p. 562).

194

Anacreontic

I must
Not trust
Here to any;
Bereaved,
Deceived   5
By so many:
As one
Undone
By my losses,
Comply   10
Will I
With my crosses.
Yet still
I will
Not be grieving,   15
Since thence
And hence
Comes relieving.
But this
Sweet is   20
In our mourning:
Times bad
And sad
Are a turning;
And he   25
Whom we
See dejected
Next day
We may
See erected.   30

195

Upon Love, by Way of Question and Answer

I bring ye love. *Question.* What will love do?
   Answer. Like and dislike ye.
I bring ye love. *Question.* What will love do?
   Answer. Stroke ye to strike ye.
I bring ye love. *Question.* What will love do?   5
   Answer. Love will be-fool ye.
I bring ye love. *Question.* What will love do?
   Answer. Heat ye to cool ye.
I bring ye love. *Question.* What will love do?
   Answer. Love-gifts will send ye.   10
I bring ye love. *Question.* What will love do?
   Answer. Stock ye to spend ye.
I bring ye love. *Question.* What will love do?
   Answer. Love will fulfil ye.
I bring ye love. *Question.* What will love do?   15
   Answer. Kiss ye, to kill ye.

196

The Vision

Methought I saw (as I did dream in bed)
A crawling vine about Anacreon's head:
Flushed was his face; his hairs with oil did shine;
And as he spake, his mouth ran o'er with wine.
Tippled he was, and tippling lisped withal,   5
And lisping reeled, and reeling like to fall.
A young enchantress close by him did stand
Tapping his plump thighs with a myrtle wand:
She smiled; he kissed; and, kissing, culled her, too;
And being cup-shot, more he could not do.   10
For which (methought) in pretty anger she
Snatched off his crown, and gave the wreath to me;
Since when (methinks) my brains about do swim,
And I am wild and wanton like to him.

---

196. 9 *culled*: embraced (Lat. *collum*, neck).   10 *cup-shot*: impotent-drunk.

197

His Hope or Sheet-Anchor

Among these tempests great and manifold,
My ship has here one only anchor-hold;
That is my hope; which if that slip, I'm one
Wildered in this vast watery region.

198

On Himself

Let me not live, if I not love,
Since I, did never prove
Where pleasures met, at last do find
All pleasures meet in womankind.

199

On Himself

I will no longer kiss,
  I can no longer stay;
The way of all flesh is
  That I must go this day;
Since longer I can't live,   5
  My frolic youths adieu;
My lamp to you I'll give,
  And all my troubles, too.

197. The sheet-anchor was the largest of a ship's anchors, used only in an
emergency. Cf. Heb. 6: 19. The anchor 'contains' a cross and was early used
as a Christian symbol.

200

The Hag

The staff is now greased,
And very well pleased
She cocks out her arse at the parting,
To an old ram goat
That rattles i' th' throat,   5
Half choked with the stink of her farting.

In a dirty hair-lace
She leads on a brace
Of black boar-cats to attend her;
Who scratch at the moon,   10
And threaten at noon
Of night from heaven for to rend her.

A hunting she goes:
A cracked horn she blows,
At which the hounds fall a bounding;   15
While the moon in her sphere
Peeps trembling for fear,
And night's afraid of the sounding.

201

The Mount of the Muses

After thy labour, take thine ease
Here with the sweet Pierides.
But if so be that men will not
Give thee the laurel crown for lot,
Be yet assured, thou shalt have one   5
Not subject to corruption.

200. See H–162 n. This and the following are the last nine poems in *Hesperides*.
They afford evidence of Herrick's sense of closure as well as of the looseness of arrangement of his poems in a structure that is never wholly out of the way nor in it.

201. Pieria was on the northern slopes of Mt. Olympus; the cult of the Muses
(Pierides) was said to have been brought from there to Mt. Helicon. The motif
of *ars longa, vita brevis* is here expressed in the Christian terms of 1 Cor. 9: 25.

202

On Himself

I'll write no more of love, but now repent
Of all those times that I in it have spent.
I'll write no more of life, but wish 'twas ended,
And that my dust was to the earth commended.

203

To His Book

Go thou forth, my book, though late;
Yet be timely fortunate.
It may chance good luck may send
Thee a kinsman, or a friend,
That may harbour thee, when I   5
With my fates neglected lie.
If thou know'st not where to dwell,
See, the fire's by: *Farewell.*

204

The End of His Work

Part of the work remains; one part is past:
And here my ship rides, having anchor cast.

205

To Crown It

My wearied bark, O let it now be crowned!
The haven reached to which I first was bound.

206

On Himself

The work is done. Young men and maidens, set
Upon my curls the myrtle coronet,
Washed with sweet ointments; thus at last I come
To suffer in the Muses' martyrdom,
But with this comfort: if my blood be shed,   5
The Muses will wear blacks when I am dead.

207

The Pillar of Fame

Fame's pillar here, at last, we set,
Out-during marble, brass, or jet,
   Charmed and enchanted so
   As to withstand the blow
     Of overthrow;   5
     Nor shall the seas
     Or outrages
     Of storms o'erbear
     What we uprear;
     Tho' kingdoms fall,   10
   This pillar never shall
   Decline or waste at all,
But stand for ever by his own
Firm and well-fixed foundation.

208

To his book's end this last line he'd have placed:
Jocund his Muse was, but his life was chaste.

---

207. Figure-poems have a long history. Poems in the shape of axe, wings, and egg (Simmias), and altar (Dosiadas), survive in Alexandrian Greek from the beginning of the third century B.C.

THOMAS CAREW
(1594/5–1640)

I

The Spring

Now that the winter's gone, the earth hath lost
Her snow-white robes; and now no more the frost
Candies the grass, or casts an icy cream
Upon the silver lake or crystal stream;
But the warm sun thaws the benumbèd earth,   5
And makes it tender, gives a sacred birth
To the dead swallow, wakes in hollow tree
The drowsy cuckoo and the humble-bee.
Now do a choir of chirping minstrels bring
In triumph to the world the youthful Spring; 10
The valleys, hills, and woods, in rich array,
Welcome the coming of the longed-for May.
Now all things smile; only my love doth lour,
Nor hath the scalding noonday sun the power
To melt that marble ice which still doth hold   15
Her heart congealed, and makes her pity cold.
The ox which lately did for shelter fly
Into the stall doth now securely lie
In open fields, and love no more is made
By the fireside; but in the cooler shade   20
Amyntas now doth with his Chloris sleep
Under a sycamore, and all things keep
Time with the season; only she doth carry
June in her eyes, in her heart January.

---

1. For other treatments of 'the paradox of burgeoning earth and unhappy
lover' see Dunlap, p. 215. 3 *candies*: coats with ice. *icy cream*: 'ice[d] cream'
dates from 1688 (*OED*), but 'candies' in this line suggests an earlier date.
6–7 *a sacred birth | To the dead swallow*: swallows are said to have been 'sacred
unto the *Penates* or household gods of the ancients' (Sir Thomas Browne,
Pseudodoxia Epidemica, 1646, v. xxiii. 3). Some texts read 'second' for 'sacred',
a plausible but easier and probably sophisticated reading. 21 *Amyntas . . .
Chloris*: conventional names for shepherd and shepherdess in pastoral literature.
Thomas Randolph's *Amyntas* was performed in 1631.

2

To A. L.

Persuasions to Love

Think not 'cause men flattering say
Y' are fresh as April, sweet as May,
Bright as is the morning star,
That you are so; or though you are
Be not therefore proud, and deem   5
All men unworthy your esteem.
For, being so, you lose the pleasure
Of being fair, since that rich treasure
Of rare beauty and sweet feature
Was bestowed on you by nature   10
To be enjoyed, and 'twere a sin
There to be scarce where she hath been
So prodigal of her best graces;
Thus common beauties and mean faces
Shall have more pastime, and enjoy   15
The sport you lose by being coy.
Did the thing for which I sue
Only concern myself, not you;
Were men so framed as they alone
Reaped all the pleasure, women none;   20
Then had you reason to be scant:
But 'twere a madness not to grant
That which affords (if you consent),
To you the giver, more content
Than me the beggar. Oh, then be   25
Kind to yourself, if not to me!
Starve not yourself because you may
Thereby make me pine away,
Nor let brittle beauty make
You your wiser thoughts forsake;   30

2. Suckling wrote '*Non est mortale quod opto*: Upon Mrs. A. L.' presumably to the same person, who has not been identified. A manuscript title, 'An Admonition to Coy Acquaintance', anticipates Marvell's 'To His Coy Mistress'. Musical setting (ll. 37–48 only): Henry Lawes. 29–84 a 'free translation' of a canzone by Marino (Dunlap, p. 216).

For that lovely face will fail:
Beauty's sweet, but beauty's frail;
'Tis sooner past, 'tis sooner done,
Than summer's rain or winter's sun;
Most fleeting when it is most dear,   35
'Tis gone while we but say 'tis here.
These curious locks so aptly twined,
Whose every hair a soul doth bind,
Will change their abroun hue, and grow
White and cold as winter's snow.   40
That eye which now is Cupid's nest
Will prove his grave, and all the rest
Will follow; in the cheek, chin, nose,
Nor lily shall be found nor rose.
And what will then become of all   45
Those whom now you servants call?
Like swallows when your summer's done,
They'll fly and seek some warmer sun.
Then wisely choose one to your friend,
Whose love may, when your beauties end,   50
Remain still firm; be provident,
And think before the summer's spent
Of following winter; like the ant,
In plenty hoard for time of scant.
Cull out, amongst the multitude   55
Of lovers that seek to intrude
Into your favour, one that may
Love for an age, not for a day;
One that will quench your youthful fires,
And feed in age your hot desires.   60
For when the storms of time have moved
Waves on that cheek which was beloved,
When a fair lady's face is pined
And yellow spread where red once shined;
When beauty, youth, and all sweets leave her,   65
Love may return, but lover never;
And old folks say there are no pains
Like itch of love in aged veins.

---

39 *abroun*: auburn.   44 *lily . . . rose*: the 'garden in her face, / Where roses and
white lilies grow' (Campion), was a commonplace of Renaissance imagery.

O love me then, and now begin it;
Let us not lose this present minute: 70
For time and age will work that wrack
Which time or age shall ne'er call back.
The snake each year fresh skin resumes,
And eagles change their aged plumes;
The faded rose each spring receives   75
A fresh red tincture on her leaves:
But if your beauties once decay,
You never know a second May.
O then be wise, and whilst your season
Affords you days for sport, do reason: 80
Spend not in vain your life's short hour,
But crop in time your beauty's flower,
Which will away, and doth together
Both bud and fade, both blow and wither.

3

Secrecy Protested

Fear not, dear love, that I'll reveal
Those hours of pleasure we two steal;
No eye shall see, nor yet the sun
Descry, what thou and I have done.
No ear shall hear our love, but we   5
Silent as the night will be.
The God of Love himself (whose dart
Did first wound mine, and then thy heart)
Shall never know that we can tell
What sweets in stol'n embraces dwell.   10
This only means may find it out:
If when I die, physicians doubt
What caused my death, and, there to view
Of all their judgements which was true,

---

81 *live*[']*s*: i.e. 'life's', a phonetic spelling enforcing a variant pronunciation.

3. Musical settings: Henry Lawes, William Lawes, and anonymous.   6 Perhaps this should read '*As* silent', since this is the only acephalous line in the poem; if not, 'silent' is well placed.   12–16 *If when I die*, etc.: an adaptation of Donne's 'The Damp', ll. 1–4.

Rip up my heart. Oh then I fear   15
The world will see thy picture there.

4

Song

Mediocrity in Love Rejected

Give me more love, or more disdain;
    The torrid or the frozen zone
Bring equal ease unto my pain;
    The temperate affords me none:
Either extreme, of love or hate,   5
Is sweeter than a calm estate.

Give me a storm: if it be love,
    Like Danae in that golden shower
I swim in pleasure; if it prove
    Disdain, that torrent will devour   10
My vulture-hopes; and he's possessed
Of heaven that's but from hell released.
    Then crown my joys, or cure my pain:
    Give me more love, or more disdain.

4. Variations on the theme of 'all or nothing at all' are perennial in love poems. Dunlap cites Renaissance antecedents, parallels, and imitations, and draws attention to Lovelace's extended adaptation of 'A la Bourbon' (L–23). Also cf. Sidney Godolphin's 'Song', 'Or love me less, or love me more'. Musical setting: Henry Lawes. *Mediocrity*: moderation. 8 *Danae*: see G.

5

Song

Good Counsel to a Young Maid

Gaze not on thy beauty's pride,
Tender maid, in the false tide
That from lovers' eyes doth slide.

Let thy faithful crystal show
How thy colours come and go: 5
Beauty takes a foil from woe.

Love, that in those smooth streams lies
Under pity's fair disguise,
Will thy melting heart surprise.

Nets of passion's finest thread,   10
Snaring poems, will be spread,
All to catch thy maidenhead.

Then beware, for those that cure
Love's disease, themselves endure
For reward a calenture.   15

Rather let the lover pine,
Than his pale cheek should assign
A perpetual blush to thine.

5. Musical setting: Henry Lawes. 4 *crystal*: mirror, but especially apt in the original sense, 'clear ice' (Greek 'Krustallos'). 6 *foil*: (1) background leaf of metal setting off a jewel's brilliancy; (2) defeat. 15 *calenture*: a tropical fever or delirium causing victims to leap into the sea.

6

To My Mistress Sitting by a River's Side

An Eddy

Mark how yon eddy steals away
From the rude stream into the bay;
There locked up safe, she doth divorce
Her waters from the channel's course,
And scorns the torrent that did bring   5
Her headlong from her native spring.
Now doth she with her new love play,
Whilst he runs murmuring away.
Mark how she courts the banks, whilst they
As am'rously their arms display,   10
T' embrace and clip her silver waves:
See how she strokes their sides, and craves
An entrance there, which they deny;
Whereat she frowns, threatening to fly
Home to her stream, and 'gins to swim   15
Backward, but from the channel's brim
Smiling returns into the creek,
With thousand dimples on her cheek.
    Be thou this eddy, and I'll make
My breast thy shore, where thou shalt take   20
Secure repose, and never dream
Of the quite forsaken stream:
Let him to the wide ocean haste,
There lose his colour, name, and taste;
Thou shalt save all, and safe from him   25
Within these arms for ever swim.

---

6. An adaptation of ll. 21–34 of Donne's Elegy VI. *Eddy*: water running
contrary to the direction of tide or current; a small whirlpool.

7

Song

To My Inconstant Mistress

When thou, poor excommunicate
    From all the joys of love, shalt see
The full reward and glorious fate
    Which my strong faith shall purchase me,
    Then curse thine own inconstancy.   5

A fairer hand than thine shall cure
    That heart which thy false oaths did wound;
And to my soul a soul more pure
    Than thine shall by Love's hand be bound,
    And both with equal glory crowned.   10

Then shalt thou weep, entreat, complain
    To Love, as I did once to thee;
When all thy tears shall be as vain
    As mine were then, for thou shalt be
    Damned for thy false apostasy.   15

8

Song

Persuasions to Enjoy

If the quick spirits in your eye
Now languish, and anon must die;

---

7. The theme is that of Catullus, *Carm.* viii. 12–19, and Propertius, III. xxv, and cf. Donne, 'The Apparition'. Musical setting: Henry Lawes.

8. The sophistical argument, presented more succinctly by Ronsard, is the traditional one from change and loss, of which Herrick's 'To the Virgins' (H–73) presents a Christian sacramentalized version. Musical settings: Henry Lawes and Giovanni Giacomo Gastoldi di Carravaggio.   1 *quick*: vivid, vital. *spirits*: see G.

If every sweet, and every grace,
Must fly from that forsaken face:
    Then, Celia, let us reap our joys,   5
    Ere Time such goodly fruit destroys.

Or if that golden fleece must grow
For ever free from aged snow;
If those bright suns must know no shade,
Nor your fresh beauties ever fade: 10
Then fear not, Celia, to bestow
What, still being gathered, still must grow.
    Thus, either Time his sickle brings
    In vain, or else in vain his wings.

9

A Deposition from Love

I was foretold your rebel sex
    Nor love nor pity knew,
And with what scorn you use to vex
    Poor hearts that humbly sue;
Yet I believed, to crown our pain,   5
    Could we the fortress win,
The happy lover sure should gain
    A paradise within:
I thought Love's plagues like dragons sate,
Only to fright us at the gate.   10

7 *golden fleece*: alluding to the object of Jason's quest in the *Argonautica*.
13–14 *Thus, either*, etc.: loving, we triumph in time or eternity.

9. Most of the imagery of the poem is that of the siege, which Suckling exploits
in 'Love's Siege' (S–24); it was a Caroline inheritance from the Petrarchan
tradition. Musical setting: Henry Lawes. 9 *Love's plagues like dragons sate*:
alluding to the guardian monsters of medieval romance and classical mythology,
notably the dragon (Ladon) or dragons that guarded the golden apples in the
garden of the Hesperides, a type of paradise.

But I did enter, and enjoy
   What happy lovers prove;
For I could kiss, and sport, and toy,
   And taste those sweets of love,
Which, had they but a lasting state,   15
   Or if in Celia's breast
The force of love might not abate,
   Jove were too mean a guest.
But now her breach of faith far more
Afflicts than did her scorn before.   20

Hard fate! to have been once possessed,
   As victor, of a heart
Achieved with labour, and unrest,
   And then forced to depart.
If the stout foe will not resign,   25
   When I besiege a town,
I lose but what was never mine;
   But he that is cast down
From enjoyed beauty feels a woe
Only deposèd kings can know.   30

10

Ingrateful Beauty Threatened

Know, Celia (since thou art so proud),
   'Twas I that gave thee thy renown:
Thou hadst, in the forgotten crowd
   Of common beauties, lived unknown,
Had not my verse exhaled thy name,   5
And with it imped the wings of Fame.

10. Dunlap notes a translation of this poem into Latin elegiacs by Henry Jacob and refers to the expression of the same theme in Propertius, II. xi. 1–4. Musical setting: Henry Lawes. 6 *imp*[*ed*]: technically, 'repair' (falconry). The process involves grafting a moulted feather onto the stump of an injured feather.

That killing power is none of thine;
 I gave it to thy voice and eyes:
Thy sweets, thy graces, all are mine;
 Thou art my star, shin'st in my skies;   10
Then dart not from thy borrowed sphere
Lightning on him that fixed thee there.

Tempt me with such affrights no more,
 Lest what I made I uncreate;
Let fools thy mystic forms adore,
 I'll know thee in thy mortal state: 15
Wise poets, that wrapped Truth in tales,
Knew her themselves, through all her veils.

11

Disdain Returned

He that loves a rosy cheek,
 Or a coral lip admires,
Or from star-like eyes doth seek
 Fuel to maintain his fires;
As old Time makes these decay,   5
So his flames must waste away.

But a smooth and steadfast mind,
 Gentle thoughts and calm desires,
Hearts with equal love combined,
 Kindle never-dying fires.   10
Where these are not, I despise
Lovely cheeks, or lips, or eyes.

10–12 *Thou art my star*, etc.: and also my falcon, continuing the metaphor
suggested in l. 6. 11 *sphere*: see NRC. 17–18 *Wise poets, that wrapped Truth in
tales*. Dunlap cites Thomas Stanley's translation of Pico della Mirandola's
Platonik Discourse upon Love: 'The ancient ethnic theologians . . . cast poetical
veils over the face of their mysteries' (p. 222); Renaissance mythography was
characteristically allegorical.

11. Musical settings: Walter Porter (1632) and Henry Lawes. The last stanza
does not occur in Porter's setting, printed in Carew's lifetime, and it is often
omitted by anthologists. The first two stanzas are entirely complementary and
self-subsistent as a poem.

No tears, Celia, now shall win
    My resolved heart to return;
I have searched thy soul within,   15
    And find nought but pride and scorn;
I have learned thy arts, and now
Can disdain as much as thou.
Some power, in my revenge convey
That love to her I cast away.   20

12

A Looking-Glass

That flattering glass whose smooth face wears
Your shadow, which a sun appears,
Was once a river of my tears.

About your cold heart they did make
A circle, where the briny lake   5
Congealed into a crystal cake.

Gaze no more on that killing eye,
For fear the native cruelty
Doom you, as it doth all, to die;

For fear lest the fair object move   10
Your froward heart to fall in love:
Then you yourself my rival prove.

Look rather on my pale cheeks pined:
There view your beauties; there you'll find
A fair face, but a cruel mind.   15

19 *power*: i.e. supernatural power, or deity; some MSS. read 'god'.

12. It is uncertain whether this or the following version of the poem, if either, was finally preferred by Carew; this one appeared in the posthumous *Poems*, 1640. Thomas Randolph has a poem 'To One Admiring Herself in a Looking-Glass'. Musical setting: anonymous, for solo voice, in British Museum MS. Egerton 2013. 2 *shadow*: i.e. image, but with a turn on 'shadow' in relation to the 'sun'. 6 *crystal*: clear ice; cf. C–1: 3–4.

Be not for ever frozen, coy;
One beam of love will soon destroy
And melt that ice to floods of joy.

13

On His Mistress Looking in a Glass

This flattering glass, whose smooth face wears
Your shadow, which a sun appears,
Was once a river of my tears.

About your cold heart they did make
A circle, where the briny lake   5
Congealed into a crystal cake.

This glass and shadow seem to say,
Like us the beauties you survey
Will quickly break or fly away.

Since then my tears can only show   10
You your own face, you cannot know
How fair you are but by my woe.

Nor had the world else known your name,
But that my sad verse spread the fame
Of thee, most fair and cruel dame.   15

Forsake but your disdainful mind,
And in my song the world shall find
That you are not more fair than kind.

Change but your scorn, my verse shall chase
Decay far from you, and your face   20
Shall shine with an immortal grace.

---

13. An alternative version of 'A Looking-Glass' preceding, from manuscripts
(see Dunlap, p. 273); the first six lines are the same except for the first word.

14

To My Mistress in Absence

Though I must live here, and by force
Of your command suffer divorce;
Though I am parted, yet my mind
(That's more myself) still stays behind;
I breathe in you, you keep my heart;   5
'Twas but a carcass that did part.
Then, though our bodies are disjoined,
As things that are to place confined,
Yet let our boundless spirits meet,
And in love's sphere each other greet;   10
There let us work a mystic wreath,
Unknown unto the world beneath;
There let our clasped loves sweetly twin;
There let our secret thoughts unseen
Like nets be weaved and intertwined,   15
Wherewith we'll catch each other's mind;
There, whilst our souls do sit and kiss,
Tasting a sweet and subtle bliss
(Such as gross lovers cannot know,
Whose hands, and lips, meet here below),   20
Let us look down, and mark what pain
Our absent bodies here sustain,
And smile to see how far away
The one doth from the other stray,
Yet burn and languish with desire   25
To join, and quench their mutual fire.
There let us joy to see, from far,
Our em'lous flames at loving war,
Whilst both with equal lustre shine,
Mine bright as yours, yours bright as mine.   30

---

14. 5–6 *I breathe in you,* etc. It was a commonplace of the mysteries of love that
'the soul of a lover lives in another body' (marginal note in Sir Thomas North's
translation of Plutarch's 'Life of Mark Antony'). Cf. Donne, 'A Valediction:
Forbidding Mourning' and 'The Ecstasy', and Lovelace, 'To Lucasta: Going
Beyond the Seas' (L–1).

There seated in those heavenly bowers,
We'll cheat the lag and lingering hours,
Making our bitter absence sweet,
Till souls, and bodies both, may meet.

15

To Her in Absence

A Ship

Tossed in a troubled sea of griefs, I float
Far from the shore, in a storm-beaten boat,
Where my sad thoughts do (like the compass) show
The several points from which cross winds do blow.
My heart doth, like the needle, touched with love,   5
Still fixed on you, point which way I would move.
You are the bright pole-star, which in the dark
Of this long absence guides my wandering bark.
Love is the pilot, but o'ercome with fear
Of your displeasure dares not homewards steer;   10
My fearful hope hangs on my trembling sail;
Nothing is wanting but a gentle gale,
Which pleasant breath must blow from your sweet lip:
Bid it but move, and quick as thought this ship
Into your arms, which are my port, will fly,   15
Where it for ever shall at anchor lie.

32 *lag*: lagging, tardy.

15. The navigational conceit is a commonplace of Petrarchan love poetry. Cf.,
for example, Petrarch, *Rime*, 80, 164, 177, 189, 235, 237, and 272; and also
Wyatt, 'My galley charged with forgetfulness', and Drayton, *Idea*, 1, 'Like an
adventurous seafarer am I'.

16

Upon Some Alterations in My Mistress,
After My Departure into France

O gentle Love, do not forsake the guide
Of my frail bark, on which the swelling tide
      Of ruthless pride
Doth beat, and threaten wrack from every side.
Gulfs of disdain do gape to overwhelm   5
This boat, nigh sunk with grief, whilst at the helm
      Despair commands;
    And round about, the shifting sands
Of faithless love, and false inconstancy,
      With rocks of cruelty,   10
Stop up my passage to the neighbour lands.

My sighs have raised those winds whose fury bears
My sails o'erboard, and in their place spreads tears,
      And from my tears
This sea is sprung, where nought but death appears;   15
A misty cloud of anger hides the light
Of my fair star, and everywhere black night
      Usurps the place
    Of those bright rays which once did grace
My forth-bound ship: but when it could no more   20
      Behold the vanished shore,
In the deep flood she drowned her beamy face.

17

Good Counsel to a Young Maid

When you the sunburnt pilgrim see
    Fainting with thirst, haste to the springs,
Mark how at first with bended knee
    He courts the crystal nymph, and flings
    His body to the earth, where he   5
Prostrate adores the flowing deity.

17. Musical setting: Henry Lawes.

But when his sweaty face is drenched
  In her cool waves, when from her sweet
Bosom his burning thirst is quenched,
    Then mark how with disdainful feet   10
    He kicks her banks, and from the place
That thus refreshed him moves with sullen pace.

So shalt thou be despised, fair maid,
  When by the sated lover tasted;
What first he did with tears invade   15
    Shall afterwards with scorn be wasted;
    When all thy virgin-springs grow dry,
When no streams shall be left but in thine eye.

18

To T. H., a Lady Resembling My Mistress

Fair copy of my Celia's face,
Twin of my soul, thy perfect grace
Claims in my love an equal place.

Disdain not a divided heart;
Though all be hers, you shall have part: 5
Love is not tied to rules of art.

For as my soul first to her flew,
Yet stayed with me, so now 'tis true
It dwells with her, though fled to you.

Then entertain this wandering guest,   10
And if not love, allow it rest:
It left not, but mistook, the nest.

Nor think my love or your fair eyes
Cheaper, 'cause from the sympathies
You hold with her these flames arise.   15

18. 6 *art*: logic, which with grammar and rhetoric constituted the *trivium* ('art'
was used of both whole and parts). 11 *not*: so *CP 40* Errata and Dunlap;
CP 40 text reads 'it'.

To lead, or brass, or some such bad
Metal, a prince's stamp may add
That value which it never had;

But to the pure refinèd ore
The stamp of kings imparts no more   20
Worth than the metal held before.

Only the image gives the rate
To subjects; in a foreign state
'Tis prized as much for its own weight.

So though all other hearts resign   25
To your pure worth, yet you have mine
Only because you are her coin.

19

To Saxham

Though frost and snow locked from mine eyes
That beauty which without door lies,
Thy gardens, orchards, walks, that so
I might not all thy pleasures know,
Yet, Saxham, thou within thy gate   5
Art of thyself so delicate,
So full of native sweets that bless
Thy roof with inward happiness,
As neither from nor to thy store
Winter takes aught, or spring adds more.   10
The cold and frozen air had starved
Much poor, if not by thee preserved,
Whose prayers have made thy table blest
With plenty, far above the rest.

16–27 *To lead, or brass*, etc.: Cf. Donne, Elegy X ('The Dream'), ll. 1–6, and
'The Second Anniversary', ll. 223–5.

19. This topographical poem belongs to the specific genre of the Country-House
Poem (see G) and owes much to the first English poem in the genre, Jonson's
'To Penshurst'. On 'Saxham' see G s.v. 'Sir John Crofts'.

The season hardly did afford   15
Coarse cates unto thy neighbours' board,
Yet thou hadst dainties as the sky
Had only been thy volary;
Or else the birds, fearing the snow
Might to another Deluge grow,   20
The pheasant, partridge, and the lark
Flew to thy house as to the Ark.
The willing ox of himself came
Home to the slaughter, with the lamb,
And every beast did thither bring   25
Himself to be an offering.
The scaly herd more pleasure took,
Bathed in thy dish, than in the brook.
Water, earth, air, did all conspire
To pay their tributes to thy fire,   30
Whose cherishing flames themselves divide
Through every room, where they deride
The night and cold abroad; whilst they,
Like suns within, keep endless day.
Those cheerful beams send forth their light   35
To all that wander in the night,
And seem to beckon from aloof
The weary pilgrim to thy roof;
Where if, refreshed, he will away,
He's fairly welcome, or if stay   40
Far more, which he shall hearty find,
Both from the master and the hind.
The stranger's welcome each man there
Stamped on his cheerful brow doth wear;
Nor doth this welcome or his cheer   45
Grow less 'cause he stays longer here:
There's none observes (much less repines)
How often this man sups or dines.
Thou hast no porter at the door
T' examine, or keep back the poor;   50

---

18 *volary*: large bird-cage, aviary.   27 *scaly herd*: a type of periphrasis—for fish
—that became widespread in the eighteenth century. Cf. S–9: 7, 'scaly fry'.
33 *abroad*: afar.   42 *hind*: farm servant.

Nor locks nor bolts: thy gates have been
Made only to let strangers in;
Untaught to shut, they do not fear
To stand wide open all the year;
Careless who enters, for they know   55
Thou never didst deserve a foe;
And as for thieves, thy bounty's such,
They cannot steal, thou giv'st so much.

20

Upon a Ribband

This silken wreath, which circles in mine arm,
Is but an emblem of that mystic charm
Wherewith the magic of your beauties binds
My captive soul, and round about it winds
Fetters of lasting love. This hath entwined   5
My flesh alone, that hath impaled my mind:
Time may wear out these soft weak bands, but those
Strong chains of brass Fate shall not discompose.
This holy relic may preserve my wrist,
But my whole frame doth by that power subsist: 10
To that my prayers and sacrifice, to this
I only pay a superstitious kiss:
This but the idol, that's the deity;
Religion there is due, here cer'mony.
That I receive by faith, this but in trust;   15
Here I may tender duty, there I must.
This order as a layman I may bear,
But I become Love's priest when that I wear.
This moves like air, that as the centre stands;
That knot your virtue tied, this but your hands;   20
That Nature framed, but this was made by Art;
This makes my arm your prisoner, that my heart.

20. 1 ff. *This silken wreath*, etc.: bracelet of hair used as a love token; cf. Donne, 'The Funeral' and 'The Relic'.   6 *impaled*: enclosed (strictly, with pales or stakes).   19 *centre*: i.e. earth (see NRC).

21

To the King, at His Entrance into Saxham

By Master John Crofts

Sir,
Ere you pass this threshold, stay,
And give your creature leave to pay
Those pious rites which unto you,
As to our household gods, are due.
Instead of sacrifice, each breast   5
Is like a flaming altar drest
With zealous fires, which from pure hearts
Love mixed with loyalty imparts.
   Incense nor gold have we, yet bring
As rich and sweet an offering;   10
And such as doth both these express,
Which is our humble thankfulness,
By which is paid the All we owe
To gods above, or men below.
The slaughtered beast, whose flesh should feed   15
The hungry flames, we for pure need
Dress for your supper, and the gore
Which should be dashed on every door
We change into the lusty blood
Of youthful vines, of which a flood   20
Shall sprightly run through all your veins,
First to your health, then your fair train's.
   We shall want nothing but good fare
To show your welcome and our care;
Such rarities that come from far   25
From poor men's houses banished are;
Yet we'll express in homely cheer
How glad we are to see you here.
We'll have whate'er the season yields,
Out of the neighb'ring woods and fields;   30

21. This declamatory poem was written to be recited by Sir John Crofts's (see G) son John at one of James I's visits to Saxham in 1620 and 1621. 17-18 *The gore* etc.: after Exod. 12: 7.

For all the dainties of your board
Will only be what those afford;
And, having supped, we may perchance
Present you with a country dance.
  Thus much your servants, that bear sway   35
Here in your absence, bade me say,
And beg, besides, you'ld hither bring
Only the mercy of a king,
And not the greatness, since they have
A thousand faults must pardon crave,   40
But nothing that is fit to wait
Upon the glory of your state.
Yet your gracious favour will,
They hope, as heretofore, shine still
On their endeavours, for they swore,   45
Should Jove descend, they could no more.

22

A New-Year's Sacrifice

To Lucinda

Those that can give, open their hands this day;
Those that cannot, yet hold them up to pray,
That health may crown the seasons of this year,
And mirth dance round the circle; that no tear
(Unless of joy) may with its briny dew   5
Discolour on your cheek the rosy hue;
That no access of years presume t' abate
Your beauty's ever-flourishing estate.
  Such cheap and vulgar wishes I could lay
As trivial offerings at your feet this day,   10
But that it were apostacy in me
To send a prayer to any deity
But your divine self, who have power to give
Those blessings unto others, such as live

---

22. Dated 1633 by a MS. text, this poem is addressed to Lucy, Countess of
Carlisle (see G).   9 verse-paragraph supplied.

Like me, by the sole influence of your eyes,   15
Whose fair aspects govern our destinies.
  Such incense, vows, and holy rites, as were
To the involvèd serpent of the year
Paid by Egyptian priests, lay I before
Lucinda's sacred shrine, whilst I adore   20
Her beauteous eyes, and her pure altars dress
With gums and spice of humble thankfulness.
  So may my goddess from her heaven inspire
My frozen bosom with a Delphic fire,
And then the world shall by that glorious flame   25
Behold the blaze of thy immortal name.

23

Song

The Willing Prisoner to His Mistress

Let fools great Cupid's yoke disdain,
  Loving their own wild freedom better;
Whilst proud of my triumphant chain
  I sit, and court my beauteous fetter.

Her murdering glances, snaring hairs,   5
  And her bewitching smiles so please me,
As he brings ruin that repairs
  The sweet afflictions that disease me.

Hide not those panting balls of snow
  With envious veils from my beholding;   10

15–16 *influence . . . aspects*: her eyes are implicitly made stars by these astro-nomical and astrological terms. Cf. C–23: 13–14.   18 *the involved serpent of the year*: 'the Egyptian symbol of endless time as a snake devouring its own tail' (Dunlap, p. 229).   24 *Delphic fire*: inspiring prophetic and poetic 'rage', as coming from the hearth of the shrine of the Oracle of Delphi, Apollo's prophetess. 26 *the blaze*, etc.: aptly, since her name is derived from Latin *lux* '(sun)light'.

23. The figure is a commonplace in Petrarchan and earlier love poetry; Dunlap cites Propertius, I. vi. 27–8, and notes that Carew's first two stanzas may have been specifically copied from a chançon by Pontus de Tyard (p. 231). Musical setting: Henry Lawes.   4 *beauteous fetter*: probably a wreath of 'snaring hair' (l. 5), as in 'Upon a Ribband' (C–20).

Unlock those lips, their pearly row
  In a sweet smile of love unfolding.

And let those eyes, whose motion wheels
  The restless fate of every lover,
Survey the pains my sick heart feels,   15
  And wounds themselves have made discover.

24

A Fly That Flew into My Mistress's Eye

When this fly lived, she used to play
In the sunshine all the day;
Till, coming near my Celia's sight,
She found a new and unknown light
So full of glory as it made   5
The noonday sun a gloomy shade.
Then this amorous fly became
My rival, and did court my flame;
She did from hand to bosom skip,
And from her breath, her cheek, and lip   10
Sucked all the incense and the spice,
And grew a bird of paradise.
At last into her eye she flew;
There scorched in flames and drowned in dew,
Like Phaeton from the sun's sphere   15
She fell, and with her dropped a tear,
Of which a pearl was straight composed,
Wherein her ashes lie enclosed.
Thus she received from Celia's eye
Funeral flame, tomb, obsequy.   20

13–14 *those eyes*, etc.: see C–22: 15–16 n.

24. The theme was a commonplace at least from Petrarch's time on (Dunlap
quotes Guarini's Madrigal No. 37, p. 231), and, under the influence of a
medieval poem misattributed to Ovid, such flea/fly poems proliferated in the
sixteenth and early seventeenth centuries; the most famous of these poems is
Donne's 'Flea'. There is evidence that this poem was written in 1619–23, and
it occurs in a number of manuscript miscellanies. Musical setting: Henry Lawes.
12 *Bird of Paradise*: the 'incense' and 'spice' suggest that phoenix (see **G**) is
intended.   15–16 *Like Phaeton*, etc.: see **G**.

25

Boldness in Love

Mark how the bashful morn in vain
Courts the amorous marigold
With sighing blasts and weeping rain,
Yet she refuses to unfold.
But when the planet of the day   5
Approacheth with his powerful ray,
Then she spreads, then she receives
His warmer beams into her virgin leaves.
So shalt thou thrive in love, fond boy;
If thy tears and sighs discover   10
Thy grief, thou never shalt enjoy
The just reward of a bold lover;
But when with moving accents thou
Shalt constant faith and service vow,
Thy Celia shall receive those charms   15
With open ears, and with unfolded arms.

26

A Pastoral Dialogue

Shepherd   Nymph   Chorus

Shepherd. This mossy bank they pressed. *Nymph.* That aged oak
          Did canopy the happy pair
          All night from the dank air.

Chorus. Here let us sit, and sing the words they spoke,
          Till the day breaking their embraces broke.   5

25. This poem turns on the poetical commonplace that the marigold opens when the sun shines. Musical setting: Nicholas Lanier (?), or possibly Charles I (see Dunlap, pp. 291–2).

26. 'In general conception and a few details this poem shows the influence of *Rom.* III. v. 1–36, which also portrays the reluctant parting of lovers at dawn' (Dunlap, p. 234), making it a dialogue aubade.   3 *dank*: so *CP 40* text and MSS.; *CP 40* Errata and Dunlap read 'damp'.

Shepherd. See, love, the blushes of the morn appear,
   And now she hangs her pearly store
   (Robbed from the Eastern shore)
   I' th' cowslip's bell and rose's ear:
   Sweet, I must stay no longer here.   10

Nymph. Those streaks of doubtful light usher not day,
   But show my sun must set; no morn
   Shall shine till thou return;
   The yellow planets and the grey
   Dawn shall attend thee on thy way.   15

Shepherd. If thine eyes gild my paths, they may forbear
   Their useless shine. *Nymph.* My tears will quite
   Extinguish their faint light.

Shepherd. Those drops will make their beams more clear;
   Love's flames will shine in every tear.   20

Chorus. They kissed and wept, and from their lips and eyes,
   In a mixed dew of briny sweet,
   Their joys and sorrows meet,
   But she cries out. *Nymph.* Shepherd, arise!
   The sun betrays us else to spies.   25

Shepherd. The wingèd hours fly fast whilst we embrace,
   But when we want their help to meet
   They move with leaden feet.
Nymph. Then let us pinion Time, and chase
   The day for ever from this place.   30

Shepherd. Hark! *Nymph.* Ay me, stay! *Shepherd.* For ever! *Nymph.*
   No, arise!
   We must be gone. *Shepherd.* My nest of spice!
Nymph. My soul! *Shepherd.* My paradise!

Chorus. Neither could say farewell, but through their eyes
   Grief interrupted speech with tears' supplies. 35

---

9 *ear*: *Poems*, 1670, MSS., Dunlap, and *MND* II. i. 14–15; '[roses] rare'
in *CP 40* and Howarth. 29–30 Cf. Marvell, 'To His Coy Mistress', ll. 38–46,
especially the last two lines. 35 i.e. grief supplies interrupted speech with tears.

27

A Lover, upon an Accident Necessitating
His Departure, Consults with Reason

Lover

Weep not, nor backward turn your beams,
    Fond eyes; sad sighs, lock in your breath,
Lest on this wind, or in those streams,
    My grieved soul fly or sail to death.
Fortune destroys me if I stay,   5
Love kills me if I go away:
Since Love and Fortune both are blind,
Come, Reason, and resolve my doubtful mind.

Reason

Fly, and blind Fortune be thy guide,
    And gainst the blinder god rebel: 10
Thy lovesick heart shall not reside
    Where Scorn and self-willed Error dwell,
Where entrance unto Truth is barred,
Where Love and Faith find no reward;
For my just hand may sometime move   15
The wheel of Fortune, not the sphere of Love.

---

27. Musical setting: Henry Lawes.   3 *wind . . . streams*: conventional Petrarchan
hyperboles.

28

A Rapture

I will enjoy thee now, my Celia, come
And fly with me to Love's Elysium:
The giant, Honour, that keeps cowards out,
Is but a masquer, and the servile rout
Of baser subjects only bend in vain   5
To the vast idol, whilst the nobler train
Of valiant soldiers daily sail between
The huge Colossus' legs, and pass unseen
Unto the blissful shore. Be bold and wise,
And we shall enter: the grim Swiss denies   10
Only tame fools a passage, that not know
He is but form, and only frights in show
The duller eyes that look from far; draw near,
And thou shalt scorn what we were wont to fear.
We shall see how the stalking pageant goes   15
With borrowed legs, a heavy load to those
That made and bear him; not as we once thought
The seed of gods, but a weak model wrought
By greedy men that seek t' enclose the common
And within private arms impale free woman.   20

28. Carew's principal models were Donne's Elegy XIX ('Going to Bed'), the second of the *Basia* of Johannes Secundus, and a chorus from Tasso's *Aminta*, Act I. 'A Rapture' may be dated before 1624 if, as Dunlap argues (pp. 236–7), *The Tragedy of Nero, Newly Written*, printed anonymously in 1624 and reprinted in 1633, is patterned in part after 'A Rapture' rather than the other way round. 2 *Elysium*: see G.   3 *The giant, Honour*: cf. Donne, 'The Damp', ll. 11–12; and Suckling, S–24: 35–6.   4 *masquer*: masquerader, pretended 'giant'.   7 *soldiers*: so *CP 40* text; Dunlap reads 'lovers' with the Errata; 'soldiers' belongs more strictly to the vehicle, 'lovers' to the tenor, of the conceit.   8 *the huge Colossus' legs*: alluding to the Colossus of Rhodes, one of the seven wonders of the ancient world; it was Chares' huge bronze statue of Apollo, whose legs were said (as here) to have straddled the entrance of the harbour. *CP 40* reads 'Collosse[']s', a common English form.   10–13 *the grim Swiss* etc.: i.e. 'Swiss guard'; these mercenary soldiers were used as a special body-guard by continental monarchs; cf. Claudius' 'Switzers' (*Ham.* IV. v. 97); Marvell's 'Upon Appleton House', l. 336. Dunlap cites Donne, Elegy IV ('The Perfume'), ll. 31–4 (which also include 'the great Rhodian Colossus').   15 *the stalking pageant*: a piece of stage machinery, or a mechanical contrivance or machine generally (*OED* 2b), here specifically a mechanical giant; allusion to the Hindu 'juggernaut' seems possible (*OED*, 1638).   20 *impale*: enclose (within pales or stakes).

Come, then, and mounted on the wings of Love
We'll cut the flitting air, and soar above
The monster's head, and in the noblest seats
Of those blest shades quench and renew our heats.
There shall the Queen of Love, and Innocence,   25
Beauty, and Nature, banish all offence
From our close ivy-twines; there I'll behold
Thy barèd snow and thy unbraided gold;
There my enfranchised hand on every side
Shall o'er thy naked polished ivory slide.   30
No curtain there, though of transparent lawn,
Shall be before thy virgin-treasure drawn;
But the rich mine, to the enquiring eye
Exposed, shall ready still for mintage lie,
And we will coin young Cupids. There a bed   35
Of roses and fresh myrtles shall be spread
Under the cooler shade of cypress groves,
Our pillows of the down of Venus' doves,
Whereon our panting limbs we'll gently lay
In the faint respites of our active play,   40
That so our slumbers may in dreams have leisure
To tell the nimble fancy our past pleasure;
And so our souls, that cannot be embraced,
Shall the embraces of our bodies taste.
Meanwhile the bubbling stream shall court the shore;   45
Th' enamoured chirping wood-choir shall adore
In varied tunes the deity of Love;
The gentle blasts of western winds shall move
The trembling leaves, and through their close boughs breathe
Still music, whilst we rest ourselves beneath   50
Their dancing shade; till a soft murmur, sent
From souls entranced in am'rous languishment,
Rouse us, and shoot into our veins fresh fire,
Till we in their sweet ecstasy expire.

33–5 *the rich mine* etc.: cf. Donne, 'Love's Alchemy', l. 1, and Elegy XIX, ll. 29 ff.
34 *mintage*: coinage, here with reference specifically to the stamping of images.
36 *myrtles*: sacred to Venus and an emblem of love, like the doves of l. 37.

Then, as the empty bee, that lately bore   55
Into the common treasure all her store,
Flies 'bout the painted field with nimble wing,
Deflow'ring the fresh virgins of the spring,
So will I rifle all the sweets that dwell
In my delicious paradise, and swell   60
My bag with honey, drawn forth by the power
Of fervent kisses, from each spicy flower.
I'll seize the rose-buds in their perfumed bed,
The violet knots, like curious mazes spread
O'er all the garden, taste the ripened cherry,   65
The warm firm apple, tipped with coral berry;
Then will I visit, with a wandering kiss,
The vale of lilies and the bower of bliss;
And, where the beauteous region doth divide
Into two milky ways, my lips shall slide   70
Down those smooth alleys, wearing as I go
A tract for lovers on the printed snow;
Thence climbing o'er the swelling Apennine
Retire into thy grove of eglantine,
Where I will all those ravished sweets distil   75
Through love's alembic, and with chemic skill

55–62 *the empty bee*: cf. Suckling, S–20: 16–25. Herrick is fond of bee conceits
(see *A Concordance to the Poems of Robert Herrick*, comp. Malcolm MacLeod, 1936).
61 *bag*: worker bees store nectar sucked from flowers in their sacs, removing it
when they return to the hive.   63–78 A visitation of flowers symbolizing an
expedition of sexual arousal culminates in a 'great elixir' ready 'for the hive'
(l. 78), but it is doubtful whether there is a consistent allegory of relatively
simple anatomical equivalences here. Carew's impressionism of equivalences
seems to be intermittent and sometimes indirect here, as it is certainly direct
and consistent in ll. 85 ff. In any case, the anatomical possibilities are obvious
enough.   64 *violet knots . . . curious mazes*: as found in the elaborate gardens of
the period. Elizabeth Burton notes that James I 'clipped hedges, put in neat
linden avenues, fountains, *a mount of Venus set within a labyrinth*, and he encircled
the park with miles of high wall' ('Of Gardens and Gardeners' in *The Jacobeans
at Home*, London: Secker and Warburg, 1962, p. 381, my italics).   65–6 *cherry
. . . apple . . . coral berry*: so *CP 40* and Dunlap; most MSS. read 'cherries . . .
apples . . . crimson berries'. Such variants complicate attempts at anatomical
identification. 'Cherries' were ordinarily lips, in Petrarchan symbology; apples
figure breasts.   68 *vale of lilies*: cf. S. of S. 2: 16.   *bower of bliss*: after *Faerie
Queene*, II. xii, the garden of sensual pleasure.   73 *Apennine*: to be identified with
the *mons Veneris*?   74 *eglantine*: or sweetbrier, a species of rose having prickles,
pink single flowers, and small aromatic leaves.   76 *love's alembic*: an alchemical
distilling apparatus so shaped as to be able to represent either the womb (as
in Donne's 'Love's Alchemy') or the penis (as here).

From the mixed mass one sovereign balm derive,
Then bring that great elixir to thy hive.
   Now in more subtile wreaths I will entwine
My sin'wy thighs, my legs and arms, with thine;   80
Thou like a sea of milk shalt lie displayed,
Whilst I the smooth, calm oceän invade
With such a tempest as when Jove of old
Fell down on Danae in a storm of gold:
Yet my tall pine shall in the Cyprian strait   85
Ride safe at anchor, and unlade her freight;
My rudder with thy bold hand, like a tried
And skilful pilot, thou shalt steer, and guide
My bark into love's channel, where it shall
Dance, as the bounding waves do rise or fall.   90
Then shall thy circling arms embrace and clip
My willing body, and thy balmy lip
Bathe me in juice of kisses, whose perfume
Like a religious incense shall consume,
And send up holy vapours to those powers   95
That bless our loves and crown our sportful hours,
That with such halcyon calmness fix our souls
In steadfast peace as no affright controls.
There no rude sounds shake us with sudden starts;
No jealous ears, when we unrip our hearts,   100
Suck our discourse in; no observing spies
This blush, that glance, traduce; no envious eyes
Watch our close meetings; nor are we betrayed
To rivals by the bribèd chambermaid.
No wedlock bonds unwreathe our twisted loves;   105
We seek no midnight arbour, no dark groves,

---

77 *balm*: a medicinal ointment; here a sexual panacea, like the 'elixir' in the following line.　78 *elixir*: a supposed essence capable of prolonging life indefinitely; in alchemy, a supposed preparation able to change baser metals into gold. Cf. Donne's 'Love's Alchemy' (ll. 7–10), and Elegy VIII, ll. 35–8. 79–90 The vehicle changes. He becomes first a kind of tree ('subtle wreaths', 'sin'wy thighs'), then a ship (cf. Catullus, *Carm.* iv, 'Phasellus ille'); she becomes the Sea (cf. Donne, Elegy XVIII, 'Love's Progress'; and Shakespeare, *Tro.*, i. iii. 34–45).　84 *Danae*: see G.　85 *pine*: a common synecdoche for ship (like *trabs* in Catullus, *Carm.* iv. 3), with obvious anatomical application.　*Cyprian*: Venus' birthplace was Cyprus.　92 *willing*: so *CP 40* and Dunlap; 'naked' in most MSS.　100 *unrip*: open; the word originally meant 'strip (a house or roof) of tiles' (*SOED*).　103 *close*: secret; perhaps also intimate.

To hide our kisses; there the hated name
Of husband, wife, lust, modest, chaste, or shame,
Are vain and empty words, whose very sound
Was never heard in the Elysian ground.   110
All things are lawful there that may delight
Nature or unrestrainèd appetite;
Like and enjoy, to will and act, is one:
We only sin when Love's rites are not done.
    The Roman Lucrece there reads the divine   115
Lectures of love's great master, Aretine,
And knows as well as Lais how to move
Her pliant body in the act of love.
To quench the burning ravisher, she hurls
Her limbs into a thousand winding curls,   120
And studies artful postures, such as be
Carved on the bark of every neighb'ring tree
By learned hands that so adorned the rind
Of those fair plants, which as they lay entwined
Have fanned their glowing fires. The Grecian Dame,   125
That in her endless web toiled for a name
As fruitless as her work, doth there display
Herself before the Youth of Ithaca,
And th' amorous sport of gamesome nights prefer
Before dull dreams of the lost Traveller.   130
Daphne hath broke her bark, and that swift foot
Which th' angry gods had fastened with a root

---

115 *Lucrece*: Lucretia, a Roman matron (wife of Collatinus) legendary for her fidelity in refusing the advances of Tarquin and killing herself when raped by him. 116 *lectures of . . . Aretine*: presumably the erotic sonnets Pietro Aretino (1492–1556) wrote to accompany the sixteen engravings Marcantonio Raimondi made for Giulio Romano. Burton wrote that 'Aretine's Lucretia sold her maidenhead a thousand times before she was twenty-four years old' (*Anatomy of Melancholy*, Part. III, Sect. II, Mem. I, Subs. II). 117 *Lais*. There were three celebrated Greek courtesans of this name. The most famous (b. *c.* 420 B.C.) was the daughter of Alcibiades' mistress, Timandra; she was patronized by men of all stations, but she charged too much for Demosthenes. 119 *the burning ravisher*: Tarquin. 125–30 *the Grecian dame*: Penelope, the faithful wife of 'the lost Traveller' (l. 130), Odysseus; she is here said to have woven her 'endless web' (woven by day, unravelled by night) not to put off suitors but 'for a name' ('Penelope' *is* eponymous for patient fidelity). 128 *youth of Ithaca*: probably plural for all the suitors, but possibly a singular referring to Antinous, the most arrogant. 131–9 *Daphne*: a nymph pursued by Apollo and turned to a bay tree.

To the fixed earth doth now unfettered run
To meet th' embraces of the youthful Sun:
She hangs upon him like his Delphic lyre;   135
Her kisses blow the old and breathe new fire;
Full of her god, she sings inspired lays,
Sweet odes of love, such as deserve the bays,
Which she herself was. Next her, Laura lies
In Petrarch's learned arms, drying those eyes   140
That did in such sweet smooth-paced numbers flow
As made the world enamoured of his woe.
These, and ten thousand beauties more, that died
Slave to the tyrant, now enlarged deride
His cancelled laws, and for their time mis-spent   145
Pay into Love's exchequer double rent.
    Come then, my Celia, we'll no more forbear
To taste our joys, struck with a Panic fear,
But will depose from his imperious sway
This proud usurper and walk free as they,   150
With necks unyoked; nor is it just that he
Should fetter your soft sex with chastity,
Which Nature made unapt for abstinence;
When yet this false impostor can dispense
With human justice, and with sacred right,   155
And maugre both their laws command me fight
With rivals, or with em'lous loves, that dare
Equal with thine their mistress' eyes or hair:
If thou complain of wrong, and call my sword
To carve out thy revenge, upon that word   160
He bids me fight and kill, or else he brands
With marks of infamy my coward hands;
And yet Religion bids from bloodshed fly,
And damns me for that act. Then tell me why
    This goblin Honour, which the world adores,   165
    Should make men atheists, and not women whores.

139–40 *Laura . . . Petrarch*: the famous beloved (d. 1348) of the famous
poet-lover (1304–74); she has a traditional identification as a wife, but 'her
identity is totally uncertain' except as Petrarch recreates it in his sonnets.
144 *tyrant*: Honour. 146 *Love's exchequer*: from Donne's Elegy XVIII ('Love's
Progress'), ll. 91–4. 156 *maugre*: despite.

29

Epitaph on the Lady Mary Villiers

The Lady Mary Villiers lies
Under this stone; with weeping eyes
The parents that first gave her birth,
And their sad friends, laid her in earth.
If any of them, Reader, were   5
Known unto thee, shed a tear;
Or if thyself possess a gem
As dear to thee, as this to them,
Though a stranger to this place,
Bewail in theirs thine own hard case;   10
For thou, perhaps, at thy return
May'st find thy darling in an urn.

30

Another

The purest soul that e'er was sent
Into a clayey tenement
Informed this dust, but the weak mould
Could the great guest no longer hold;
The substance was too pure, the flame   5
Too glorioüs, that thither came:
Ten thousand Cupids brought along
A grace on each wing, that did throng
For place there, till they all oppressed
The seat in which they sought to rest;   10
So the fair model broke, for want
Of room to lodge th' inhabitant.

---

29. Presumably the daughter of Christopher Villiers, Earl of Anglesey, although
her death at two years old is recorded (4 August 1630) as after her father's
(3 April 1630), who could not literally have 'laid her in earth' (l. 4: see Dunlap,
pp. 239 and 248). Carew wrote a consolatory poem 'To the Countess of
Anglesey' on the Earl's death.

30. 5–10 C. L. Powell (*MLR* xi, 1916, 286–7) preferred an alternative text he
found in British Museum MS. Harleian 6917 (see Dunlap, p. 240).

31

Another

This little vault, this narrow room,
Of love and beauty is the tomb;
The dawning beam that gan to clear
Our clouded sky lies darkened here,
For ever set to us, by death   5
Sent to inflame the world beneath;
'Twas but a bud, yet did contain
More sweetness than shall spring again,
A budding star that might have grown
Into a sun, when it had blown.   10
This hopeful beauty did create
New life in Love's declining state;
But now his empire ends, and we
From fire and wounding darts are free:
His brand, his bow, let no man fear;   15
The flames, the arrows, all lie here.

32

Maria Wentworth,
Thomae Comitis Cleveland Filia Praemortua Prima Virgineam Animam
Exhalavit: Anno Domini 1632. Aetatis Suae 18

And here the precious dust is laid,
Whose purely tempered clay was made
So fine that it the guest betrayed.

32. 'Mary Wentworth, daughter of Thomas, Earl of Cleveland, having died prematurely, exhaled her virgin spirit in [January] 1632 [i.e. 1633], aged 18.' Her grandfather was Sir John Crofts (see G) of Saxham. Mary's tomb in St. George's Church, Toddington, Beds., has the first six stanzas of Carew's epitaph inscribed on it along with a sculptured portrait of her seated with a sewing basket; 'local tradition says that she died from pricking her finger while sewing on Sunday' (Dunlap, p. 243). Carew wrote, An Hymeneal Song' (C–48) on the marriage of Mary's younger sister, Anne, to John Lord Lovelace (1638).

Else the soul grew so fast within
It broke the outward shell of sin,   5
And so was hatched a cherubin.

In heighth it soared to God above;
In depth it did to knowledge move,
And spread in breadth to general love.

Before, a pious duty shined   10
To parents; courtesy behind;
On either side, an equal mind.

Good to the poor, to kindred dear,
To servants kind, to friendship clear,
To nothing but herself severe.   15

So, though a virgin, yet a bride
To every grace, she justified
A chaste polygamy, and died.

Learn from hence, Reader, what small trust
We owe this world, where virtue must,   20
Frail as our flesh, crumble to dust.

4–6 *else the soul grew*, etc.: Dunlap notes the borrowing from Donne's 'Second Anniversary', ll. 183–4. 5–9 The 'shell', hatching a cherubim, and flight described suggest the dove of the Holy Ghost as something of a visual image.

33

To Ben Jonson

Upon Occasion of His Ode of Defiance Annexed to His Play of
The New Inn

'Tis true, dear Ben, thy just chastising hand
Hath fixed upon the sotted age a brand
To their swoll'n pride and empty scribbling due;
It can nor judge nor write; and yet 'tis true
Thy comic Muse, from the exalted line   5
Touched by thy *Alchemist,* doth since decline
From that her zenith, and foretells a red
And blushing evening, when she goes to bed;
Yet such as shall outshine the glimmering light
With which all stars shall gild the following night.   10
Nor think it much (since all thy eaglets may
Endure the sunny trial) if we say
This hath the stronger wing, or that doth shine
Tricked up in fairer plumes, since all are thine.
Who hath his flock of cackling geese compared   15
To thy tuned choir of swans? Or else who dared
To call thy births deformed? But if thou bind
By city-custom, or by gavelkind,
In equal shares thy love on all thy race,
We may distinguish of their sex and place;   20

---

33. Jonson's *New Inn* was hooted off the stage before its conclusion at its first performance in 1629; this prompted Jonson's splendidly splenetic 'Ode to Himself', which was appended to the 1631 quarto of the play. There is a copy of this poem in Carew's own hand in the Public Record Office, which is 'to be dated about 1631' (Dunlap, p. lxviii). Its few variants are insignificant. 11–12 *all thy eaglets,* etc.: proverbially 'only the eagle can gaze at the sun' (Tilley E 3). 16 *tuned choir of swans.* There is an ancient fable that the swan sings just (and only) before it dies. The Greek legend that Apollo (god of music) passed into a swan led to a generalized myth about the souls of poets passing into swans at their death; cf. 'Swan of Avon' for Shakespeare. 18 *city-custom*: or Custom of London, by which the possessions of a deceased citizen and freeman were to be divided into equal parts for the widow, the executors, and the children unprovided for (Dunlap, pp. 246–7). *gavelkind*: land tenure, especially in Kent, involving equal division of an intestate's property among all his sons (*OED*).

Though one hand form them, and though one brain strike
Souls into all, they are not all alike.
Why should the follies then of this dull age
Draw from thy pen such an immodest rage
As seems to blast thy (else-immortal) bays,   25
When thine own tongue proclaims thy itch of praise?
Such thirst will argue drouth. No, let be hurled
Upon thy works by the detracting world
What malice can suggest; let the rout say
The running sands that, ere thou make a play,   30
Count the slow minutes, might a Goodwin frame,
To swallow when th' hast done thy shipwracked name.
Let them the dear expense of oil upbraid,
Sucked by thy watchful lamp, that hath betrayed
To theft the blood of martyred authors, spilt   35
Into thy ink, whilst thou grow'st pale with guilt.
Repine not at the taper's thrifty waste
That sleeks thy terser poems; nor is haste
Praise, but excuse; and if thou overcome
A knotty writer, bring the booty home;   40
Nor think it theft, if the rich spoils so torn
From conquered authors be as trophies worn.
Let others glut on the extorted praise
Of vulgar breath; trust thou to after days:
Thy laboured works shall live, when Time devours   45
Th' abortive offspring of their hasty hours.
Thou art not of their rank; the quarrel lies
Within thine own verge; then let this suffice:
The wiser world doth greater Thee confess
Than all men else, than Thyself only less.   50

21 *though one brain strike*, etc.: is there a glance here at Jonson's elegy on
Shakespeare (1623), ll. 59–61? 28 *works*: alluding to the so-called *Works* of
1616, which some thought presumptuous; see S–26: 20 n. 31 *a Goodwin*: 'the
dangerous Goodwin Sands, seven miles off Ramsgate' (Dunlap, p. 247).
34–6, 41–2 *thy watchful lamp, that hath betrayed*, etc.: as Dryden put it in 'An
Essay of Dramatic Poesy', Jonson 'invades authors like a monarch; and
what would be theft in other poets is only victory in him.' 36 *pale with guilt*: a
turn on 'gilt/guilt'; see S–9: 4 n. 48 *verge*: 'an area . . . defined as extending
to a distance of twelve miles round the King's court' (*OED*). 49, 50 *Thee . . .
Thyself*: the capitals in *CP 40* seem more than accidental.

34

An Elegy upon the Death of the Dean of Paul's,
Doctor John Donne

Can we not force from widowed poetry,
Now thou art dead, great Donne, one elegy
To crown thy hearse? Why yet dare we not trust,
Though with unkneaded dough-baked prose, thy dust,
Such as th' unscissored churchman, from the flower   5
Of fading rhetoric, short-lived as his hour,
Dry as the sand that measures it, should lay
Upon thy ashes on the funeral day?
Have we no voice, no tune? Didst thou dispense
Through all our language both the words and sense?   10
    'Tis a sad truth. The pulpit may her plain
And sober Christian precepts still retain;
Doctrines it may, and wholesome uses, frame,
Grave homilies and lectures; but the flame

34. Donne died on 31 March 1631, and Carew's elegy was first printed, with other elegies, in Donne's *Poems* (1633). Dunlap (p. 250): 'Grierson noted of Carew's *Elegie* in his edition of Donne (ii. 257) that "the 1633 text is so much better that it seems probable that the poem was printed in 1640 from an early unrevised version". With this impression I concur, and have accordingly' followed the 1633 text, as I follow Dunlap's. As Dunlap argues, the elegy 'seems to have been written a considerable period before its publication'. To the verse paragraphs of *CP 40* I add those of ll. 11, 25, and 45. 1 *widowed poetry*: by analogy with the Church as the bride of Christ, Donne is the husband of poetry. 3–8 Commentators' silence suggests more syntactical ease and evident sense than are readily found. Lines 3–4 seem to govern the rest, with syntactical ambiguity *en passant* (the first sense is assimilated to the second): (1) 'dare we not trust . . . thy dust[?]', i.e. believe that you are dead; and/or (2) 'dare we not [en]trust . . . thy dust' with something of an elegy, or funeral eulogy, 'Though [made] with [nothing more fitting or needed than] unkneaded . . . prose . . . such as th' unscissored churchman . . . should lay upon thy ashes on the funeral day?' The rest of the sentence describes and imitates a 'force[d] . . . elegy' (ll. 1–2) and the 'dough-baked prose' that is made 'from the flower [and 'flour'] / Of fading rhetoric' and is as ephemeral as the eulogy's reading time and as dry as the sand in the hour-glass that measures it. 4 *dough-baked*. Cf. Donne, 'A Letter to the Lady Carey, and Mistress Essex Rich, from Amiens', ll. 16–21 (especially 'tasteless flat humility / In dough-baked men'). 5 *unscissored*: with uncut hair, as in 'curled unscissored Bacchus' (C–39: 64); untonsured (John Buxton's suggestion).

Of thy brave soul—that shot such heat and light   15
As burnt our earth, and made our darkness bright,
Committed holy rapes upon our will,
Did through the eye the melting heart distil,
And the deep knowledge of dark truths so teach,
As sense might judge what fancy could not reach—   20
Must be desired for ever. So the fire
That fills with spirit and heat the Delphic choir,
Which, kindled first by thy Promethean breath,
Glowed here awhile, lies quenched now in thy death.

    The Muses' garden, with pedantic weeds   25
O'erspread, was purged by thee; the lazy seeds
Of servile imitation thrown away,
And fresh invention planted; thou didst pay
The debts of our penurious bankrupt age;
Licentious thefts, that make poetic rage   30
A mimic fury, when our souls must be
Possessed, or with Anacreon's ecstasy
Or Pindar's, not their own; the subtle cheat
Of sly exchanges, and the juggling feat
Of two-edged words, or whatsoever wrong   35
By ours was done the Greek or Latin tongue,
Thou hast redeemed, and opened us a mine
Of rich and pregnant fancy; drawn a line

22 *Delphic choir*: poets, since Delphi was an oracular shrine and precinct sacred to Apollo, god of music and poetry.   23 *Promethean breath*: Prometheus was the titan who stole fire (often symbolic light) from the gods and gave it to men.   30 *rage*: inspiration.   32–3 *Anacreon's ecstasy . . . or Pindar's*: these ancient Greek lyric poets are made to stand for slavish imitation of classical verse of the types, respectively, of racily informal and ceremonious public expression, or familiar and formal. 33–7 *the subtle cheat*, etc. Whatever the specific abuses are, they have to do with the 'banking' of impoverished imagination on classical resources; 'sly exchanges and the juggling feat / Of two-edged words' seems more likely to refer to using Latin and Greek derivatives in original and non-current as well as current senses, and perhaps to Latinate neologisms, than to syllepsis or Metaphysical ambiguity ('puns'), which Donne uses 'all the time' and Carew often. Carew is certainly referring in ll. 35–6 to the misuse of Greek and Latin in or through English by various (not clearly specified) kinds of imitation and affectation. Donne paid off the debt by perfecting the vernacular tongue and his own matchless idiom.

Of masculine expression, which had good
Old Orpheus seen, or all the ancient brood   40
Our superstitious fools admire, and hold
Their lead more precious than thy burnished gold,
Thou hadst been their exchequer, and no more
They each in other's dust had raked for ore.
   Thou shalt yield no precedence, but of time,   45
And the blind fate of language whose tuned chime
More charms the outward sense; yet thou may'st claim
From so great disadvantage greater fame,
Since to the awe of thy imperious wit
Our stubborn language bends, made only fit   50
With her tough thick-ribbed hoops to gird about
Thy giant fancy, which had proved too stout
For their soft melting phrases. As in time
They had the start, so did they cull the prime
Buds of invention many a hundred year,   55
And left the rifled fields, besides the fear
To touch their harvest; yet from those bare lands
Of what is purely thine thy only hands
(And that thy smallest work) have gleanèd more
Than all those times and tongues could reap before.   60
   But thou art gone, and thy strict laws will be
Too hard for libertines in poetry.
They will repeal the goodly exiled train
Of gods and goddesses, which in thy just reign
Were banished nobler poems; now with these   65
The silenced tales o' th' *Metamorphoses*
Shall stuff their lines and swell the windy page,
Till verse, refined by thee, in this last age

39 *masculine expression*: downright 'strong lines', in the case of Donne and his
imitators; in general, complex, vigorous, and conceptual, rather than simple,
sensuous, and conventionally passionate, or fancifully decorative.   40 *Orpheus*:
see G.   46 *tuned chime*: euphonious and regular verse (cf. l. 71).   58 *thy only
hands*: thy hands, alone, no one else's.   62 *libertines*: certainly with specific
allusion to the French *Libertin* poets and their English imitators, of whom Carew
himself was often one.   66 *Metamorphoses*: Ovid's collection of wittily narrated
myths, much imitated in the Renaissance and translated by Arthur Golding
(1565–7) and by one whose Psalm-translations Carew praised (C–41), George
Sandys (1621–6).

Turn ballad-rhyme, or those old idols be
Adored again with new apostasy.   70
   O pardon me, that break with untuned verse
The reverend silence that attends thy hearse,
Whose awful solemn murmurs were to thee
More than these faint lines a loud elegy,
That did proclaim in a dumb eloquence   75
The death of all the arts, whose influence,
Grown feeble, in these panting numbers lies
Gasping short-winded accents, and so dies:
So doth the swiftly turning wheel not stand
In th' instant we withdraw the moving hand,   80
But some small time maintain a faint weak course
By virtue of the first impulsive force;
And so, whilst I cast on thy funeral pile
Thy crown of bays, oh, let it crack awhile,
And spit disdain, till the devouring flashes   85
Suck all the moisture up, then turn to ashes.
   I will not draw thee envy to engross
All thy perfections, or weep all our loss:
Those are too num'rous for an elegy,
And this too great to be expressed by me.   90
Though every pen should share a distinct part,
Yet art thou theme enough to tire all art;
Let others carve the rest; it shall suffice
I on thy tomb this epitaph incise:

     Here lies a king, that ruled as he thought fit   95
     The universal monarchy of wit;
     Here lie two flamens, and both those the best:
     Apollo's first, at last the true God's priest.

---

69 *ballad-rhyme*: the matter in the manner of street-ballads, presumably;
doggerel narratives of sensational events, or scurrilous fictions, in traditional
ballad-measure: quatrains of alternating four- and three-stress lines.   71 *untuned
verse*: as though in Donne's idiom (cf. l. 46).   84 *bays*: see G.   *crack*: (1) crackle;
(2) wax sarcastic ('crack a joke').   87 *thee*: an emendation proposed by Grierson
in his edition of Donne (ii. 257); cf. Jonson's elegy on Shakespeare, ll. 1–2. 'To
engross' would have been used interchangeably with 'by engrossing' in Carew's
time (see Abbott, sec. 356).   97 *flamens*: pagan-Roman priests, appropriately
personifying the image of triumphant fire in the poem (e.g. ll. 21 ff. and 83 ff.).

35

Upon Master Walter Montagu's
Return from Travel

Lead the black bull to slaughter, with the boar
And lamb, then purple with their mingled gore
The ocean's curlèd brow, that so we may
The sea-gods for their careful waftage pay;
Send grateful incense up in pious smoke   5
To those mild spirits that cast a curbing yoke
Upon the stubborn winds that calmly blew
To the wished shore our longed-for Montagu.
Then, whilst the aromatic odours burn
In honour of their darling's safe return,   10
The Muses' choir shall thus with voice and hand
Bless the fair gale that drove his ship to land:

    Sweetly breathing vernal air,
    That with kind warmth dost repair
    Winter's ruins, from whose breast   15
    All the gums and spice of th' East
    Borrow their perfumes, whose eye
    Gilds the morn and clears the sky,
    Whose dishevelled tresses shed
    Pearls upon the violet bed,   20
    On whose brow with calm smiles dressed
    The halcyon sits and builds her nest:
    Beauty, youth, and endless spring
    Dwell upon thy rosy wing.
    Thou, if stormy Boreas throws   25
    Down whole forests when he blows,
    With a pregnant flowery birth
    Canst refresh the teeming earth;

35. On 'Wat' Montagu (1603?–77) see S–26: 88 n. This poem cannot be dated,
but Montagu's religious proclivities (turned Roman Catholic in 1635) may
account for some of the imagery of sacrifice and incensation at the beginning
of the poem, and for the reference to his 'deal[ing] your body 'mongst your
friends' at the end. Musical setting (ll. 13–24): Henry Lawes.   22 *halcyon*: see
G.   25 *Boreas*: the north wind.

If he nip the early bud,
If he blast what's fair or good,   30
If he scatter our choice flowers,
If he shake our hills or bowers,
If his rude breath threaten us:
Thou canst stroke great Aeolus,
And from him the grace obtain   35
To bind him in an iron chain.

Thus, whilst you deal your body 'mongst your friends,
And fill their circling arms, my glad soul sends
This her embrace; thus we of Delphos greet:
As laymen clasp their hands, we join our feet.   40

36

For a Picture Where a Queen Laments over
the Tomb of a Slain Knight

Brave youth, to whom Fate in one hour
Gave death and conquest, by whose power
Those chains about my heart are wound
With which the foe my kingdom bound,
Freed and captived by thee, I bring   5
For either act an offering:
For victory, this wreath of bay;
In sign of thraldom, down I lay
Sceptre and crown. Take from my sight
Those royal robes; since Fortune's spite   10
Forbids me live thy virtue's prize,
I'll die thy valour's sacrifice.

34 *Aeolus*: god of winds, who is depicted in *Aeneid* i. 50–9 as keeping the winds imprisoned in a cave.   37–40 There seem to be allusions to rites and rituals here, and to different kinds of priesthood, sacred and secular, like those of the last lines of the elegy on Donne (C–34). Montagu eventually became a Roman priest (whether before or after this poem was written is uncertain), and Carew and his fellow poets might be said to be Greek or Apollonian priests, as 'we of Delphos', who join not hands but 'feet', in a very parochial drollery alluding to metrical verse.   39 *we of Delphos*: i.e. poets (see C–34: 22 n.).

36. 'Poems of this genre were more popular on the Continent than in England; Marino published a whole *Galeria*' (Dunlap, p. 254).

37

To a Lady That Desired I Would Love Her

Now you have freely giv'n me leave to love,
What will you do?
Shall I your mirth or pastime move
When I begin to woo?
Will you torment, or scorn, or love me too? 5

Each petty beauty can disdain, and I,
Spite of your hate,
Without your leave can see, and die;
Dispense a nobler fate:
'Tis easy to destroy; you may create. 10

Then give me leave to love, and love me too,
Not with design
To raise, as Love's curst rebels do
When puling poets whine,
Fame to their beauty from their blubbered eyne. 15

Grief is a puddle, and reflects not clear
Your beauty's rays;
Joys are pure streams; your eyes appear
Sullen in sadder lays;
In cheerful numbers they shine bright with praise, 20

Which shall not mention to express you fair
Wounds, flames, and darts,
Storms in your brow, nets in your hair,
Suborning all your parts
Or to betray or torture captive hearts. 25

37. 3 *pastime*: the reading of *CP 40* text (= amusement, entertainment, sport); Errata, 'passion'. 21–30 A collection of Petrarchisms, almost the verbal counterpart of an engraving by M. van Lochem after Chrispin de Passe, 'La Belle Charité', who has in her hair, however, not nets but little angling rods with hearts suspended from them.

H

I'll make your eyes like morning suns appear,
  As mild and fair;
  Your brow as crystal smooth and clear;
   And your dishevelled hair
Shall flow like a calm region of the air.   30

Rich Nature's store (which is the poet's treasure)
  I'll spend to dress
  Your beauties, if your mine of pleasure
   In equal thankfulness
You but unlock, so we each other bless.   35

38

Upon My Lord Chief Justice's Election of My Lady Anne Wentworth for His Mistress

  Hear this and tremble, all
  Usurping Beauties that create
  A government tyrannical
   In Love's free state:
Justice hath to the sword of your edged eyes   5
His equal balance joined; his sage head lies
In Love's soft lap, which must be just and wise.

  Hark how the stern Law breathes
  Forth am'rous sighs, and now prepares
  No fetters but of silken wreaths   10
   And braided hairs;
His dreadful rods and axes are exiled,
Whilst he sits crowned with roses: Love hath filed
His native roughness; Justice is grown mild.

---

38. The Lord Chief Justice (16 October 1634) was Sir John Finch, Baron Finch of Fordwich, mentioned in 1637 by the Earl of Strafford, the father of 'His Mistress', as 'the best Courtier of them all'; he must have 'elected' Anne Wentworth between 1634 and 1638, when she married John Lord Lovelace; Carew celebrated the marriage, too (C–48).

The Golden Age returns: 15
Love's bow and quiver useless lie;
His shaft, his brand, nor wounds nor burns,
        And cruelty
Is sunk to hell; the fair shall all be kind;
Who loves shall be beloved; the froward mind   20
To a deformèd shape shall be confined.

Astraea hath possessed
An earthly seat, and now remains
In Finch's heart, but Wentworth's breast
        That guest contains;   25
With her she dwells, yet hath not left the skies,
Nor lost her sphere, for, new-enthron'd, she cries,
'I know no Heaven but fair Wentworth's eyes.'

39

To My Friend G. N., from Wrest

I breathe, sweet Gib, the temperate air of Wrest,
Where I no more, with raging storms oppressed,
Wear the cold nights out by the banks of Tweed,
On the bleak mountains where fierce tempests breed

---

22 *Astraea*: goddess of justice, returned with 'the Golden Age' (l. 15).

39. A Country-House Poem (see G), this, like 'To Saxham', shows the influence of Martial (III. lviii) and of Jonson's 'To Penshurst'; it takes the form-of-address of a verse epistle. The allusion in ll. 2–8 to the first Bishops' War (concluded by the treaty of Berwick in June 1639) dates it as having been written not long before Carew died. Dunlap has persuasively argued that the 'Gib' of l. 1 is Gilbert North, like Carew a Gentleman of the Privy Chamber. An elder brother was Dudley, third Baron North, whose association with Suckling has been established and who wrote an interesting essay 'Concerning Petty [lyric] Poetry'; a manuscript of his poems was acquired by the Bodleian Library in 1976.   *Wrest*: the manor at Wrest Park, Bedfordshire, passed to Anthony de Grey (d. 1643) in 1631; it had been in the possession of the family, earls of Kent, for over six centuries.   3 *Tweed*: the river in southern Scotland and northern England where the encounters of the first Bishops' War took place in 1639 (see Suckling's letters, Nos. 39–42, OET *Non-Dramatic Works*, pp. 144–8).

And everlasting Winter dwells, where mild   5
Favonius and the vernal winds exiled
Did never spread their wings, but the wild North
Brings sterile fern, thistles, and brambles forth.
Here, steeped in balmy dew, the pregnant Earth
Sends from her teeming womb a flowery birth,   10
And cherished with the warm sun's quickening heat,
Her porous bosom doth rich odours sweat;
Whose perfumes through the ambient air diffuse
Such native aromatics as we use
No foreign gums, nor essence fetched from far,   15
No vol'tile spirits, nor compounds that are
Adult'rate, but at Nature's cheap expense
With far more genuine sweets refresh the sense.
Such pure and uncompounded beauties bless
This mansion with an useful comeliness   20
Devoid of art, for here the architect
Did not with curious skill a pile erect
Of carvèd marble, touch, or porphyry,
But built a house for hospitality;
No sumptuous chimney-piece of shining stone   25
Invites the stranger's eye to gaze upon
And coldly entertains his sight, but clear
And cheerful flames cherish and warm him here;
No Doric nor Corinthian pillars grace
With imagery this structure's naked face.   30
The lord and lady of this place delight
Rather to be in act than seem in sight:
Instead of statues to adorn their wall,
They throng with living men their merry hall,
Where at large tables filled with wholesome meats   35
The servant, tenant, and kind neighbour eats.
Some of that rank, spun of a finer thread,
Are with the women, steward, and chaplain fed

6 *Favonius*: the west wind (also called Zephyrus) associated with spring.
23 *touch*: 'touchstone', as applied to black marble (*OED*). 29 *Doric nor Corinthian
pillars*: the most severe and the most ornate, respectively, of the three Grecian
orders of architecture, here as types of decorative superfluity (l. 54).

With daintier cates; others of better note,
Whom wealth, parts, office, or the herald's coat   40
Have severed from the common, freely sit
At the lord's table, whose spread sides admit
A large access of friends to fill those seats
Of his capacious circle, filled with meats
Of choicest relish, till his oaken back   45
Under the load of piled up dishes crack.
Nor think, because our pyramids and high
Exalted turrets threaten not the sky,
That therefore Wrest of narrowness complains
Or straitened walls, for she more num'rous trains   50
Of noble guests daily receives, and those
Can with far more conveniency dispose
Than prouder piles, where the vain builder spent
More cost in outward gay embellishment
Than real use, which was the sole design   55
Of our contriver, who made things not fine,
But fit for service. Amalthea's horn
Of plenty is not in effigy worn
Without the gate, but she within the door
Empties her free and unexhausted store.   60
Nor, crowned with wheaten wreaths, doth Ceres stand
In stone, with a crook'd sickle in her hand;
Nor, on a marble tun, his face besmeared
With grapes, is curled unscissored Bacchus reared.
We offer not in emblems to the eyes   65
But to the taste those useful deities:
We press the juicy god and quaff his blood,
And grind the yellow goddess into food.
Yet we decline not all the work of Art,
But where more bounteous Nature bears a part   70
And guides her handmaid, if she but dispense
Fit matter, she with care and diligence

---

40 *herald's coat*: i.e. coat of arms.   45 *his*: its (the table's).   53 *piles*: large buildings.   57 *Amalthea*: a nymph who refreshed Zeus with goat's milk; in return he gave her the horn known in Latin (and English) as the *cornucopia*, or horn of 'unexhausted store' (see l. 60).   61 *Ceres*: Roman goddess of grain and the harvest.   65-8 *We offer not*, etc.: an Epicurean eucharist, with emphasis on the Real Presence of food and drink.

Employs her skill, for where the neighbour source
Pours forth her waters she directs their course
And entertains the flowing streams in deep   75
And spacious channels, where they slowly creep
In snaky windings as the shelving ground
Leads them in circles, till they twice surround
This island mansion, which i' th' centre placed
Is with a double crystal heaven embraced,   80
In which our watery constellations float,
Our fishes, swans, our waterman and boat,
Envied by those above, which wish to slake
Their star-burnt limbs in our refreshing lake;
But they stick fast, nailed to the barren sphere,   85
Whilst our increase in fertile waters here
Disport, and wander freely where they please
Within the circuit of our narrow seas.
       With various trees we fringe the water's brink,
Whose thirsty roots the soaking moisture drink,   90
And whose extended boughs in equal ranks
Yield fruit, and shade, and beauty to the banks.
On this side young Vertumnus sits, and courts
His ruddy-cheeked Pomona; Zephyr sports
On th' other with loved Flora, yielding there   95
Sweets for the smell, sweets for the palate here.
But did you taste the high and mighty drink
Which from that fountain flows, you'ld clearly think
The god of wine did his plump clusters bring,
And crush the Falerne grape into our spring;   100
Or else disguised in watery robes did swim
To Ceres' bed, and make her big of him,
Begetting so himself on her: for know
Our vintage here in March doth nothing owe

---

73 ff. *where the neighbour source*, etc.: on the gardens of the period see ref. cit. in
C–28: 64 n.   80 *double crystal heaven*: see NRC.   85 *they stick fast*, etc.: as fixed
stars (see NRC).   93–4 *Vertumnus . . . Pomona*: the Roman god of orchards, who
presided over the year's changes, and his wife, a Roman goddess of fruit, whom
he had courted in a variety of shapes, as a reaper, ploughman, pruner of vines,
etc. (Ovid, *Met.* xiv. 623–771).   94–5 *Zephyrus . . . Flora*: an *ad hoc* allegorical
myth; Zephyrus was a personification of the west wind, Flora a goddess of
fertility and flowers.   100 *Falerne*: 'Falernian' was a classic wine of the
Campania celebrated by Horace and other Roman poets.

To theirs in Autumn, but our fire boils here   105
As lusty liquor as the sun makes there.
   Thus I enjoy myself, and taste the fruit
Of this blest peace, whilst toiled in the pursuit
Of bucks and stags, th' emblem of war, you strive
To keep the memory of our arms alive.   110

40

To the New Year

For the Countess of Carlisle

Give Lucinda pearl nor stone,
Lend them light who else have none,
Let her beauty shine alone.

Gums nor spice bring from the East,
For the phoenix in her breast   5
Builds his funeral pile, and nest.

No attire thou canst invent
Shall to grace her form be sent;
She adorns all ornament.

Give her nothing, but restore   10
Those sweet smiles which heretofore
In her cheerful eyes she wore.

Drive those envious clouds away,
Veils that have o'ercast my day,
And eclipsed her brighter ray.   15

109 *th' emblem*: i.e. 'the pursuit', not the 'bucks and stags' (Dunlap, p. 257).

40. On the Countess see G ('Carlisle'). This poem must have been written before 1 January 1632, when Gustavus Adolphus died (see l. 16 n.). 2 *lend them light*, etc.: 'Lucinda' has light in the Latin root of her name, *lux*. 5 *phoenix*: see G.

Let the royal Goth mow down
This year's harvest with his own
Sword, and spare Lucinda's frown.

Janus, if when next I trace
Those sweet lines, I in her face   20
Read the charter of my grace,

Then from bright Apollo's tree
Such a garland wreath'd shall be
As shall crown both her and thee.

41

To My Worthy Friend Master George Sandys,
On His Translation of the Psalms

I press not to the quire, nor dare I greet
The holy place with my unhallowed feet;
My unwashed Muse pollutes not things divine,
Nor mingles her profaner notes with thine;
Here humbly at the porch she listening stays,   5
And with glad ears sucks in thy sacred lays.

---

16 *the royal Goth*: probably Gustavus Adolphus (1594–1632), King of Sweden and
commander-in-chief of the protestant forces during part of the Thirty Years'
War (1618–48). 20 *Janus*: the Roman god of beginnings (and of January), the
doors of whose temple stood open in time of war and closed in time of peace.
22 *bright Apollo's tree*: the laurel, which provided bays (see G) for the victor's
crown.

41. This poem was first printed in the second edition of Sandys's *Paraphrase upon
the Divine Poems* (1638). Sandys (1578–1644) is remembered mainly for his
translation of Ovid's *Metamorphoses* (1621–6); his Psalms were set to music by
Henry Lawes. Carew's commendation is based on a conceit that expresses his
unworthiness and Sandys's distinction in terms of a church's interior—'choir',
sanctuary ('holy place'), 'porch', 'font'—and a book's bibliographical make-up
and literary contents: a 'choir', or 'quire' (now the standard spelling for the
printer's term), is a gathering of sheets as well as a part of a church (between
nave and sanctuary) and a body of choristers; Carew's commendatory poem
is found in the preliminaries (analogous to the porch) before the Psalms, and
the 'unhallowed feet' are in part those of his verses. 1 *quire*: see general note;
this spelling was common for the musical as well as the bibliographical sense
in Carew's day. 2 *feet*: with reference also to Carew's secular metrics.

So devout penitents of old were wont,
Some without door and some beneath the font,
To stand and hear the Church's liturgies,
Yet not assist the solemn exercise: 10
Sufficeth her that she a lay-place gain,
To trim thy vestments or but bear thy train;
Though nor in tune nor wing she reach thy lark,
Her lyric feet may dance before the Ark.
Who knows but that her wandering eyes, that run   15
Now hunting glow-worms, may adore the sun?
A pure flame may, shot by Almighty Power
Into her breast, the earthy flame devour.
My eyes in penitential dew may steep
That brine which they for sensual love did weep.   20
So (though gainst Nature's course) fire may be quenched
With fire, and water be with water drenched.
Perhaps my restless soul—tired with pursuit
Of mortal beauty, seeking without fruit
Contentment there, which hath not, when enjoyed,   25
Quenched all her thirst, nor satisfied, though cloyed—,
Weary of her vain search below, above
In the first Fair may find th' immortal Love.
Prompted by thy example then, no more
In moulds of clay will I my God adore,   30
But tear those idols from my heart, and write
What His blest Sp'rit, not fond love, shall indite;
Then I no more shall court the verdant bay,
But the dry leaveless trunk on Golgotha;
And rather strive to gain from thence one thorn,   35
Than all the flour'shing wreaths by laureates worn.

---

13 *lark*: because of its high flight and its singing only when in flight toward
heaven, the lark has been taken as a symbol of the humility of the priesthood.
Cf. George Herbert, 'Easter-Wings', ll. 7–8.   14 *Ark*: the Ark of the Covenant,
containing the tables of the law and placed in the holiest place in a tabernacle.
16 *glow-worms . . . sun*: mortals (notably women) and the Son, partly as
representative of secular and sacred verse, respectively.   28 *fair*: fair one (here,
God).   33 *bay*: the tree supplying the laurel wreath of the conqueror or poet,
with a probable quibble on the maritime connection; see 'A Rapture' (C–28),
ll. 81–90.

42

To the Reader of Master William Davenant's
Play, The Wits

It hath been said of old that plays are feasts,
Poets the cooks, and the spectators guests,
The actors waiters: from this simile
Some have derived an unsafe liberty
To use their judgements as their tastes, which choose   5
Without control this dish, and that refuse.
But wit allows not this large privilege:
Either you must confess, or feel, its edge;
Nor shall you make a current inference
If you transfer your reason to your sense: 10
Things are distinct, and must the same appear
To every piercing eye, or well-tuned ear.
Though sweets with yours, sharps best with my taste meet,
Both must agree this meat's or sharp or sweet;
But if I scent a stench, or a perfume,   15
Whilst you smell nought at all, I may presume
You have that sense imperfect: so you may
Affect a sad, merry, or hum'rous play,
If, though the kind distaste or please, the good
And bad be by your judgement understood;   20
But if, as in this play, where with delight
I feast my Epicurean appetite
With relishes so curious as dispense
The utmost pleasure to the ravished sense,
You should profess that you can nothing meet   25
That hits your taste, either with sharp or sweet,

42. This poem was first printed with Davenant's play, *The Wits* (1636), which
was written in 1633 and first acted in 1634. Davenant became in effect the poet
laureate of England after Ben Jonson's death in 1637. *1–3 It hath been said of*
old, etc.: by Horace (*Epistles,* II. ii. 58–64) and many others. *5–12 their*
judgements as their tastes: the source of a perennial argument is rooted in literal
and figurative uses of 'taste', as in *de gustibus non est disputandum*; as Coleridge
puts it, there are significant differences between the respective 'tastes' for Milton
and Virgil and for mutton and venison ('On the Principles of Genial Criticism').
9–10 current . . . reason: integral syllepsis, since currants and raisins (homonymous
at the time) are types of fruits.

But cry out, "'Tis insipid!', your bold tongue
May do its master, not the author, wrong;
For men of better palate will by it
Take the just elevation of your wit.   30

43

On Sight of a Gentlewoman's Face in the Water

Stand still, you floods, do not deface
    That image which you bear:
So votaries from every place
    To you shall altars rear.

No winds but lovers' sighs blow here   5
    To trouble these glad streams,
On which no star from any sphere
    Did ever dart such beams.

To crystal then in haste congeal,
    Lest you should lose your bliss;   10
And to my cruel fair reveal
    How cold, how hard she is.

But if the envious nymphs shall fear
    Their beauties will be scorned,
And hire the ruder winds to tear   15
    That face which you adorned,

Then rage and foam amain, that we
    Their malice may despise;
When from your froth we soon shall see
    A second Venus rise.   20

43. Musical setting: Henry Lawes. 5, 7 *blow here* ... *no star from any sphere*. Four
MSS. read 'draw nigh ... nor star nor the world's eye' (the Lawes MS. reads
'no star').

44

A Song

Ask me no more where Jove bestows,
When June is past, the fading rose;
For in your beauty's orient deep
These flowers, as in their causes, sleep.

Ask me no more whither doth stray   5
The golden atoms of the day;
For in pure love heaven did prepare
Those powders to enrich your hair.

Ask me no more whither doth haste
The nightingale when May is past;   10
For in your sweet dividing throat
She winters and keeps warm her note.

Ask me no more where those stars light
That downwards fall in dead of night;
For in your eyes they sit, and there   15
Fixèd become as in their sphere.

Ask me no more if east or west
The phoenix builds her spicy nest;
For unto you at last she flies,
And in your fragrant bosom dies.   20

---

44. Dunlap gives alternative versions of this poem, including one that looks like an 'early draft', as well as imitations, answers, parodies, and satirical adaptations (pp. 263–5). Like Donne's 'Song', 'Go and catch a falling star', this poem rings changes on 'impossibilities', an exercise in hyperbole found in many Petrarchan love poems. Musical settings: Henry Lawes, John Wilson, and anonymous. 4 *their causes*: i.e. their four Aristotelian causes, the material, efficient, formal, and final (*Physics*, ii. 3; *Metaphysics*, i. 3–7), all of which seem pertinent; *she* is, or is as it were, 'their causes': the means, the matter, and the end as well as form of beauty's manifest being. 8 Radiant or resplendent with reference to the 'orient' (rising) as the land of the sunrise, by contrast with that implied by 'the fading rose'. 11 *dividing*: performing 'divisions', or rapid melodic passages. 15–16 *For in your eyes*, etc.: 'falling stars' finding their 'sphere' in her eyes is Petrarchan hyperbole and Christian-Ptolemaic astronomy (see NRC). 18 *phoenix*: see G.

45

The Second Rapture

No, worldling, no, 'tis not thy gold,
Which thou dost use but to behold;
Nor fortune, honour, nor long life,
Children, or friends, nor a good wife,
That makes thee happy: these things be   5
But shadows of felicity.
Give me a wench about thirteen,
Already voted to the queen
Of lust and lovers, whose soft hair,
Fanned with the breath of gentle air,   10
O'erspreads her shoulders like a tent,
And is her veil and ornament;
Whose tender touch will make the blood
Wild in the aged and the good;
Whose kisses, fastened to the mouth   15
Of threescore years and longer slouth,
Renew the age, and whose bright eye
Obscures those lesser lights of sky;
Whose snowy breasts (if we may call
That snow that never melts at all)   20
Makes Jove invent a new disguise,
In spite of Juno's jealousies;
Whose every part doth re-invite
The old decayèd appetite;
And in whose sweet embraces I   25
May melt myself to lust, and die.
    This is true bliss, and I confess
    There is no other happiness.

---

45. 7 *about thirteen*: 'hardly yet fifteen' (Thomas Randolph, in 'Acolastus, a
Voluptuous Epicure') helps suggest 13–15 as the ideal age for the inamoratas
of paedophiles; Capulet says that Juliet, short of fourteen, should see two more
summers before she marries, but 'younger than she are happy mothers made'
(Paris; see *Rom.* i. ii. 1 ff.).   16 *slouth*: sloth.   21 *Makes Jove invent a new
disguise*: beyond the metamorphoses of classical mythology, in which he
consorted with Europa as a bull, Leda as a swan, and Danaë as a shower of
gold, for example.   26 *die*: experience orgasm (a common but *not* invariable
figurative sense in Tudor-Stuart times).

46

The Tinder

Of what mould did Nature frame me?
Or was it her intent to shame me,
That no woman can come near me,
Fair, but her I court to hear me?
Sure that mistress to whose beauty   5
First I paid a lover's duty
Burnt in rage my heart to tinder,
That nor prayers nor tears can hinder,
But wherever I do turn me,
Every spark let fall doth burn me.   10
Women, since you thus inflame me,
Flint and steel I'll ever name ye.

47

Upon a Mole in Celia's Bosom

That lovely spot which thou dost see
In Celia's bosom was a bee,
Who built her am'rous spicy nest
I' th' Hyblas of her either breast;
But from close ivory hives she flew   5
To suck the aromatic dew
Which from the neighbour vale distils,
Which parts those two twin-sister hills.
There feasting on ambrosial meat,
A rolling file of balmy sweat   10
(As in soft murmurs before death
Swan-like she sung) choked up her breath;

---

46. 'Tinder' poems clearly had some currency, probably in the 1630s. 'The Guiltless Inconstant', ascribed to both Suckling and Carew, but almost certainly by Walton Poole, is probably the 'major' poem of the type.

47. 4 *Hybla[s]*: a town in Sicily famous for the honey distilled from the thyme and fragrant herbs that grew on Mt. Etna.   5 *close*: (1) 'private, secluded, snug' (*OED*); (2) proximate.   10 *file*: 'thread' or course.   12 *Swan-like*: the 'swan-song', sung just before death, is proverbial (Tilley S 1028).

So she in water did expire,
More precious than the phoenix' fire.
  Yet still her shadow there remains   15
Confined to those Elysian plains
With this strict law: that who shall lay
His bold lips on that milky way
The sweet and smart from thence shall bring
Of the bee's honey and her sting.   20

48

An Hymeneal Song on the Nuptials of the
Lady Anne Wentworth and the Lord Lovelace

Break not the slumbers of the bride,
But let the sun in triumph ride,
      Scattering his beamy light;
When she awakes, he shall resign
His rays, and she alone shall shine   5
      In glory all the night.
For she till day return must keep
An am'rous vigil, and not steep
Her fair eyes in the dew of sleep.

14 *phoenix' fire*: the fire from the ashes of which the unique phoenix (see G) was born.   16 *Elysian*: heavenly (see G, 'Elysium').

48. Lady Anne and John, second Baron Lovelace of Hurley, were married on 9 July 1638. The groom's cousin Richard, the poet, dedicated *Lucasta* to her in 1649. It is possible that Suckling's 'Ballad upon a Wedding' also is associated with this wedding. The poem is divided into tercets in *Poems*, 1642, but the rhymes suggest four nine-line stanzas (the present arrangement) or stanzas of *rime couée* (the stanza-form of Suckling's 'Ballad') alternating with triplets. *Hymeneal*: after Hymen, god of marriage.

Yet gently whisper, as she lies,   10
And say her lord waits her uprise,
    The priests at th' altar stay;
With flowery wreaths the virgin crew
Attend, while some with roses strew
    And myrtles trim the way.   15
Now to the temple and the priest
See her conveyed, thence to the feast;
Then back to bed, though not to rest:

For now, to crown his faith and truth,
We must admit the noble youth   20
    To revel in Love's sphere;
To rule as chief Intelligence
That orb, and happy time dispense
    To wretched lovers here.
For they're exalted far above   25
All hope, fear, change, as they do move
The wheel that spins the fates of love.

They know no night nor glaring noon,
Measure no hours of sun or moon,
    Nor mark Time's restless glass;   30
Their kisses measure, as they flow,
Minutes, and their embraces show
    The hours as they pass.
Their motions the year's circle make,
And we from their conjunctions take   35
Rules to make love an almanac.

21–3 *To revel in Love's sphere*, etc.: cf. Donne, 'The Ecstasy', ll. 50–2: 'Our bodies why do we forbear? / They are ours, though they are not we; we are / The intelligences, they the sphere.' 'Love's sphere' is technically Venus's, the third, sphere; here the 'intelligence' is the groom, the 'sphere' the bride (see NRC). 23–4 *happy time dispense / To wretched lovers here*. The sense that, thus translated into heavenly bodies and celestial motions, the bride and groom and their love will beneficently influence earth-bound lovers is enlarged upon in the remainder of the poem. The whole notion owes much to Donne, 'The Canonization', especially ll. 35–45, and to Renaissance Neoplatonism generally. 26 *as. CP 42* reads 'or', which makes no sense.

49

Love's Force

In the first ruder age, when love was wild,
Not yet by laws reclaimed, not reconciled
To order, nor by reason manned, but flew
Full-summed by nature, on the instant view,
Upon the wings of appetite at all   5
The eye could fair or sense delightful call,
Election was not yet: but as their cheap
Food from the oak or the next acorn-heap,
As water from the nearest spring or brook,
So men their undistinguished females took   10
By chance, not choice; but soon the heavenly spark
That in man's bosom lurked broke through this dark
Confusion; then the noblest breast first felt
Itself for its own proper object melt.

50

A Lady's Prayer to Cupid

Since I must needs into thy school return,
Be pitiful, O Love, and do not burn
Me with desire of cold and frozen age,
Nor let me follow a fond boy or page.
But, gentle Cupid, give me, if you can,   5
One to my love whom I may call a man;
Of person comely, and of face as sweet,
Let him be sober, secret, and discreet,
Well practised in Love's school; let him within
Wear all his beard, and none upon his chin.   10

49. The opening lines of Dryden's *Absalom and Achitophel*, in which Charles II's promiscuousness is rationalized, are reminiscent of this poem, whose conception of a 'first ruder age' is reminiscent of Lucretius, v. 925 ff., as Dunlap notes (p. 271). A tacit controlling metaphor for the domesticating of wild love is based on falconry: 'manned', for example, is a technical term for a complex process that the synonym 'tamed', though accurate as far as it goes, cannot do justice to. 3–5 *flew* . . . *at*: attacked (falconry). 4 *full-summed*: with feathers fully grown (falconry). 7 *election*: the exercise of deliberate choice. 10 *undistinguished*: un-differentiated from each other. 14 *proper object*: peculiarly appropriate mate.

51

An Excuse of Absence

You'll ask, perhaps, wherefore I stay,
Loving so much, so long away.
O do not think 'twas I did part,
It was my body, not my heart;
For like a compass in your love   5
One foot is fixed and cannot move;
Th' other may follow the blind guide
Of giddy Fortune, but not slide
Beyond your service, nor dares venture
To wander far from you, the centre.   10

51. 5–10 *For like a compass*, etc.: a variation on the famous compass imagery of Donne's 'Valediction: Forbidding Mourning', ll. 25–36.

SIR JOHN SUCKLING
(1609–1641)

I

A Barley-Break

Love, Reason, Hate, did once bespeak
Three mates to play at Barley-break;
Love, Folly took; and Reason, Fancy;
And Hate consorts with Pride; so dance they:
Love coupled last, and so it fell   5
That Love and Folly were in hell.

They break, and Love would Reason meet,
But Hate was nimbler on her feet;
Fancy looks for Pride, and thither
Hies, and they two hug together: 10
Yet this new coupling still doth tell
That Love and Folly were in hell.

The rest do break again, and Pride
Hath now got Reason on her side;
Hate and Fancy meet, and stand   15
Untouched by Love in Folly's hand:
Folly was dull, but Love ran well,
So Love and Folly were in hell.

The poems by Suckling are arranged as far as possible in the order in which
they were probably written. For the ordering, see Clayton, pp. cxxxii–vii.

1. Games of the type of barley-break (see G) easily lend themselves to allegorical
treatment, as here (cf. H–47 and H–129). This poem was probably written
when Suckling was seventeen or younger.

2

A Pedlar of Small-Wares

A pedlar I am, that take great care
And mickle pains for to sell small-ware;
I had need do so, when women do buy,
That in small wares trade so unwillingly.

L. W.

A Looking-glass will 't please you, madam, buy?   5
A rare one 'tis indeed, for in it I
Can show what all the world besides can't do,
A face like to your own, so fair, so true.

L. E.

For you a girdle, madam? But I doubt me
Nature hath ordered there's no waste about ye;   10
Pray therefore be but pleased to search my pack,
There's no ware that I have that you shall lack.

L. E. L. M.

You, ladies, want you pins? If that you do,
I have those will enter, and that stiffly, too.
It's time you choose, in troth; you will bemoan   15
Too late your tarrying, when my pack's once gone.

L. B. L. A.

As for you, ladies, there are those behind
Whose ware perchance may better take your mind:
One cannot please ye all; the pedlar will draw back,
And wish, against himself, that they may have the knack.   20

---

2. The transparently fictionalized pedlar apostrophizes a series of ladies ('L') whose initials don't much assist identification. The metre seems to be four-stress in ll. 1–3, 14, and 16. *Small-Wares*: small textile-articles (strictly of the tape kind), buttons, hooks and eyes, etc. (*SOED*; first recorded use, 1617), and also toilet-articles, as the poem makes clear; 'notions' (U.S.).   2 *mickle*: great. 10 *waste*: waste/waist, a favourite pun of the period.   20 *knack*: (1) knick-knack, toy, trinket, of the 'small-ware' kind; (2) trick, craft, device, skill.

3

The Metamorphosis

The little Boy, to show his might and power,
Turned Io to a cow, Narcissus to a flower;
Transformed Apollo to a homely swain,
And Jove himself into a golden rain.
    These shapes were tolerable, but by th' mass   5
    H'as metamorphosed me into an ass!

4

To B. C.

When first, fair mistress, I did see your face,
I brought but carried no eyes from the place;
And since that time God Cupid hath me led,
In hope that once I shall enjoy your bed.
    But I despair; for now alas I find,   5
    Too late for me, the blind does lead the blind.

3. 1 *little Boy*: Cupid, Eros, made the master-deity personifying love's transcendent force. In traditional mythology, Hera, jealous of Zeus's love for Io, did the immediate turning. Narcissus pined away for love of his reflection in the water, and the flower grew where he died. 3 *Transformed Apollo to a homely swain*: when as a shepherd he sported with Isse; Ovid, *Met.* vi. 124. 4 *Jove himself*, etc.: when he wooed Danaë (see G), a myth referred to in the same passage in *Met.* (vi. 113). 5 *by th' mass*: a common oath but especially apt, since transubstantiation is a species of metamorphosis.

4. The proverb of l. 6 (Tilley B 452) is made literal in association with Cupid's conventional blindness.

5

Upon Sir John Lawrence's Bringing Water over the
Hills to My Lord Middlesex's House at Wiston

And is the water come? Sure't cannot be,
It runs too much against philosophy;
For heavy bodies to the centre bend,
Light bodies only naturally ascend.
How comes this then to pass? The good knight's skill   5
Could nothing do without the water's will:
  Then 'twas the water's love that made it flow,
  For love will creep where well it cannot go.

6

A Song to a Lute

Hast thou seen the down i' th' air,
  When wanton blasts have tossed it?
Or the ship on the sea,
  When ruder winds have crossed it?
Hast thou marked the crocodile's weeping,   5
  Or the fox's sleeping?
Or hast viewed the peacock in his pride,
  Or the dove by his bride,
  When he courts for his lechery?
Oh so fickle, oh so vain, oh so false, so false is she!   10

---

5. Written in September 1630 to celebrate a feat of engineering accomplished by Lawrence at the Wiston estate of Suckling's uncle, the Earl of Middlesex. 1 *And is the water come?* Cf. the proverb, 'If the mountain will not come to Mahomet, let Mahomet go to the mountain' (Tilley M 1213). 2 *philosophy*: natural philosophy, here the (gravitational) law of physics. 8 *For love*, etc.: proverbial (Tilley K 49). *well* does double duty, as adverb ('properly') and as noun; Lawrence had written that he could 'make the dainty spring which runs out of the bottom of the well to mount up to the castle'.

6. Suckling parodies stanza 3 of a song by Ben Jonson first printed in *The Devil is an Ass* (1631) and later in *The Under-Wood* (1641; No. 4, 'Her Triumph', in 'A Celebration of Charis'). Other parodies were written by James Shirley, the Duke of Newcastle, and (possibly but not certainly) the Earl of Rochester. The birds and animals were proverbial for their offices in the poem.

7

*Upon My Lady Carlisle's Walking in
Hampton-Court Garden*

Dialogue

T. C.   J. S.

T. C.

Didst thou not find the place inspired,
And flowers, as if they had desired
No other sun, start from their beds,
And for a sight steal out their heads?
Heardst thou not music when she talked?   5
And didst not find that as she walked
She threw rare perfumes all about,
Such as bean-blossoms newly out
Or chafèd spices give?——

J. S.

I must confess those perfumes, Tom,   10
I did not smell, nor found that from
Her passing by aught sprung up new:
The flowers had all their birth from you;
For I passed o'er the selfsame walk,
And did not find one single stalk   15
Of any thing that was to bring
This unknown-after after-spring.

T. C.

Dull and insensible, couldst see
A thing so near a deity
Move up and down, and feel no change?   20

7. On Lady Carlisle see G. The friendly antagonists of the dialogue are Thomas
Carew, an infatuated admirer, and John Suckling, a cynical detractor.
17 *This unknown-after after-spring*: probably 'this second spring still unknown
after its supposed occurrence'. A variant MS.-text reads 'News of this unknown
after-spring', certainly an acceptable reading, but also an 'easier' and quite
probably editorial one.

J. S.

None and so great were alike strange:
I had my thoughts, but not your way;
All are not born, sir, to the bay.
Alas, Tom, I am flesh and blood,
And was consulting how I could   25
In spite of masks and hoods descry
The parts denied unto the eye;
I was undoing all she wore,
And had she walked but one turn more,
Eve in her first state had not been   30
More naked, or more plainly seen.

T. C.

'Twas well for thee she left the place,
For there's great danger in that face;
But hadst thou viewed her leg and thigh,
And upon that discovery   35
Searched after parts that are more dear
(As fancy seldom stops so near),
No time or age had ever seen
So lost a thing as thou hadst been.

J. S.

Troth, in her face I could descry   40
No danger, no divinity.
But since the pillars were so good
On which the lovely fountain stood,
Being once come so near, I think
I should have ventured hard to drink.   45
What ever fool like me had been
If I'd not done as well as seen?
There to be lost why should I doubt,
Where fools with ease go in and out?

23 *bay*: see G.   39 In the first printed text (*FA* **46**) the poem ends here; ll. 40–9 are found in the MS. text, Bodleian MS. Rawl. Poet. 19.   48–9 A rather wicked turn on the idea of Pope's 'fools rush in where angels fear to tread' ('Essay on Criticism', l. 625).

8

The Miracle

If thou be'st ice, I do admire
How thou couldst set my heart on fire;
Or how thy fire could kindle me,
Thou being ice, and not melt thee;
But even my flames, light at thy own,   5
Have hardened thee into a stone!
Wonder of love, that canst fulfil,
Inverting nature thus, thy will;
Making ice another burn,
Whilst itself doth harder turn!   10

9

On King Richard the Third,
Who Lies Buried under Leicester Bridge

What means this watery canop' 'bout thy bed,
These streaming vapours o'er thy sinful head?
Are they thy tears? Alas, in vain they're spilt;
'Tis now too late to wash away thy guilt:
Thou still art bloody Richard, and 'tis much   5
The water should not from thy very touch
Turn quite Egyptian, and the scaly fry
Fear to be killed, and so thy carcass fly.

8. The ice–fire antithesis is a conventional Petrarchism with ancient antecedents.   5 *light*: lighted (participle with -ed omitted; see Abbott, sec. 342).

9. This poem belongs to the minor genre of the imprecation. Suckling elsewhere makes Richard the type of the evil king, a usual characterization of him in the Renaissance.   4 *guilt*: punning on 'gilt', in the manner of *Mac.* II. ii. 54–6. 6 *thy very touch*: scrofula, the 'king's evil', was supposedly cured by the royal touch, a custom introduced into England by Edward the Confessor, the 'most pious Edward' whose miraculous curative powers are described in *Macbeth* (IV. iv. 140–59). Here Edward's touch of grace is transformed into the source of the king's evil.   7 *turn quite Egyptian*: with reference to the proverbial (Biblical) cowardice and treachery of the Egyptians, and probably alluding to Exod. 14: 27.

Bathe, bathe thy fill, and take thy pleasure now
In this cold bed; yet guilty Richard know   10
Judgement must come, and water then will be
A heaven to thee in hellish misery.

10

Against Fruition I

Stay here, fond youth, and ask no more, be wise:
Knowing too much long since lost Paradise;
The virtuous joys thou hast, thou wouldst should still
Last in their pride; and wouldst not take it ill
If rudely from sweet dreams (and for a toy)   5
Th'wert waked? He wakes himself that does enjoy.

Fruition adds no new wealth, but destroys,
And, while it pleases much the palate, cloys;
Who thinks he shall be happier for that
As reasonably might hope he should grow fat   10
By eating to a surfeit: this once past,
What relishes? Ev'n kisses lose their taste.

Urge not 'tis necessary. Alas, we know
The homeliest thing which mankind does is so;
The world is of a vast extent we see,   15
And must be peopled: children then must be;
So must bread, too; but since there are enough
Born to the drudgery, what need we plough?

---

10. Poems for and against fruition—and answer poems in general—were popular in the earlier seventeenth century, and Edmund Waller and Henry Bold wrote answers to this poem, for example. The purported speaker is a man of some age and worldly experience; he addresses the 'fond youth' in much the same terms as the speaker of 'Why so pale and wan, fond lover?' (S–23). The senses of 'fruition' as commercial success, propagation, and sexual consummation as such are all present in the poem, with Gen. 1 : 22 providing the sub-text: 'be fruitful, and multiply'.   2 *Knowing too much*: the forbidden fruit of the tree of the knowledge of good and evil condensed to carnal knowledge.   6 *He wakes himself*, etc.: probably a reference to awakenings from completed sexual dreams.

Women enjoyed (whats'e'er before th'ave been)
Are like romances read, or sights once seen;   20
Fruition's dull, and spoils the play much more
Than if one read or knew the plot before;
'Tis expectation makes a blessing dear:
It were not heaven, if we knew what it were.

And as in prospects we are there pleased most   25
Where something keeps the eye from being lost
And leaves us room to guess, so here restraint
Holds up delight, that with excess would faint.
They who know all the wealth they have are poor;
He's only rich that cannot tell his store.   30

11

To Master Davenant for Absence

Wonder not if I stay not here:
Hurt lovers (like to wounded deer)
Must shift the place; for standing still
Leaves too much time to know our ill.
Where there is a traitor eye   5
That lets in from th' enemy
All that may supplant an heart,
'Tis time the chief should use some art:
Who parts the object from the sense
Wisely cuts off intelligence.   10
Oh how quickly must men die,
Should they stand all Love's battery!
Persinda's eyes great mischief do,
So does (we know) the cannon, too;
But men are safe at distance still: 15
Where they reach not, they cannot kill.
Love is a fit, and soon is past;
Ill diet only makes it last:
Who is still looking, gazing ever,
Drinks wine i' th' very height o' th' fever.   20

11. This is the counterpart of 'To Mr. W. M. Against Absence', a poem printed as
Davenant's but possibly also by Suckling (see Clayton, pp. cxi–iii, 94, and 296–8).

12

Against Absence

My whining lover, what needs all
These vows of life monastical?
Despairs, retirements, jealousies,
And subtle sealing up of eyes?
Come, come, be wise, return again,   5
A finger burnt's as great a pain;
And the same physic, selfsame art,
Cures that would cure a flaming heart,
Wouldst thou whiles yet the fire is in
But hold it to the fire again.   10
If you, dear sir, the plague have got,
What matter is 't whether or not
They let you in the same house lie,
Or carry you abroad to die?
He whom the plague, or love, once takes,   15
Every room a pest-house makes.
Absence were good if 'twere but sense
That only held th' intelligence:
Pure love alone no hurt would do.
But love is love, and magic, too;   20
Brings a mistress thousand miles,
And the sleight of locks beguiles;
Makes her entertain thee there,
And the same time your rival here;
And (oh, the devil!) that she should   25
Say finer things now than she would;
So nobly fancy doth supply
What the dull sense lets fall and die.
Beauty like man's old enemy's known
To tempt him most when he's alone: 30
The air of some wild o'ergrown wood
Or pathless grove is the Boy's food.

12. 16 *pest-house*: hospital for persons suffering from infectious diseases, especially the plague. 18 *only*: alone. 21 *thousand*: 'a thousand' in modern usage. 29 *man's old enemy*: Satan, who approached Eve alone in the garden of Eden, but here Cupid, 'the Boy'.

Return then back, and feed thine eye,
Feed all thy senses, and feast high.
Spare diet is the cause love lasts,   35
For surfeits sooner kill than fasts.

13

To a Lady That Forbad To Love Before Company

What, no more favours? Not a ribbon more,
No fan, nor muff, to hold as heretofore?
Must all those little blisses then be left,
And every kiss we have become a theft?
May we not look ourselves into a trance,   5
Let our souls parley at our eyes, not glance,
Not touch the hand, nor by soft wringing there
Whisper a love that none but eyes can hear?
Not free a sigh, a sigh that's there for you?
Dear, must I love you, yet not love you, too?   10
Be not so nice, fair; sooner shall they trace
The feathered travellers from place to place
By prints they leave i' th' air, and sooner say
By what right line the last star made his way
That fled from heaven to us, than guess or know   15
How our loves first did spring, or how they grow.
Love is all spirit; fairies sooner may
Be taken tardy when they night-tricks play
Than we; we are too safe, I fear—that rather
Would they could find us both in bed together!   20

13. The text of this poem in general circulation is unusually corrupt (from
LR 59, published eighteen years posthumously from very mixed copy). The
present text is based in part on British Museum MS. Harleian 6917.

14

Sonnet I

Dost see how unregarded now
    That piece of beauty passes?
There was a time when I did vow
    To that alone;
    But mark the fate of faces: 5
That red-and-white works now no more on me
Than if it could not charm or I not see.

And yet the face continues good,
    And I have still desires,
Am still the selfsame flesh and blood,   10
        As apt to melt
        And suffer from those fires;
Oh, some kind power unriddle where it lies,
Whether my heart be faulty, or her eyes.

She every day her man doth kill,   15
    And I as often die;
Neither her power, then, nor my will
        Can questioned be;
        What is the mystery?
Sure Beauty's empires, like to greater states,   20
Have certain periods set, and hidden fates.

14. Musical settings: Henry Lawes and John Goodgroome. *Sonnet*: diminutive
of 'song' and a term of much more general application than at present. 6 *red-
and-white*: i.e. 'that piece of beauty', with reference to cosmetic effects of art and
nature; MacLean pertinently quotes Marvell's 'Garden', ll. 17–18. 20
beauties' empires, etc.: related to the *sententia*, 'States have their . . . periods as
well as natural bodies' (Tilley S 832).

15

Sonnet II

Of thee, kind boy, I ask no red and white
          To make up my delight,
          No odd becoming graces,
Black eyes, or little know-not-whats, in faces;
Make me but mad enough, give me good store   5
Of love, for her I court,
                    I ask no more:
'Tis love in love that makes the sport.

There's no such thing as that we beauty call,
          It is mere cozenage all;   10
          For though some long ago
Liked certain colours mingled so and so,
That doth not tie me now from choosing new;
If I a fancy take
                    To black and blue,   15
That fancy doth it beauty make.

'Tis not the meat, but 'tis the appetite
          Makes eating a delight,
          And if I like one dish
More than another, that a pheasant is;   20
What in our watches, that in us is found,
So to the height and nick
                    We up be wound,
No matter by what hand or trick.

16

Sonnet III

Oh for some honest lover's ghost,
    Some kind unbodied post
    Sent from the shades below!
    I strangely long to know
Whether the nobler chaplets wear   5
Those that their mistress' scorn did bear,
    Or those that were used kindly.

For whatsoe'er they tell us here
    To make those sufferings dear,
    'Twill there I fear be found   10
    That to the being crowned
T' have loved alone will not suffice,
Unless we also have been wise,
    And have our loves enjoyed.

What posture can we think him in,   15
    That here, unloved again,
    Departs, and's thither gone
    Where each sits by his own?
Or how can that Elysium be
Where I my mistress still must see   20
    Circled in others' arms?

16. Cf. Donne's 'Love's Deity', ll. 1 ff. *2 post*: messenger. 5–7 i.e. whether those (l. 6) or those (l. 7) wear the nobler chaplets. 16 *again*: in turn, reciprocally. 19 *Elysium*: see G. 23 *Sophonisba*. Daughter of the Carthaginian general Hasdrubal, she was the wife of Syphax, but she became enamoured of Masinissa when he overthrew Syphax. Scipio Africanus prevented her from marrying Masinissa by sending her captive to Rome; unable to save her otherwise, Masinissa sent her poison, which she readily took, according to Livy (*Hist.* xxx. 12–15). In short, Sophonisba was married to Syphax, but she loved Masinissa.

For there the judges all are just,
And Sophonisba must
Be his whom she held dear,
Not his who loved her here;   25
The sweet Philoclea, since she died,
Lies by her Pirocles's side,
Not by Amphialus.

Some bays (perchance) or myrtle bough
For difference crowns the brow   30
Of those kind souls that were
The noble martyrs here;
And if that be the only odds
(As who can tell), ye kinder gods,
Give me the woman here.   35

17

Love's Offence

If when Don Cupid's dart
Doth wound a heart,
We hide our grief
And shun relief,
The smart increaseth on that score;   5
For wounds unsearched but rankle more.

Then if we whine, look pale,
And tell our tale,
Men are in pain
For us again;   10
So, neither speaking doth become
The lover's state, nor being dumb.

26–8 *Philoclea . . . Pirocles . . . Amphialus*: from Sidney's *Arcadia*. The point in context is obvious. Both Pyrocles and Amphialus loved Philoclea, but she loved Pyrocles. 29 *bays . . . myrtle*: as types of symbolic as opposed to tangible reward (cf. l. 35); the myrtle, associated with Venus, was an emblem of—here unrequited—love; on 'bays' see G.

17. 1 *Don Cupid*: obviously suggested by Don Quixote, the celebrated tilter at windmills more literal than that of the poem, where the effects of heartburn mock the usual hyperboles associated with the supposed seat of affection. 10 *again*: in turn.

When this I do descry,
Then thus think I,
     Love is the fart   15
     Of every heart:
It pains a man when 'tis kept close,
And others doth offend when 'tis let loose.

18

The Constant Lover

Out upon it, I have loved
   Three whole days together,
And am like to love three more,
   If it hold fair weather.

Time shall moult away his wings   5
   Ere he shall discover
In the whole wide world again
   Such a constant lover.

But a pox upon 't, no praise
   There is due at all to me: 10
Love with me had made no stay,
   Had it any been but she.

Had it any been but she
   And that very very face,
There had been at least ere this   15
   A dozen dozen in her place.

18. This poem is best known in the corrupt text of *LR 59*. There are many variant texts in manuscripts and printed miscellanies, and it is doubtful whether there was a definitive authorial version. An answer to this poem was headed 'Sir Toby Mathew', presumably the putative speaker rather than the author, in *LR 59*. Musical setting: Henry Lawes.   4 *hold*: *LR 59* alone reads 'prove'. 6 *shall*: some texts read 'can', which may be 'right', although it smacks of elegant variation.   9 *a pox upon 't*: the more robust and in some respects quite pertinent reading. The traditional reading is 'the spite on 't is', from *LR 59* (also in the Henry Lawes MS. of songs); there is something to be said for each. 13 The Lawes MS. and one at Harvard read 'Had it not been she alone'.

19

Loving and Beloved

There never yet was honest man
   That ever drove the trade of love;
It is impossible, nor can
   Integrity our ends promove:
For kings and lovers are alike in this,   5
That their chief art in reign dissembling is.

Here we are loved, and there we love:
   Good nature now and passion strive
Which of the two should be above,
   And laws unto the other give.   10
So we false fire with art sometimes discover,
And the true fire with the same art do cover.

What rack can fancy find so high?
   Here we must court, and here engage,
Though in the other place we die.   15
   Oh, 'tis torture all, and cozenage;
And which the harder is I cannot tell,
To hide true love, or make false love look well.

19–20. These are companion-pieces on the character of men and women in love; the speaker in both cases is manifestly a man.

19. 2 *drove*: pursued vigorously, practised. 4 *promove*: promote. The argument is that integrity is disadvantageous in love, business, and politics. 11–12 *false fire*, etc.: *SOED* (a) a blank discharge of arms, (b) a fire made to deceive an enemy, or as a signal by night: we show 'false fire' to deceive, sometimes to mislead, sometimes to conceal; feigning love, we are thought actually to love that person and not to love the person really loved. 13 *rack*: an instrument of torture (so too 'brands', l. 21) on which the limbs were stretched by the rotation of rollers at each end. 14–15 *here . . . the other place we die*: part of the wit seems to depend upon 'die' as also meaning 'achieve sexual consummation', a sense assisted by the military and amatory senses of 'engage'.

Since it is thus, God of Desire,
    Give me my honesty again,   20
And take thy brands back, and thy fire;
    I'm weary of the state I'm in:
Since (if the very best should now befall)
Love's triumph must be Honour's funeral.

20

Woman's Constancy

There never yet was woman made,
    Nor shall, but to be curst;
And oh, that I, fond I, should first
    Of any lover
This truth at my own charge to other fools discover!   5

You that have promised to yourselves
    Propriety in love,
Know women's hearts like straws do move,
    And what we call
Their sympathy is but love to jet in general.   10

All mankind are alike to them,
    And though we iron find
That never with a lodestone joined,
    'Tis not its fault:
It is because the lodestone yet was never brought.   15

24 That is, succeeding in mercenary 'love', one loses personal integrity; succeeding in true love, one loses 'public' honour, status. Cf. 'when love puts in friendship is gone' (Tilley L 549: 1576), but the relationship is not very direct. In the end, what the poem proves to be about is the dilemma of having to court one person—prompted by the demands of rank and the state of one's fortune—while loving another.

20. 8–10 *women's hearts like straws*, etc.: i.e. what we suppose deliberate love is sheer instinct. Cf. Jonson, *Every Man in His Humour* (1598), III. iii. 24–5; *OED*, citing this passage, explains 'jet' as a form of coal that 'has the property of attracting light bodies when electrified by rubbing'.   13 *lodestone*: magnet, but with a more directly available sexual application (cf. l. 20).

If where a gentle bee hath fallen
   And laboured to his power,
A new succeeds not to that flower,
   But passes by,
'Tis to be thought the gallant elsewhere loads his thigh.   20

For still the flowers ready stand:
   One buzzes round about,
One lights, one tastes, gets in, gets out;
   All, all ways use them,
Till all their sweets are gone, and all again refuse them.   25

21

Love's Clock

That none beguiled be by time's quick flowing,
Lovers have in their hearts a clock still going;
   For though time be nimble, his motions
      Are quicker
      And thicker   5
   Where Love hath his notions:

Hope is the mainspring on which moves desire,
And these do the less wheels, fear, joy, inspire;
   The balance is thought, evermore
      Clicking   10
      And striking,
   And ne'er giving o'er;

Occasion's the hand which still's moving round,
Till by it the critical hour may be found;
   And when that falls out, it will strike   15
      Kisses,
      Strange blisses,
   And what you best like.

20 *the gallant . . . loads his thigh*: bees load their thighs with pollen.

21. The clock and its works are a favourite conceit of Suckling; cf. 'What in
our watches, that in us is found' in S–15: 21–4.   13 *Occasion's the hand*, etc.: a
condensed form of a number of proverbial notions; e.g. 'strike while the iron
is hot' (Tilley I 94) and many of the proverbs with 'time' in them (T 290–343).

22

Song

No, **no**, fair heretic, it needs must be
     But an ill love in me,
     And worse for thee;
For were it in my power
To love thee now, this hour,   5
     More than I did the last,
'Twould then so fall
I might not love at all:
  Love that can flow, and can admit increase,
  Admits as well an ebb, and may grow less.   10

True love is still the same; the torrid zones,
     And those more frigid ones,
     It must not know;
For love grown cold or hot
Is lust, or friendship, not   15
     The thing we have;
For that's a flame would die
Held down or up too high:
  Then think I love more than I can express,
  And would love more, could I but love thee less.   20

22. This song was first printed in Suckling's *Aglaura* (IV. iv. 4–23) in 1638. Like Carew's 'Mediocrity in Love Rejected' (C–4), it deals, in relation to love, with the Aristotelian degrees of too much, too little, and enough. Musical setting: Henry Lawes.

23

Song

Why so pale and wan, fond lover?
          Prithee why so pale?
Will, when looking well can't move her,
          Looking ill prevail?
          Prithee why so pale?   5

Why so dull and mute, young sinner?
          Prithee why so mute?
Will, when speaking well can't win her,
          Saying nothing do't?
          Prithee why so mute?   10

Quit, quit, for shame, this will not move,
          This cannot take her;
If of herself she will not love,
          Nothing can make her:
          The Devil take her.   15

24

Love's Siege

'Tis now since I sat down before
     That foolish fort, a heart,
(Time strangely spent) a year, and more,
     And still I did my part:

---

23. First printed in *Aglaura* (IV. ii. 14–28) in 1638. Its continuing popularity is attested by at least five musical settings (T. A. Arne, William Lawes, Lewis Ramondon, and two anonymous).   14 *make her*: make her love (elliptical). 15 *the Devil take her*: (1) let her go to the devil; (2) let the devil 'take' her sexually.

24. The imagery of warfare is common in Petrarchan love poetry, but this is an unusually detailed and extended use of it. There is an anonymous musical setting in a manuscript in the New York Public Library.   1 *sat down before*: began the siege of (military-idiomatic).

Made my approaches, from her hand   5
   Unto her lip did rise,
And did already understand
   The language of her eyes;

Proceeded on with no less art,
   My tongue was engineer: 10
I thought to undermine the heart
   By whispering in the ear.

When this did nothing, I brought down
   Great canon-oaths, and shot
A thousand thousand to the town,   15
   And still it yielded not.

I then resolved to starve the place
   By cutting off all kisses,
Praising and gazing on her face,
   And all such little blisses.   20

To draw her out, and from her strength,
   I drew all batteries in,
And brought myself to lie at length
   As if no siege had been.

When I had done what man could do,   25
   And thought the place mine own,
The enemy lay quiet, too,
   And smiled at all was done.

I sent to know from whence, and where,
   These hopes, and this relief?   30
A spy informed, Honour was there,
   And did command in chief.

---

14 *Canon-oaths*: (1) canonical, in accordance with Church law; (2) cannon; in context, loud, vaunting. Cf. Shakespeare, *Cor.* III. i. 90.

'March, march', quoth I, 'the word straight give,
  Let's lose no time, but leave her:
That Giant upon air will live,   35
  And hold it out for ever.

'To such a place our camp remove
  As will no siege abide;
I hate a fool that starves her love
  Only to feed her pride.'   40

25

Farewell to Love

Well-shadowed landskip, fare-ye-well:
How I have loved you, none can tell,
      At least so well
    As he that now hates more
    Then e'er he loved before.   5

But my dear nothings, take your leave;
No longer must you me deceive,
      Since I perceive
    All the deceit, and know
    Whence the mistake did grow.   10

As he whose quicker eye doth trace
A false star shot to a marked place
      Does run apace,
    And thinking it to catch
    A jelly up does snatch,   15

---

35 *Giant*: Carew has this in 'A Rapture' (C–28), l. 3. In 'The Damp' Donne has
the 'Giant . . . Disdain' and 'th' Enchantress Honour'. Honour, like the
chameleon, will live on 'mere air' and needs no substantial nourishment; as it
is for Falstaff, honour is vanity to the speaker.

25. Suckling's poem was clearly influenced by Donne's 'Farewell to Love' and
also his 'Eclogue 1613', especially ll. 11–15. 12–15 *A false star*, etc.: falling
star, false because 'he that sees a star fall runs apace / And finds a jelly in the
place' (Donne, 'Eclogue 1613', ll. 204–5).

So our dull souls, tasting delight
Far off, by sense, and appetite,
    Think that is right
  And real good, when yet
  'Tis but the counterfeit.   20

Oh, how I glory now that I
Have made this new discovery!
    Each wanton eye
  Enflamed before; no more
  Will I increase that score.   25

If I gaze now, 'tis but to see
What manner of death's-head 'twill be,
    When it is free
  From that fresh upper skin,
  The gazer's joy, and sin.   30

The gum and glistening which with art
And studied method in each part
    Hangs down the hair—'t
  Looks just as if that day
  Snails there had crawled the hay.   35

The locks that curled o'er each ear be
Hang like two master-worms to me,
    That (as we see)
  Have tasted to the rest
  Two holes, where they like 't best.   40

---

27 *death's-head*: skull as *memento mori*, a reminder of mortality.   33 *hair—'t*: in
the OET *Non-Dramatic Works* I followed *FA 46* in reading 'heart', but I now
accept A. H. Thompson's emendation (1910, developed from Hazlitt's 'hair',
1874).   35 *had crawled the hay*: (1) lit.: crawled over hay, leaving a 'glistening'
trail; (2) in allusion to dancing the (antic) hay, a country dance having a
serpentine movement.   36 *locks*: lovelocks of hair, but small quantities of hay
were also referred to as locks, as by Herrick in 'The New-Year's Gift' (ll. 4–6).
37 *master-worms*: probably a nonce-coinage by analogy from 'master-keys' in
consonance with 'locks' (l. 36) and 'holes' (l. 40).

A quick corse methinks I spy
In every woman; and mine eye,
    At passing by,
Checks, and is troubled, just
As if it rose from dust.   45

They mortify not heighten me;
These of my sins the glasses be:
    And here I see
How I have loved before.
And so I love no more.   50

26

The Wits

(A Sessions of the Poets)

A sessions was held the other day,
And Apollo himself was at it, they say;
The laurel that had been so long reserved
Was now to be given to him best deserved.
    And
Therefore the wits of the Town came thither;   5
'Twas strange to see how they flocked together:
Each, strongly confident of his own way,
Thought to carry the laurel away that day.

There was Selden, and he sat hard by the chair;
Wenman not far off, which was very fair;   10
Sandys with Townsend, for they kept no order;
Digby and Chillingworth a little further;

41 *quick*: living.

26. Manuscript texts make clear that 'The Wits' is authoritative, but the traditional title, 'A Sessions of the Poets' (from *FA 46*), dies hard. 1 *sessions*: trial. 5 *Town*: London. 9 *Selden*: John Selden (1584–1654), a scholar of 'stupendous' (Clarendon) erudition. 10 *Wenman*: Sir Francis Wenman (*post* 1596–?;*fl.* 1615–40). 11 *Sandys and Townsend*: George Sandys (1578–1644) and Aurelian Townsend (*fl.* 1601–43). 12 *Digby and Chillingworth*: Sir Kenelm Digby (1603–65) and William Chillingworth (1602–44).

And
There was Lucan's Translator, too, and he
That makes God speak so big in's poetry;
Selwin and Waller, and Berkeleys, both the brothers;   15
Jack Vaughan and Porter, with divers others.

The first that broke silence was good old Ben,
Prepared before with Canary wine,
And he told them plainly he deserved the bays,
For his were called *Works*, where others were but plays;   20
And
Bid them remember how he had purged the stage
Of errors that had lasted many an age;
And he hoped they did think *The Silent Woman*,
The Fox, and *The Alchemist* outdone by no man.

Apollo stopped him there and bad him not go on;   25
'Twas merit, he said, and not presumption
Must carry it; at which Ben turned about
And in great choler offered to go out;
But
Those that were there thought it not fit
To discontent so ancient a wit,   30
And therefore Apollo called him back again,
And made him mine host of his own *New Inn*.

13 *Lucan's translator*: Thomas May (1595–1650).   13–14 *he that makes God speak so big*, etc.: one thinks of Milton despite the date, but his associations were not with the circles of 'The Wits'; other unconvincing suggestions have been made, notably Quarles, Wither, and Phineas Fletcher.   15 *Selwin and Waller*: Selwin is unidentified; Edmund Waller (1606–87).   15 *Berkeleys*: John Berkeley, first Baron Berkeley of Stratton (d. 1678) and Sir William Berkeley (d. 1677). 16 *Jack Vaughan and Porter*: Sir John Vaughan (1603–74) and Endymion Porter (1587–1644).   17 *good old Ben*: Ben Jonson (1572–1637).   20 The folio *Workes of Beniamin Jonson* (1616) came in for a good deal of lampooning on account of the author's 'presumption' (l. 26). Carew refers to Jonson's 'laboured works' in 'To Ben Jonson' (C–33), and an anonymous set of epigrams clarifies: 'Pray tell me, Ben, where does the mystery lurk, / What others call a play you call a work?' Reply: 'The author's friend thus for the author says: / Ben's plays are works, when others' works are plays.'   26 *'Twas merit*, etc.: repeating ll. 3–4 in paraphrase.   32 *mine host* [i.e. innkeeper] *of his own New Inn*: a failure; see C–33 n.

Tom Carew was next, but he had a fault
That would not well stand with a laureate:
His muse was hard bound, and th' issue of 's brain   35
Was seldom brought forth but with trouble and pain;
        And
All that were present there did agree,
A laureate's muse should be easy and free,
Yet sure 'twas not that; but 'twas thought that his grace
Considered he was well he had a cup-bearer's place.   40

Will Davenant, ashamed of a foolish mischance
That he had got lately travelling in France,
Modestly hoped the handsomness of 's muse
Might any deformity about him excuse;
        And
Surely the company would have been content,   45
If they could have found any precedent;
But in all their records, either in verse or prose,
There was not one laureate without a nose.

To Will Berkeley sure all the wits meant well,
But first they would see how his snow would sell;   50
Will smiled and swore in their judgements they went less
That concluded of merit upon success;
        So
Sullenly taking his place again,
He gave way to Selwin, that straight stepped in;
But alas! he had been so lately a wit   55
That Apollo himself hardly knew him yet.

---

35 *hard bound*: constipated.   40 *a cup-bearer's place*: Carew was a Sewer in Ordinary
to Charles I, hence an official *serving* Ganymede, perhaps to Apollo. A 'sewer'
(from OF *asseoir* 'to cause to sit, seat') superintended the arrangement of the
table, the seating of guests, and the tasting and serving of food and drink.
41 *Will Davenant*: Sir William Davenant (1606–68).   48 *without a nose*: owing
to syphilis, which he had got figuratively 'travelling in France', since the 'great
pox' was conventionally the 'French disease'. On 13 December 1638 Davenant
received a royal grant 'which is generally assumed to mark the beginning of'
his 'appointment as Poet Laureate'; A. M. Gibbs, ed., *Sir William Davenant: The
Shorter Poems* (1972), p. xxv.   50 *how his snow would sell*. No one knows what this
means; R. C. Bald suggested the possibility of reference 'to the frigidity, or
purity, of [Berkeley's play,] *The Lost Lady*' (printed 1638); *MLN* lviii (1943),
551.

Tobiè Mathew (pox on 't! how came he there?)
Was busily whispering somebody i' th' ear,
When he had the honour to be named i' the court:
But sir, you may thank my Lady Carlisle for 't;   60
                    For
Had not her Character furnished you out
With something of handsome, without all doubt
You and your sorry Lady Muse had been
In the number of those that were not to come in.

In haste two or three from the Court came in,   65
And they brought letters (forsooth) from the Queen;
'Twas discreetly done, too, for if they had come
Without them, they had scarce been let into the room.
                    This
Made a dispute, for 'twas plain to be seen
Each man had a mind to gratify the Queen;   70
But Apollo himself could not think it fit;
There was difference, he said, 'twixt fooling and wit.

Suckling next was called, but did not appear,
And straight one whispered Apollo in's ear,
That of all men living he cared not for 't,   75
He loved not the Muses so well as his sport;
                    And
Prized black eyes, or a lucky hit
At bowls, above all the trophies of wit;
But Apollo was angry, and publicly said
'Twere fit that a fine were set on his head.   80

Wat Montagu now stood forth to his trial,
And did not so much as suspect a denial;
Wise Apollo then asked him first of all
If he understood his own pastoral;

57 [Sir] *Tobie Mathew* (1577–1655). 61 *her Character*: i.e. Mathew's 'Character of the Most Excellent Lady, Lucy, Countess of Carliele', circulating in 1636 but first printed in Mathew's *Collection of Letters* (1660). On Lady Carlise see G. The picture-in-context is clear: the seeking and conferring of powerful patronage through literary flattering (cf. l. 66). 66 *the Queen*: Henrietta Maria (1609–69). 72 *fooling*: (1) buffoonery; (2) sexual play. 81 *Wat Montagu*: Walter Montagu (1603?–77). 84 *his own pastoral*: *The Shepherd's Paradise*, acted at Court on 8 January 1633, printed 1659.

For
If he could do it, 'twould plainly appear   85
He understood more than any man there,
And did merit the bays above all the rest;
But the Monsieur was modest, and silence confessed.

During these troubles, in the crowd was hid
One that Apollo soon missed, little Sid;   90
And, having spied him, called him out of the throng,
And advised him in his ear not to write so strong.
Then
Murray was summoned, but 'twas urged that he
Was chief already of another company.

Hales, set by himself, most gravely did smile   95
To see them about nothing keep such a coil;
Apollo had spied him, but knowing his mind
Passed by, and called Falkland that sat just behind;
But
He was of late so gone with divinity,
That he had almost forgot his poetry,   100
Though to say the truth (and Apollo did know it)
He might have been both his priest and his poet.

88 *the Monsieur*: in reference to Montagu's French connections, 1624 and 1627–
33, on secret service; he turned Roman Catholic in 1635, and upon his exile in
1649 he became Abbot of St. Martin near Pontoise. *silence*. Some texts read
'silent', which is an equally good reading (a MS. that reads 'silene' could point
paleographically in either direction). 90 *little Sid*: Sidney Godolphin (1610–
43); 'little Cid' (*FA 46*), alluding to the hero of the twelfth-century Spanish
epic, has its attraction, since the subject writes 'so strong'. 93 *Murray*: William
Murray, first Earl of Dysart (1600?–51). 94 *another company*. The poem is
missing a couplet of the pattern in all surviving texts, so that is probably how
Suckling left it. 95 *Hales*: John Hales (1584–1656). 98 *Falkland*: Lucius
Cary, second Viscount Falkland (1610?–43). He entertained many learned
friends, including many of 'The Wits', in his house at Great Tew in Oxford-
shire. 102 *both his priest and his poet*: as, in Carew's elegy, Donne was, as 'two
flamens, and both those the best: Apollo's first, at last the true God's priest'
(C–34: 97–8).

At length, who but an alderman did appear,
At which Will Davenant began to swear;
But wiser Apollo bad him draw nigher,   105
And when he was mounted a little higher
          He
Openly declared that 'twas the best sign
Of good store of wit to have good store of coin,
And without a syllable more or less said
He put the laurel on the alderman's head.   110

At this all the wits were in such a maze
That for a good while they did nothing but gaze
One upon another: not a man in the place
But had discontent writ in great in his face.
          Only
The small-poets cleared up again,   115
Out of hope (as 'twas thought) of borrowing;
But sure they were out, for he forfeits his crown
When he lends any poet about the Town.

---

103 *an alderman*: a fittingly ironical choice for the crown of wit, as explained
in ll. 107–8.   104 *Will Davenant*, etc.: presumably because he was ambitious
and hopeful of the laureateship.   107–8 *He | Openly declared*, etc.: 'He that
is wise is rich' (Tilley W 534) easily becomes the cynical—and not unsound
—'he that is rich is wise'. Suckling echoes Jonson, *Poetaster*, I. ii. 253–6. Jonson
in turn draws on Ovid, *Amores*, III. viii. 3–4.   111 *a maze*: state of bewilderment
(with or without allusion to the mythical labyrinth); also a poetical form of
'amaze' (bewilderment).   114 *in great*: 'in large letters' (*OED*, citing this
passage only, but it seems reasonable).   115 *small-poets*: insignificant poets; see
G, 'small-'.

27

A Ballad upon a Wedding

I tell thee, Dick, where I have been,
Where I the rarest things have seen,
    Oh, things beyond compare!
Such sights again cannot be found
In any part of English ground,   5
    Be it at wake or fair.

At Charing Cross, hard by the way
Where we (thou know'st) do sell our hay,
    There is a house with stairs;
And there did I see coming down   10
Such folk as are not in our town,
    Forty, at least, in pairs.

Amongst the rest, one pest'lent fine
(His beard no bigger though than thine)
    Walked on before the rest;   15
Our landlord looks like nothing to him;
The King (God bless him), 'twould undo him,
    Should he go still so dressed.

27. Suckling's speaker is 'zome honest plain West-Country-mon' (Thomas Jordan, *Triumphs of London,* 1678, cited in *OED*), if we believe those variant texts that have 'volk' in l. 11 and 'Vorty' in l. 12. 'A Ballad' could not have been written after mid 1639, because Suckling is lampooned in two poems that deal with events of that time in the verse-form (*rime couée* or tail rhyme) and with a paraphrase of the first line of 'A Ballad'. Carew wrote 'An Hymeneal Song on the Nuptials of the Lady Anne Wentworth and the Lord Lovelace' in a verse-form like Suckling's (C–48), and it has been suggested that it would be pleasant and reasonable to view the poems as celebrating the same wedding in very different idioms, one in the courtly vein of Carew's hard-bound muse, the other in a country vein by 'natural, easy Suckling'. 6 *wake*: annual village parish-festival, originally associated with the patron saint. 8 *where we . . . do sell our hay*: the Haymarket in London. 9 *a house with stairs*: especially impressive to one accustomed to cottages.

At Course-a-park, without all doubt,
He should have first been taken out   20
          By all the maids i' th' town;
Though lusty Roger there had been,
Or little George upon the Green,
          Or Vincent of the Crown.

But wot you what? The youth was going   25
To make an end of all his wooing;
          The Parson for him stayed;
Yet by his leave (for all his haste)
He did not wish so much all past
          (Perchance) as did the maid.   30

The maid (and thereby hangs a tale,
For such a maid no Whitsun-ale
          Could ever yet produce)—
No grape that's kindly ripe could be
So round, so plump, so soft as she,   35
          Nor half so full of juice.

Her fingers were so small, the ring
Would not stay on which they did bring,
          It was too wide a Peck;
And to say truth (for out it must),   40
It looked like the great collar (just)
          About our young colt's neck.

---

19 *Course-a-park*: 'a country game in which a girl called out one of the other sex
to chase her'; *OED*, citing William Browne of Tavistock, *Brittania's Pastorals*, I.
iii. 19 f.   22–4 *lusty Roger . . . little George . . . Vincent of the Crown*: ostensibly
these are accomplished village lads; 'as good as George of Green' was proverbial
(Tilley G 83).   32 *Whitsun-ale*: an 'ale' was a country festival at which the
drinking of ale was pre-eminent in the merry-making; this one, celebrated at
Whitsuntide, the week of Whit Sunday (the seventh after Easter), was associated
with sheep-shearing.   37 *fingers were*: two texts read this, two read 'finger was';
Suckling probably wrote the plural.

Her feet beneath her petticoat
Like little mice stole in and out,
    As if they feared the light;   45
But oh, she dances such a way!
No sun upon an Easter day
    Is half so fine a sight.

He would have kissed her once or twice,
But she would not, she was so nice,   50
    She would not do 't in sight;
And then she looked as who should say,
'I will do what I list to day,
    And you shall do 't at night.'

Her cheeks so rare a white was on   55
No daisy makes comparison
    (Who sees them is undone);
For streaks of red were mingled there,
Such as are on a Katherine pear
    (The side that's next the sun).   60

Her mouth so small when she doth speak,
Thou'dst swear her teeth her words did break
    That they might passage get;
But she so handles still the matter,
They come as good as ours, or better,   65
    And are not spoiled one whit.

Her lips were red, and one was thin,
Compared to that was next her chin
    (Some bee had stung it newly);
But, Dick, her eyes so guard her face,   70
I durst no more upon her gaze,
    Than on the sun in July.

43–4 *her feet . . . like little mice*, etc.: cf. H–142.   47 *No sun upon an Easter day*: see
H–187: 7 n.   52 *as who should say*: as if to say.   61 *her mouth* [being] *so small*,
etc.: absolute construction.   71 *her.* Two manuscripts with independent
authority read 'her'; *FA 46* reads 'them'.

If wishing should be any sin,
The parson self had guilty been
    (She looked that day so purely);   75
And did the youth so oft the feat
At night as some did in conceit,
    It would have spoiled him, surely.

Passion o' me, how I run on!
There's that that would be thought upon,   80
    I trow, besides the bride:
The business of the kitchen great;
For it is fit that men should eat,
    Nor was it there denied.

Just in the nick the cook knocked thrice,   85
And all the waiters in a trice
    His summons did obey:
Each serving man with dish in hand
Marched boldly up, like our trainband,
    Presented, and away.   90

When all the meat was on the table,
What man of knife, or teeth, was able
    To stay to be entreated?
And this the very reason was,
Before the parson could say grace,   95
    The company was seated.

Now hats fly off, and youths carouse;
Healths first go round, and then the house,
    The bride's came thick and thick;
And when 'twas named another's health,   100
Perhaps he made it hers by stealth.
    (And who could help it, Dick?)

---

74 *Parson self:* editorial (an archaic and perhaps dialectal uninflected genitive);
FA 46 reads 'Parson himself'; two MSS. read 'Parson[']s self'; one MS. reads
'Parson sure'; all together, they suggest an original and 'difficult' reading of
both 'Parson' and 'self'.   89 *trainband:* a division of citizen soldiers or militia.

O' th' sudden up they rise and dance,
Then sit again and sigh, and glance,
     Then dance again and kiss;   105
Thus several ways the time did pass,
Whilst every woman wished her place,
     And every man wished his.

By this time all were stol'n aside
To counsel and undress the bride,   110
     But that he must not know;
But yet 'twas thought he guessed her mind,
And did not mean to stay behind
     Above an hour or so.

When in he came, Dick, there she lay   115
Like new-fall'n snow melting away
     ('Twas time I trow to part);
Kisses were now the only stay,
Which soon she gave, as who should say,
     'God b'w'y', with all my heart.'   120

But just as heavens would have to cross it,
In came the bridemaids with the posset;
     The bridegroom eat in spite;
For had he left the women to 't,
It would have cost two hours to do 't,   125
     Which were too much that night.

At length the candle's out, and now
All that they had not done they do:
     What that is, who can tell?
But I believe it was no more   130
Than thou and I have done before
     With Bridget and with Nell.

---

120 *God b'w'y'*: like 'good-bye' a contraction of 'God be with you'.   122 *posset*: see G.   123 *eat*: once common as the past tense where 'ate' is now usual.

28

Upon My Lord Brohall's Wedding

Dialogue

S.　　　B.

S.　　　　　In bed, dull man?
When Love and Hymen's revels are begun,
And the church ceremonies past and done?

B.　　　　Why, who's gone mad today?

S.　　　　Dull Heretic, thou'dst say　　　　5
He that is gone to heaven's gone astray;
　　　Brohall our gallant friend
Is gone to church as martyrs to the fire.

B.　　　Who marry differ but i' th' end,
　　　　Since both do take　　　　10
The hardest way to what they most desire.

S.　　Nor stayed he till the formal priest had done,
But ere that part was finished, his begun.

B.　　　　Which did reveal
The haste and eagerness men have to seal　　　15
　　　That long to tell the money.

---

28. This poem is associated with the marriage of Lady Margaret Howard to
Roger Boyle, Baron Broghill, on 27 January 1641, with which 'A Ballad upon
a Wedding' (S–27) was long thought to be associated. Six or seven months
later Suckling was dead, and this is his last poem, so far as we know. The
fictional dialogue is between *S*[uckling], presumably, and a 'Jack' friend of
Suckling who has been conjecturally identified as either a Berry or a Bond; both
had some connection with bride or groom, and the latter is mentioned by name
in Suckling's poem, 'A Summons to Town', ll. 9–10. In the *FA 46* text there
are speech-prefixes only at ll. 1, 4, and 5, but the dialogue was obviously
intended to be continued. The remaining speech-prefixes have been supplied,
and I have given ll. 18 and 23 to *B*, but the sense would be much the same,
although less dramatic and in character with 'Who's gone mad today?' (l. 4),
if all these were given to *S*.　2 *Hymen*: god of marriage.

S. A sprig of willow in his hat he wore,—

B. The loser's badge and livery heretofore.

S. But now so ordered that it might be taken
      By lookers-on forsaking as forsaken.   20
                    And now and then
      A careless smile broke forth, which spoke his mind,—

B. And seemed to say she might have been more kind.

S.   When this, dear Jack, I saw,
                        Thought I,   25
              How weak is lovers' law?

B. The bonds made there (like gypsies' knots) with ease
      Are fast and loose, as they that hold them please.

S. But was the fair nymph's praise or power less
      That led him captive now to happiness,   30
      'Cause she did not a foreign aid despise,
      But entered breaches made by others' eyes?
                    The gods forbid!
      There must be some to shoot and batter down,
      Others to force and to take in the town.   35
              To hawks, good Jack, and hearts
                    There may
              Be several ways and arts:
      One watches them, perchance, and makes them tame;
      Another, when they're ready, shows them game.   40

17–18 *sprig of willow . . . the loser's badge*: 'To wear the willow' (Tilley W 403)
is to be in mourning for a sweetheart or bride, to bewail a lost lover. The
association of mourning with the (weeping) willow is ancient; see, e.g. Ps. 137:
1–2, and Shakespeare, *Oth.* IV. iii. Cf. Herrick, 'The Willow Garland'.
19–20 *But now so ordered*, etc. The meaning is probably that by this celebratory
kind of wearing, the willow may be taken, by the onlookers, now to signify
forsaking as well as being forsaken.   26 *How weak is lovers' law?* Reference seems
to be made to 'a careless smile broke forth', and the tone seems amusedly
indulgent.   27–8 *gypsies' knots . . . fast and loose*: proverbial (Tilley P 401;
cf. F 78).

RICHARD LOVELACE
(1618–57)

I

Song

To Lucasta, Going Beyond the Seas

If to be absent were to be
    Away from thee;
    Or that when I am gone
    You or I were alone;
Then, my Lucasta, might I crave   5
Pity from blust'ring wind, or swall'wing wave.

But I'll not sigh one blast or gale
    To swell my sail,
    Or pay a tear to swage
    The foaming blue-god's rage;   10
For whether he will let me pass
Or no, I'm still as happy as I was.

Though seas and land be 'twixt us both,
    Our faith and troth,
    Like separated souls,   15
    All time and space controls:
Above the highest sphere we meet
Unseen, unknown, and greet as angels greet.

---

1. The identity of the historical 'Lucasta' is uncertain. Wilkinson (p. xlvii): ' "The reason", says [Anthony] Wood, "why he gave that title was, because, some time before, he had made his amours to a Gentlewoman of great beauty and fortune named Lucy Sacheverel, whom he usually called *Lux casta* [pure, or chaste, light]; but she upon a strong report that Lovelace was dead of his wound received at Dunkirk, soon after married." ' 10 *foaming blue-god*: the god of the sea, Neptune. 13 *be 'twixt*: suggested by John Buxton; *L 49* has 'betwixt' and consequent syntactical confusion. 14–16 That is, our 'faith and troth' (a compound singular) controls all time and space.

So then we do anticipate
  Our after-fate,   20
  And are alive i' th' skies:
  If thus our lips and eyes
Can speak like spirits unconfined
In heaven, their earthy bodies left behind.

2

Song

To Lucasta, Going to the Wars

Tell me not, sweet, I am unkind,
  That from the nunnery
Of thy chaste breast and quiet mind,
  To war and arms I fly.

True, a new mistress now I chase,   5
  The first foe in the field;
And with a stronger faith embrace
  A sword, a horse, a shield.

Yet this inconstancy is such
  As you too shall adore;   10
I could not love thee, dear, so much,
  Loved I not Honour more.

2. This poem figures prominently in an essay by George Fenwick Jones (see Select Bibliography: Lovelace) and in a debate on psychoanalytical interpretation and evaluation in *Literature and Psychology*, xiv (1964), 43–55 and 116–27. Musical setting: John Lanier. 1 *unkind*: perhaps sylleptic, like Hamlet's 'a little more than kin and less than *kind*' (1. ii. 65).

3

Song

To Amarantha, That She Would Dishevel Her Hair

Amarantha sweet and fair,
Ah, braid no more that shining hair!
As my curious hand or eye,
Hovering round thee, let it fly.

Let it fly as unconfined   5
As its calm ravisher, the wind,
Who hath left his darling, th' East,
To wanton o'er that spicy nest.

Every tress must be confessed
But neatly tanglèd at the best,   10
Like a clew of golden thread
Most excellently ravellèd.

Do not then wind up that light
In ribbands, and o'ercloud in night,
Like the sun in's early ray,   15
But shake your head and scatter day.

See, 'tis broke! Within this grove,
The bower and the walks of love,
Weary lie we down and rest,
And fan each other's panting breast.   20

3. In its cosmological conceits and a few specific details, this poem is reminiscent of Crashaw's 'The Weeper' (*Steps to the Temple*, 1646, rev. 1648; see l. 22 n.). The amaranth is an imaginary unfading flower. 11 *clew*: (1) ball of thread; (2) clue, like the thread given to Theseus by Ariadne that enabled him to find his way through the Labyrinth where he killed the Minotaur.

Here we'll strip and cool our fire
In cream below, in milk-baths higher;
And when all wells are drawn dry,
I'll drink a tear out of thine eye,

Which our very joys shall leave,   25
That sorrows thus we can deceive;
Or our very sorrows weep,
That joys so ripe so little keep.

4

Gratiana Dancing and Singing

See with what constant motïon,
Even and glorious as the sun,
    Gratiana steers that noble frame,
Soft as her breast, sweet as her voice
That gave each winding law and poise,   5
    And swifter than the wings of Fame.

She beat the happy pavèment
By such a star made firmament,
    Which now no more the roof envies,
But swells up high with Atlas ev'n,   10
Bearing the brighter, nobler heav'n,
    And in her all the deities.

22 *In cream below, in milk-baths higher*: the references are obviously sexual,
but cosmic references elsewhere in the poem may partly explain the paradoxical
'milk-baths higher' and 'cream below' as vehicle. Cf. 'Love Made in the First Age'
(L–36: 51–4), and Crashaw, 'The Weeper', ll. 19–22.   25 *Which*: i.e. 'tear'.

4. The Latin root, *gratia*, makes 'Gratiana' in effect a votary of the *Gratiae*, the
three Graces (see l. 24)—Aglaia, Euphrosyne, and Thalia—of favour, love-
liness, and grace. The central conceit of this poem is made fully explicit in
ll. 19–20: Gratiana is compared with the angelic Intelligences that guide the
transparent, musical, and nested spheres which surround the earth in the
geocentric universe of the Ptolemaic cosmology (see NRC).   10 *Atlas*: the
Titan compelled to support the heavens with his head and hands, and also a
mountain on the northwest coast of Africa regarded as supporting the heavens.

Each step trod out a lover's thought
And the ambitious hopes he brought,
    Chained to her brave feet with such arts,   15
Such sweet command, and gentle awe,
As, when she ceased, we sighing saw
    The floor lay paved with broken hearts.

So did she move, so did she sing,
Like the harmonious spheres that bring   20
    Unto their rounds their music's aid;
Which she performèd such a way,
As all th' enamoured world will say
    The Graces dancèd, and Apollo played.

5

The Scrutiny

Song

Why should you swear I am forsworn,
    Since thine I vowed to be?
Lady, it is already morn,
    And 'twas last night I swore to thee
That fond impossibility.   5

Have I not loved thee much and long,
    A tedious twelve hours' space?
I must all other beauties wrong,
    And rob thee of a new embrace,
Could I still dote upon thy face.   10

5. One of Lovelace's most popular songs in the seventeenth century. At least
one 'answer' poem was written in response (see Wilkinson, pp. 258–9 and
348–9), and Henry Bold twice translated it in *Latine Songs* (1685), pp. 25–7. The
poem has prominent affinities with Donne's 'Break of Day' (in which the
speaker is a woman, however) and Suckling's 'Constant Lover' (S–18), among
many others. For a psychoanalytical treatment, see L–2 n. Musical setting:
Thomas Charles.

260 CAVALIER POETS

Not but all joy in thy brown hair
    By others may be found;
But I must search the black and fair,
    Like skilful min'ralists that sound
For treasure in unploughed-up ground.   15

Then if, when I have loved my round,
    Thou prov'st the pleasant she,
With spoils of meaner beauties crowned,
    I laden will return to thee,
Ev'n sated with variety.   20

6

Orpheus to Beasts

Song

Here, here, oh here Eurydice,
    Here was she slain;
Her soul 'stilled through a vein.
    The gods knew less,
That time, divinity,   5
    Than ev'n, ev'n these
    Of brutishness.

Oh, could you view the melody
    Of every grace,
And music of her face,   10
    You'd drop a tear,
Seeing more harmony
    In her bright eye,
    Than now you hear.

14 *min'ralists*: mineralogists. *sound*: dowse; use the divining-rod.

6. On Orpheus see G. Katherine Duncan-Jones has a deft essay on this poem, 'The Lyric as Song: Lovelace's "Orpheus to Beasts" ', *Critical Survey*, iii (1966), 52–3: 'most remarkable is its exploration of the fact that it *is* a song' designed to be heard. Its opening and closing words epitomize its process: 'here, hear'. 3 *'stilled*: (1) distilled; (2) stilled. 14 *L 49*, with the archaic spelling 'Then', gives more emphasis to the expressive and certainly intended ambiguities of the last line, e.g. 'Then, now, you here'.

7

Orpheus to Woods

Song

Hark! O hark, you guilty trees,
In whose gloomy galleries
Was the cruelest murder done
That e'er yet eclipsed the sun!
Be then henceforth in your twigs   5
Blasted ere you sprout to sprigs;
Feel no season of the year
But what shaves off all your hair;
Nor carve any from your wombs
Aught but coffins, and their tombs.   10

8

The Grasshopper

To My Noble Friend Master Charles Cotton: Ode

O thou that swing'st upon the waving hair
   Of some well-fillèd oaten beard,
Drunk every night with a delicious tear
   Dropped thee from heaven, where now th' art reared:

---

7. Musical setting: 'Mr. Curtes'. 3 *murder*: by hyperbole and guilt by association, since a snake bit Eurydice (see G, 'Orpheus').

8. This poem has received more attention than any other single poem by Lovelace. It seems to owe a good deal to *Anacreontea* xxxiv, a lyric about a grasshopper which is 'as happy as a king' and 'more than half a god', and also to the fable of the ant that stores and the grasshopper that plays. The grasshopper is apostrophized, both as he was on earth and is in heaven, in sts. 1–5 as Charles Cotton is in sts. 6–10, although possible ambiguity in 'Thou be[a]st of men and friends' (l. 21) permits some fusing of symbolic grasshopper and true friend. Two important essays are Don Cameron Allen, 'Richard Lovelace: "The Grass-Hopper" ', in *Image and Meaning: Metaphoric Traditions in Renaissance Poetry* (1960), pp. 80–92; and Bruce King, 'Green Ice and a Breast of Proof', *College English*, xxvi (1965), 511–15. *Charles Cotton*: see H–191 n.

The joys of earth and air are thine entire,   5
    That with thy feet and wings dost hop and fly;
And when thy poppy works thou dost retire
    To thy carved acorn-bed to lie.

Up with the day, the sun thou welcom'st then,
    Sport'st in the gilt-plats of his beams,   10
And all these merry days mak'st merry men,
    Thyself, and melancholy streams.

But ah, the sickle! Golden ears are cropped;
    Ceres and Bacchus bid good night;
Sharp frosty fingers all your flowers have topped,   15
    And what scythes spared, winds shave off quite.

Poor verdant fool! and now green ice! Thy joys,
    Large and as lasting as thy perch of grass,
Bid us lay in gainst winter, rain, and poise
    Their floods with an o'erflowing glass.   20

Thou best of men and friends! we will create
    A genuine summer in each other's breast;
And spite of this cold time and frozen fate,
    Thaw us a warm seat to our rest.

Our sacred hearths shall burn eternally   25
    As vestal flames; the North-wind, he
Shall strike his frost-stretched wings, dissolve, and fly
    This Etna in epitome.

7 *poppy*: i.e. opium, as a soporific. 8 *acorn*: *L 49* reads 'Acron', a common contemporary spelling and pronunciation. 10 *gilt-plats*: gold patches, or 'plots', and perhaps 'folds', from 'plat' as an early form of 'plait' and 'pleat'. 11–12 'men', 'Thyself', and 'melancholy streams' are the objects of 'mak'st merry.' 16 *scythes*: punning on 'sighs' (still a common pronunciation of 'scythes') to complement 'winds' (cf. 'hearths' in l. 25 and 'reign' in l. 30). 17 *verdant*: with some of the force of Latin *ver* 'spring'. 19 *winter, rain*: editors often read 'winter rain', but 'their floods' (l. 20) demands either this plural (after *L 49*) or 'winter rains' (a plausible emendation: *L 49* reads 'Raine,'). *poise*: counterbalance. 25 *heart[h]s*: sylleptic (cf. ll. 21–2).

Dropping December shall come weeping in,
  Bewail th' usurping of his reign;   30
But when in showers of old Greek we begin,
  Shall cry he hath his crown again!

Night as clear Hesper shall our tapers whip
  From the light casements where we play,
And the dark hag from her black mantle strip,   35
  And stick there everlasting day.

Thus richer than untempted kings are we,
  That, asking nothing, nothing need:
Though lord of all what seas embrace, yet he
  That wants himself is poor indeed.   40

9

The Vintage to the Dungeon

A Song

Sing out, pent souls, sing cheerfully!
Care shackles you in liberty,
Mirth frees you in captivity:
    Would you double fetters add?
    Else why so sad?   5

Chorus
Besides your pinioned arms you'll find
Grief too can manacle the mind.

---

30 *reign*: also 'rain', complementing the 'showers of old Greek' in the following
line, and perhaps referring to the Long Parliament's turning Christmas from a
feast to a fast and banning celebration (1644). 31 *showers of old Greek*: Ana-
cre-antics, perhaps, of convivial drinking and the reciting of Anacreontic poems.
33–6 *as clear Hesper*: i.e. Hesperus, the evening star. This is ambiguous; perhaps
the primary meaning of the stanza is, 'as clear Hesper does, our tapers shall
whip night (a witch) from the light casements where we play, and we shall
replace the hag's black mantle with a "light" one of everlasting day'. Cf. 'Night:
To Lucasta' (L–28), ll. 11–12. 34 *the light casements where we play*: cf. *MND*
III. i. 55–7.
9. Musical setting: William Lawes.

K

Live then prisoners uncontrolled;
Drink o' th' strong, the rich, the old,
Till wine too hath your wits in hold;   10
    Then if still your jollity
    And throats are free—

Chorus
Triumph in your bonds and pains,
And dance to th' music of your chains.

10

To Lucasta, from Prison

An Epode

Long in thy shackles, liberty
I ask not from these walls but thee
(Left for a while another's bride),
To fancy all the world beside.

Yet ere I do begin to love,   5
See how I all my objects prove:
Then my free soul to that confine
'Twere possible I might call mine.

First I would be in love with Peace,
And her rich swelling breasts' increase;   10
But how, alas! how may that be,
Despising Earth, she will love me?

---

10. The 'epode' was invented by Archilochus (seventh century B.C.), whose
satirical iambics and mixed metres were adapted by Horace in his seventeen
epodes on a variety of subjects, political, amatory, ethical, and miscellaneous.
Lovelace was in Peterhouse Prison from October 1648 until 10 April 1649. This
poem was obviously written in 1649, since it alludes to the King's beheading
(30 January).   6 *prove*: test, try.   12 If there is no peace on earth, how can
there be good will toward Lovelace?

Fain would I be in love with War,
As my dear just avenging star;
But War is loved so everywhere,   15
Ev'n he disdains a lodging here.

Thee and thy wounds I would bemoan,
Fair thorough-shot Religion;
But he lives only that kills thee,
And whoso binds thy hands is free.   20

I would love a Parliament
As a main prop from heaven sent;
But ah! who's he that would be wedded
To th' fairest body that's beheaded?

Next would I court my Liberty,   25
And then my birthright, Property;
But can that be, when it is known
There's nothing you can call your own?

A Reformation I would have,
As for our griefs a sovereign salve;   30
That is, a cleansing of each wheel
Of state that yet some rust doth feel:

But not a Reformation so
As to reform were to o'erthrow;
Like watches by unskilful men   35
Disjointed, and set ill again.

The Public Faith I would adore,
But she is bankrupt of her store;
Nor how to trust her can I see,
For she that cozens all, must me.   40

---

24 That is, to *even* 'th' fairest body', which Parliament may not be, but it did
lose its head when Charles lost his. 30 *sovereign salve*: master-remedy, with
allusion to the King. 37 *Public Faith*: euphemism for credit coerced by Parliament.

Since then none of these can be
Fit objects for my love and me,
What then remains but th' only spring
Of all our loves and joys, the King?

He who, being the whole ball   45
Of day on earth, lends it to all;
When seeking to eclipse his right,
Blinded, we stand in our own light.

And now an universal mist
Of error is spread o'er each breast,   50
With such a fury edged as is
'Not found in th' inwards of th' Abyss.

Oh, from thy glorious Starry Wain,
Dispense on me one sacred beam,
To light me where I soon may see   55
How to serve you, and you trust me.

II

Lucasta's Fan,
with a Looking-Glass in It

Estrich, thou feathered fool and easy prey,
    That larger sails to thy broad vessel need'st:
Snakes through thy gutter-neck hiss all the day,
    Then on thy iron mess at supper feed'st.

Oh, what a glorious transmigratiön   5
    From this to so divine an edifice
Hast thou straight made! near from a wingèd stone
    Transformed into a bird of paradise.

53 *Wain*: 'Charles's Wain', or waggon (originally the Wain of Arcturus, or Arthur), a name for the constellation Ursa Major.

11. 1 *Estrich*: early form of 'ostrich'.   3 *guttur*[-*neck*]: throat.   6 *edifice*: i.e. the fan.

Now do thy plumes for hue and lustre vie
  With th' arch of heaven that triumphs o'er past wet, 10
And in a rich enamelled pinion lie,
  With sapphires, amethysts, and opals set.

Sometime they wing her side, then strive to drown
  The day's eye-piercing beams, whose am'rous heat
Solicits still, till with this shield of down 15
  From her brave face his glowing fires are beat.

But whilst a plumy curtain she doth draw,
  A crystal mirror sparkles in thy breast,
In which her fresh aspect whenas she saw,
  And then her foe retired to the west, 20

'Dear engine that o' th' sun got'st me the day,
  Spite of his hot assaults mad'st him retreat!
No wind', said she, 'dare with thee henceforth play
  But mine own breath to cool the tyrant's heat.

'My lively shade thou ever shalt retain 25
  In thy enclosèd feather-framèd glass,
And, but unto ourselves, to all remain
  Invisible, thou feature of this face!'

So said, her sad swain overheard, and cried,
  'Ye gods! For faith unstained this a reward! 30
Feathers and glass t' outweigh my virtue tried?
  Ah, show their empty strength!' The gods accord.

Now fall'n the brittle favourite lies, and burst!
  Amazed Lucasta weeps, repents, and flies
To her Alexis, vows herself accursed 35
  If hence she dress herself but in his eyes.

---

10 *arch*, etc.: rainbow.   13 *Sometime they wing her side*: Wilkinson notes that Robert Heath has in *Clarastella* (1650) a poem on a lady 'wearing a looking-glass at her girdle'.   14 *eye-piercing*. *L 49* and Wilkinson read 'eyes-piercing' (i.e. 'eye's piercing'?).   19 *whenas*: when.   25 *shade*: image.   35 *Alexis*: 'her sad swain' (l. 29) with whom she shares a 'Dialogue: Lucasta, Alexis'.

12

To Lucasta

Ode Lyric

Ah, Lucasta, why so bright,
Spread with early streakèd light?
If still veilèd from our sight,
What is 't but eternal night?

Ah, Lucasta, why so chaste,   5
With that vigour, ripeness, graced?
Not to be by man embraced
Makes that royal coin embased,
And this golden orchard waste.

Ah, Lucasta, why so great,   10
That thy crammèd coffers sweat?
Yet not owner of a seat
May shelter you from nature's heat,
And your earthly joys complete.

Ah, Lucasta, why so good,   15
Blest with an unstainèd flood
Flowing both through soul and blood?
If it be not understood,
'Tis a diamond in mud.

Lucasta, stay! Why dost thou fly?   20
Thou art not bright, but to the eye,
Nor chaste, but in the marriage-tie,
Nor great, but in this treasury,
Nor good, but in that sanctity.

Harder than the orient stone,   25
Like an apparition,
Or as a pale shadow gone,
Dumb and deaf she hence is flown.

12. 25 *orient stone*: pearl.

Then receive this equal doom:
Virgins strew no tear or bloom,   30
No one dig the Parian womb;
Raise her marble heart i' th' room,
And 'tis both her corse and tomb.

13

*To My Worthy Friend Master Peter Lely, on That
Excellent Picture of His Majesty and the Duke of
York, Drawn by Him at Hampton Court*

See what a clouded majesty, and eyes
Whose glory through their mist doth brighter rise!
See what an humble bravery doth shine,
And grief triumphant breaking through each line!
How it commands the face! So sweet a scorn   5
Never did happy misery adorn!
So sacred a contempt that others show
To this (o' th' height of all the wheel) below,
That mightiest monarchs by this shaded book
May copy out their proudest, richest look.   10
    Whilst the true eaglet this quick lustre spies,
And by his sun's enlightens his own eyes;
He cares his cares, his burthen feels, then straight
Joys that so lightly he can bear such weight;

---

31 *Parian womb*: the quarries of the isle of Paros yielded a famed white marble.
13. Sir Peter Lely (1618–80) was born near Utrecht, studied in Haarlem, and
flourished in England as a portrait-painter from 1641 until his death. He
enjoyed the patronage successively of Charles I, Cromwell, and Charles II, and
painted many of the beauties of Charles II's court. According to Wilkinson
(1930, p. 266), the picture referred to is in the possession of the Duke of
Northumberland at Syon House; there is a copy of the head of the King from
this picture in the Ashmolean Museum in Oxford. 8 *the wheel*: that is,
Charles's 'sacred contempt' shows above even those at the top of Fortune's
wheel. 11 *eaglet*: in the lore of the correspondences, the eagle is the king's
counterpart in the realm of birds as the sun is in the solar system. Proverbially,
'only the eagle can gaze at the sun' (Tilley E 3), or the suns of the King's eyes.
14 *lightly*: sylleptic; opposite of both 'heavily, gravely', and 'darkly'.

Whilst either either's passiön doth borrow,   15
And both do grieve the same victorious sorrow.
   These, my best Lely, with so bold a spirit
And soft a grace, as if thou didst inherit
For that time all their greatness, and didst draw
With those brave eyes your royal sitters saw.   20
   Not as of old, when a rough hand did speak
A strong aspect, and a fair face a weak;
When only a black beard cried villain, and
By hieroglyphics we could understand;
When crystal typified in a white spot,   25
And the bright ruby was but one red blot;
Thou dost the things orientally the same,
Not only paint'st its colour, but its flame:
Thou sorrow canst design without a tear,
And with the man his very hope or fear;   30
So that th' amazèd world shall henceforth find
None but my Lely ever drew a mind.

14

Ellinda's Glove

Sonnet

Thou snowy farm with thy five tenements!
   Tell thy white mistress here was one
   That called to pay his daily rents;
But she a gathering flowers and hearts is gone,
  And thou left void to rude possession.   5

17–20 Elliptical; the sense is 'These [thou hast drawn], my best Lely, with so bold a spirit...'   22 *aspect*: countenance, bearing, demeanour.   24 *hieroglyphics*: symbolic representations (ll. 23, 25–6) in lieu of realistically detailed, self-expressive portraiture.   27 *orientally*: Lovelace explains his own use in ll. 28–32: resplendently, radiantly, as from the east whence the sun rises.   32 *None but my Lely ever drew a mind*: the force of this is made clear in lines by Thomas Stanley appearing below an engraved portrait of Suckling in *Fragmenta Aurea* (1646): 'Drawn by the pencil here you find / His form, by his own pen his mind.'

14. 1 *tenements*: buildings, dwellings.

But grieve not, pretty ermine cabinet,
    Thy alablaster lady will come home;
    If not, what tenant can there fit
The slender turnings of thy narrow room,
But must ejected be by his own doom?   10

Then give me leave to leave my rent with thee:
    Five kisses, one unto a place;
    For though the lute's too high for me,
Yet servants knowing minikin nor base
Are still allowed to fiddle with the case.   15

15

The Lady A. L.,

My Asylum in a Great Extremity

With that delight the royal captive's brought
Before the throne, to breathe his farewell thought,
To tell his last tale, and so end with it,
Which gladly he esteems a benefit;
When the brave victor at his great soul dumb   5
Finds something there Fate cannot overcome,
Calls the chained prince, and by his glory led
First reaches him his crown, and then his head;

7 *alablaster*: alabaster.   14 *minikin*: treble string of a lute or viol; also a playful term for a woman or girl, although that sense figures only very indirectly here.
15. Wilkinson suggests that 'A. L.' is possibly Anne, Lady Lovelace, who married in 1638 and to whom *Lucasta* is dedicated; 'A. L.' also figures in L–20 and is certainly, as 'Cousin', Lady Lovelace in 24. Carew (C–2) and Suckling ('*Non est mortale quod opto*: Upon Mrs. A. L.') also have poems to a mysterious 'A. L.', but the persons need not be the same, whether real or imaginary. Carew has a poem 'Upon My Lord Chief Justice's Election of my Lady A. W. [Anne Wentworth, before her marriage to Lord Lovelace] For His Mistress' (C–38) and another '. . . on the Nuptials of the Lady Anne Wentworth and the Lord Lovelace' (C–48). In the allusion to the beheading of Charles ('the royal captive'), the King's death becomes one of many allegorical elements in this elaborate protest of inadequacy.   1 *royal captive*: Charles I, beheaded 30 January 1649.   5 *the brave victor*: death, personified.   8 *reaches him*: helps himself to.

Who ne'er till now thinks himself slave and poor,
For, though nought else, he had himself before;   10
He weeps at this fair chance, nor will allow
But that the diadem doth brand his brow,
And underrates himself below mankind,
Who first had lost his body, now his mind.

With such a joy came I to hear my doom,   15
And haste the preparation of my tomb,
When, like good angels who have heavenly charge
To steer and guide man's sudden-giddy barge,
She snatched me from the rock I was upon,
And landed me at life's pavilion,   20
Where I, thus wound out of th' immense abyss,
Was straight set on a pinnacle of bliss.

Let me leap in again, and by that fall
Bring me to my first woe, so cancel all!
Ah, 's this a quitting of the debt you owe,   25
To crush her and her goodness at one blow?
Defend me from so foul impiety
Would make fiends grieve and furies weep to see.

Now, ye sage spirits which infuse in men
That are obliged, twice to oblige again,   30
Inform my tongue in labour what to say,
And in what coin or language to repay;
But you are silent as the evening's air,
When winds unto their hollow grots repair:
Oh, then accept the all that left me is,   35
Devout oblations of a sacred wish!

When she walks forth, ye perfumed wings o' th' east,
Fan her, till with the sun she hastes to th' west,
And when her heavenly course calls up the day,
And breaks as bright, descend some glistering ray   40
To circle her, and her as-glistering hair,
That all may say a living saint shines there.

---

21 *wound*: extricated.   25–6 *Ah, 's this*, etc.: the 'you' is the speaker himself.

Slow Time, with woollen feet make thy soft pace,
And leave no tracks i' th' snow of her pure face;
But when this virtue must needs fall, to rise   45
The brightest constellation in the skies,
When we in characters of fire shall read
How clear she was alive, how spotless dead,
All you that are akin to piety
(For only you can her close mourners be),   50
Draw near, and make of hallowed tears a dearth:
Goodness and Justice both are fled the earth.

If this be to be thankful, I've a heart
Broken with vows, eaten with grateful smart,
And beside this, the vile world nothing hath   55
Worth anything, but her provokèd wrath:
So then who thinks to satisfy in time
Must give a satisfaction for that crime:
Since she alone knows the gift's value, she
Can only to herself requital be,   60
And worthily to th' life paint her own story
In its true colours and full native glory;
Which when perhaps she shall be heard to tell,
Buffoons and thieves, ceasing to do ill,
Shall blush into a virgin-innocence,   65
And then woo others from the same offence;
The robber and the murderer in spite
Of his red spots shall startle into white;
All good (rewards laid by) shall still increase
For love of her, and villainy decease;   70
Nought be ignote, not so much out of fear
Of being punished, as offending her.

So that, whenas my future, daring bays,
Shall bow itself in laurels to her praise,
To crown her conquering goodness, and proclaim   75
The due renown and glories of her name,
My wit shall be so wretched and so poor

70 *decease*: cease, desist.   71 *Nought be ignote*: wickedness be unknown, i.e. in absence, while 'all good . . . still increase[s]'.   73 *whenas*: when.   *bays*: for a wreath of 'bay(s)' (see G).

That 'stead of praising I shall scandal her,
And leave, when with my purest art I've done,
Scarce the design of what she is begun;   80
Yet men shall send me home admired, exact,
Proud that I could from her so well detract.

Where then, thou bold instinct, shall I begin
My endless task? To thank her were a sin
Great as not speak, and not to speak a blame   85
Beyond what's worst, such as doth want a name;
So thou my all, poor gratitude, ev'n thou
In this wilt an unthankful office do:
Or will I fling all at her feet I have?
My life, my love, my very soul a slave?   90
Tie my free spirit only unto her,
And yield up my affection prisoner?
Fond thought, in this thou teachest me to give
What first was hers, since by her breath I live;
And hast but showed me how I may resign   95
Possession of those things are none of mine.

16

*To My Truly Valiant, Learned Friend, Who in
His Book Resolved the Art Gladiatory into the
Mathematics*

Hark, reader! wilt be learn'd i' th' wars?
    A general in a gown?
Strike a league with arts and scars,
    And snatch from each a crown?

16. This poem was prefixed to *The Gentlemans Armorie: Wherein the right and genuine use of the Rapier and of the Sword . . . is displayed*, etc. (1639); the author, 'G. A.', is possibly George Ashwell of Wadham College, Oxford (Wilkinson, pp. 273-4).

Wouldst be a wonder? Such a one   5
   As should win with a look?
A bishop in a garrison,
   And conquer by the book?

Take then this mathematic shield,
   And henceforth by its rules   10
Be able to dispute i' th' field,
   And combat in the schools.

Whilst peaceful learning once again
   And the soldier so concord,
As that he fights now with her pen,   15
   And she writes with his sword.

17

To Althea, from Prison

Song

When Love with unconfinèd wings
   Hovers within my gates,
And my divine Althea brings
   To whisper at the grates;
When I lie tangled in her hair,   5
   And fettered to her eye,
The gods that wanton in the air
   Know no such liberty.

---

9 *this mathematic shield*: Wilkinson compares the reference to Tybalt as one 'that fights by the book of arithmetic' in *Rom.* iii. i. 99–100.

17. The references to the King in st. 3 may date this poem to late 1648 or early 1649. Musical setting: John Wilson. 7 *gods*. Four of five MSS. cited by Wilkinson that have this line read 'birds', but '**gods**' would seem to be the authoritative—perhaps later—reading. The 'gods' are probably to be taken as the little Cupids, or *putti*, so common in paintings of the period.

When flowing cups run swiftly round
   With no allaying Thames,   10
Our careless heads with roses bound,
   Our hearts with loyal flames;
When thirsty grief in wine we steep,
   When healths and draughts go free,
Fishes that tipple in the deep   15
   Know no such liberty.

When (like committed linnets) I
   With shriller throat shall sing
The sweetness, mercy, majesty,
   And glories of my King;   20
When I shall voice aloud how good
   He is, how great should be,
Enlargèd winds that curl the flood
   Know no such liberty.

Stone walls do not a prison make,   25
   Nor iron bars a cage;
Minds innocent and quiet take
   That for an hermitage;
If I have freedom in my love,
   And in my soul am free,   30
Angels alone that soar above
   Enjoy such liberty.

18

Upon the Curtain of Lucasta's Picture
It Was Thus Wrought

O stay that covetous hand! First turn all eye,
All depth and mind; then mystically spy
Her soul's fair picture, her fair soul's, in all
So truly copied from th' original
That you will swear her body by this law   5
Is but its shadow, as this its—now draw.

---

10 *allaying Thames*: diluting water (adapted from Shakespeare's 'allaying Tiber'
in *Cor.* II. i. 53).

18. *Curtain*: used as a protective dust-cover. 6 *shadow*: image.

19

Lucasta's World

Epode

Cold as the breath of winds that blow
To silver shot descending snow,
  Lucasta sighed, when she did close
  The world in frosty chains!
 And then a frown to rubies froze   5
  The blood boiled in our veins,
Yet coolèd not the heat her sphere
Of beauties first had kindled there.

Then moved, and with a sudden flame
Impatient to melt all again,   10
  Straight from her eyes she lightning hurled,
  And earth in ashes mourns;
 The sun his blaze denies the world,
  And in her lustre burns,
Yet warmèd not the hearts her nice   15
Disdain had first congealed to ice.

And now her tears nor grieved desire
Can quench this raging, pleasing fire;
  Fate but one way allows: behold
  Her smiles' divinity!   20
 They fanned this heat, and thawed that cold,
  So framed up a new sky.
Thus earth, from flames and ice reprieved,
E'er since hath in her sunshine lived.

19. On the 'epode' see L–10 n.

20

To a Lady That Desired Me I Would
Bear My Part with Her in a Song

Madam A. L.

This is the prettiest motiön:
Madam, th' alarums of a drum
That calls your lord, set to your cries,
To mine are sacred symphonies.

What though 'tis said I have a voice?   5
I know 'tis but that hollow noise
Which, as it through my pipe doth speed,
Bitterns do carol through a reed;

In the same key with monkeys' jigs,
Or dirges of proscribèd pigs,   10
Or the soft serenades above
In calm of night, when cats make love.

Was ever such a consort seen?
Fourscore and fourteen with fourteen!
Yet sooner they'll agree, one pair,   15
Than we in our spring-winter air:
They may embrace, sigh, kiss, the rest;
Our breath knows nought but east and west.
Thus have I heard to children's cries
The fair nurse 'stil such lullabies   20
That well all said, for what there lay,
The pleasure did the sorrow pay.

---

20. 4 *To mine*: compared to mine. 8 *Bitterns do carol through a reed*: according
to popular lore and the 'vulgar errors' reported on by Sir Thomas Browne, the
bittern made its peculiar booming sound by 'putting the bill in a reed', but
Browne acknowledged that he was never able to catch the bird in the act
(*Pseudodoxia Epidemica*, 1646, iii. 25). 10 *proscribed*: sentenced to death.
20 *'stil*: give forth.

Sure there's another way to save
Your fancy, madam: that's to have
('Tis but petitioning kind Fate)   25
The organs sent to Billingsgate,
Where they to that soft murm'ring choir
Shall reach you all you can admire!

Or do but hear how love-bang Kate
In pantry dark for fridge of meat   30
With edge of steel the square wood shapes,
And 'Dido' to it chants or scrapes.
The merry Phaeton o' th' car
You'll vow makes a melodious jar;
Sweeter and sweeter whistleth he   35
To unanointed axletree,
Such swift notes he and's wheels do run;
For me, I yield him Phoebus' son.

Say, fair commandress, can it be
You should ordain a mutiny?   40
For where I howl, all accents fall
As kings' harangues to one and all.

Ulysses' art is now withstood:
You ravish both with sweet and good;
Saint siren, sing, for I dare hear;   45
But when I ope, oh stop your ear!

29–31 *love-bang Kate*, etc.: Kate, a lover of resounding blows or explosive noises, 'is making a skewer to hold the meat when she scrapes or minces it' (Wilkinson, p. 291). In *L 49* 'meat' is spelled 'mate', and the double sense allowed by similar or identical pronunciation was certainly intended. 'Fridge' means 'chafe, rub', and there are clearly sexual references in the passage.   32 *Dido*: legendary queen of Carthage who detains Aeneas in Virgil's *Aeneid*; the allusion here is to the old song of 'Queen Dido', or 'The Wandering Prince of Troy' (see Wilkinson, pp. 291–2). There are equally obscure turns, in Shakespeare's *Tempest* (II. i. 73–97 passim), on 'widow Dido'; there may be puns on 'dildo' (perhaps as 'diddo') in both places. See G.   33 *Phaeton*: see G.   43–6 *Ulysses' art*, etc.: the sirens' song had the power to draw men to their destruction. In *Odyssey* xii, Odysseus (Ulysses in the *Aeneid*) tells how he filled his men's ears with wax and was able himself to listen unhurt by having himself lashed to the mast of his ship while it passed the sirens.

Far less be 't emulatiön
To pass me, or in trill or tone,
Like the thin throat of Philomel,
And the smart lute, who should excel,   50
As if her soft chords should begin,
And strive for sweetness with the pin.

Yet can I music too, but such
As is beyond all voice or touch;
My mind can in fair order chime,   55
Whilst my true heart still beats the time,
My soul so full of harmony
That it with all parts can agree;
If you wind up to th' highest fret,
It shall descend an eight from it,   60
And when you shall vouchsafe to fall,
Sixteen above you it shall call,
And yet so disassenting one,
They both shall meet an unison.

Come then, bright cherubin, begin!   65
My loudest music is within:
Take all notes with your skilful eyes;
Hark if mine do not sympathize!
Sound all my thoughts, and see expressed
The tablature of my large breast;   70
Then you'll admit that I too can
Music above dead sounds of man,
Such as alone doth bless the spheres,
Not to be reached with human ears.

49–52 *Philomel*, etc.: cf. Crashaw, 'Music's Duel'.   52 *pin*: musical pitch, with
reference to the tuning-pegs of a lute.   53 *can* . . . *music*: Wilkinson (p. 292)
notes that *OED* gives no example of 'music' as a verb earlier than 1788, but it
seems to be a verb here and in ll. 71–2, unless 'can' means 'know' in both places.
53–7 *such* [music], etc.: Lovelace rings Renaissance changes on the theme of un-
heard melodies are sweeter (see NRC).   56–8 *L 49* punctuates 'Time:', 'Har-
monie,', and 'agree:'; that leaves ll. 57–8 apparently without a verb and in an
ambiguous relationship to what precedes and what follows. Either 'soule' is in
error for 'soul[']s' or the lines stand in an absolute construction, as they are
punctuated here: 'My soul [being] so full', etc.   60 *eight*: octave.   64 *an unison*:
an identity of pitch ('in unison' is much later).   67, 69 *notes* . . . *sound*: used in
double senses.   70 *tablature*: a form of musical notation used for the lute and
other stringed instruments.

21

The Apostasy of One and But One Lady

That frantic error I adore,
   And am confirmèd the earth turns round,
Now satisfièd o'er and o'er,
   As rolling waves so flows the ground,
And as her neighbour reels the shore: 5
     Find such a woman says she loves,
     She's that fixed heaven which never moves.

In marble, steel, or porphyry,
   Who carves or stamps his arms or face,
Looks it by rust or storm must die: 10
   This woman's love no time can rase,
Hardened like ice in the sun's eye,
     Or your reflection in a glass,
     Which keeps possession though you pass.

We not behold a watch's hand   15
   To stir, nor plants or flowers to grow:
Must we infer that this doth stand,
   And therefore that those do not blow?
This she acts calmer: like heaven's brand
     The steadfast lightning, slow love's dart,   20
     She kills, but ere we feel the smart.

Oh, she is constant as the wind
   That revels in an evening's air!
Certain as ways unto the blind,
   More real than her flatteries are,   25
Gentle as chains that honour bind,
     More faithful than an Hebrew Jew,
     But as the Devil not half so true.

21. 1–2 *That frantic error*, etc.: the Copernican view that the earth rotates on
its axis. **7** *that fixed heaven*: the 'eighth' heaven of fixed stars that lay beyond
the spheres of the planets in the Ptolemaic astronomy (see NRC). **10** *Looks*:
expects that.

22

La Bella Bona-Roba

I cannot tell who loves the skeleton
Of a poor marmoset—nought but bone, bone;
Give me a nakedness with her clothes on,

Such whose white-satin upper coat of skin,
Cut upon velvet rich incarnadine,   5
Has yet a body (and of flesh) within.

Sure it is meant good husbandry in men,
Who do incorporate with airy lean,
T' repair their sides, and get their rib again.

Hard hap unto that huntsman that decrees   10
Fat joys for all his sweat, whenas he sees,
After his 'say, nought but his keeper's fees.

Then Love, I beg, when next thou tak'st thy bow,
Thy angry shafts, and dost heart-chasing go,
Pass rascal deer, strike me the largest doe.   15

---

22. The title means 'the beautiful wanton', from Italian *buona roba*, or 'service-able goods'; cf. 2 *H 4* III. ii. 21–2. In *L 49* this poem went untitled, while the present title became attached to the poem that preceded it, a poem of extravagant compliment: 'La Bella Bona Roba. *To my Lady H. Ode*'. 2 *marmoset*: monkey; like 'bona-roba', = prostitute. 3 *a nakedness with her clothes on*: a plea for pleasing plumpness (cf. l. 12) that runs counter to the proverbial notion that 'the meat is sweeter close to the bone'. 4 *incarnadine*: pink, flesh-coloured. 9 *rib*: Adam's, the one of which Eve was made (Gen. 2: 21–2). 11 *whenas*: when. 12 *'say*: assay, test of quality, taste. *keeper's fees*: shoulders and entrails, and also horns (with the usual allusion to cuckoldry). 14 *heart-chasing*: sylleptic; 'hart/heart'. 15 *rascal deer*: young, lean, or inferior deer of a herd, with pun on 'dear' (spelled 'deare' in *L 49*).

23

A la Bourbon

*Donnez moi plus de pitié ou plus de cruauté, car sans ce Je ne peux pas
vivre ni mourir*

Divine destroyer, pity me no more,
　　Or else more pity me;
Give me more love, ah, quickly give me more,
　　Or else more cruelty!
　　　　For left thus as I am,   5
　　　　My heart is ice and flame;
　　　　And languishing thus I
　　　　Can neither live nor die!

Your glories are eclipsed, and hidden in the grave
　　Of this indifferency;   10
And, Celia, you can neither altars have,
　　Nor I a deity:
　　　　They are aspects divine
　　　　That still or smile or shine,
　　　　Or like th' offended sky   15
　　　　Frown death immediately.

24

A Lady with a Falcon on Her Fist

To the Honourable My Cousin A.L.

This queen of prey (now prey to you),
　　Fast to that perch of ivory
In silver chains and silken clew,
　　Hath now made full thy victory:

---

23. *Donnez moi plus de pitié*, etc.: 'give me more pity or more cruelty, because
without it I can neither live nor die.' Cf. C–4 and n.

24. On literary falconry see 'The Hawk and the Handsaw', in T.R. Henn, *The
Living Image* (1972), pp. 21–40. *A. L.*: Lady Anne Lovelace, a cousin by
marriage, to whom *Lucasta* was dedicated.　3 *clew*: a thread of silk held by the
person carrying the hawk.

The swelling admiral of the dread   5
  Cold deep burnt in thy flames, O fair!
Was 't not enough, but thou must lead
  Bound too the princess of the air?

Unarmed of wings and scaly oar,
  Unhappy crawler on the land,   10
To what heaven fli'st? div'st to what shore,
  That her brave eyes do not command?

Ascend the chariot of the Sun
  From her bright power to shelter thee:
Her captive, fool, outgazes him;   15
  Ah, what lost wretches then are we!

Now, proud usurpers on the right
  Of sacred beauty, hear your doom:
Recant your sex, your mastery, might;
  Lower you cannot be o'ercome.   20

Repent ye e'er named he or head,
  For y' are in falcons' monarchy,
And in that just dominion bred
  In which the nobler is the she.

25

Calling Lucasta from Her Retirement

Ode

From the dire monument of thy black room
Where now that vestal flame thou dost entomb,
As in the inmost cell of all earth's womb,

5-6 *The swelling admiral*, etc.: Wilkinson suggests that the Lady's husband may
have been connected with the sea, as her husband's father had been (he died
when she was eleven).   15 *her captive, fool, outgazes him*: the falcon in this is eagle-
like (see L–13: 11 n.).   22–4 *falcons' monarchy . . . In which the nobler is the she*: the
female alone is called a 'falcon'; the male 'tercel' is the smaller bird.

Sacred Lucasta, like the powerful ray
Of heavenly truth, pass this Cimmerian way,   5
Whilst all the standards of your beams display.

Arise, and climb our whitest, highest hill:
There your sad thoughts with joy and wonder fill,
And see seas calm as earth, earth as your will.

Behold how lightning-like a taper flies   10
And gilds your chari't, but ashamèd dies,
Seeing itself outgloried by your eyes.

Threatening and boisterous tempests gently bow,
And to your steps part in soft paths, when now
There nowhere hangs a cloud but on your brow.   15

No showers but 'twixt your lids, nor gelid snow
But what your whiter, chaster breast doth owe,
Whilst winds in chains colder your sorrow blow.

Shrill trumpets now do only sound to eat,
Artillery hath loaden dish with meat,   20
And drums at every health alarums beat.

All things 'Lucasta', but 'Lucasta', call:
Trees borrow tongues, waters in accents fall,
The air doth sing, and fire's musical.

Awake from the dead vault in which you dwell;   25
All 's loyal here, except your thoughts rebel,
Which, so let loose, often their general quell.

See! she obeys! by all obeyèd thus:
No storms, heats, colds, no souls contentioüs,
Nor civil war is found—I mean, to us.   30

---

25. 5 *Cimmerian*: dark, gloomy (*Cimmerii*: people of perpetual night).   20 *dish*:
L 49's 'ev'ry [dish]' makes an anomalous hexameter and weakly duplicates the
use in l. 20; editorial omission is supported by Abbott, sec. 84 ('a' omitted
'where the noun stands for the class').

Lovers and angels, though in heaven they show
And see the woes and discords here below,
What they not feel must not be said to know.

26

To Lucasta: Her Reserved Looks

Lucasta, frown and let me die,
   But smile and see I live;
The sad indifference of your eye
   Both kills and doth reprieve.
You hide our fate within its screen,   5
   We feel our judgement ere we hear:
So in one picture I have seen
   An angel here, the Devil there.

27

In Allusion to the French Song,

N'entendez vous pas ce language

Chorus.   *Then understand you not, fair choice,*
        This language without tongue or voice?

    How often have my tears
    Invaded your soft ears,
    And dropped their silent chimes   5
    A thousand thousand times,
    Whilst echo did your eyes,
    And sweetly sympathize,
    But that the wary lid
    Their sluices did forbid!   10

26. 7–8 *in one picture*, etc.: 'curious perspectives', or anamorphic paintings, which show different images when viewed from different angles.

27. *N'entendez vous pas ce language*: do you not understand this language?

Chorus.   *Then understand you not, fair choice,*
             This language without tongue or voice?

             My arms did plead my wound,
             Each in the other bound;
             Volleys of sighs did crowd,   15
             And ring my griefs aloud;
             Groans, like a cannon ball,
             Battered the marble wall,
             That the kind neighb'ring grove
             Did mutiny for love.   20

Chorus.   *Then understand you not, fair choice,*
             This language without tongue or voice?

             The rhet'ric of my hand
             Wooed you to understand;
             Nay, in our silent walk   25
             My very feet would talk;
             My knees were eloquent,
             And spake the love I meant;
             But deaf unto that air,
             They, bent, would fall in prayer.   30

Chorus.   *Yet understand you not, fair choice,*
             This language without tongue or voice?

             No? Know then I would melt
             On every limb I felt,
             And on each naked part   35
             Spread my expanded heart,
             That not a vein of thee
             But should be filled with me;
             Whilst on thine own down I
             Would tumble, pant, and die.   40

Chorus.   *You understand not this, fair choice;*
             This language wants both tongue and voice.

13–14 *My arms*, etc.: cf. Shakespeare, *LLL* III. i. 177–9; folded arms were a
characteristic gesture of melancholy.   29 *But deaf*: i.e. but you being deaf.

28

Night

To Lucasta

Night! loathèd jailor of the locked-up sun,
   And tyrant-turnkey on committed day,
Bright eyes lie fettered in thy dungeon,
   And heaven itself doth thy dark wards obey:
      Thou dost arise our living hell;   5
      With thee groans, terrors, furies dwell,
      Until Lucasta doth awake,
And with her beams these heavy chains off shake.

Behold, with op'ning her almighty lid,
Bright eyes break rolling and with lustre spread,   10
   And captive Day his chariot mounted is;
      Night to her proper hell is beat,
      And screwèd to her ebon seat,
      Till th' earth with play oppressèd lies,
And draws again the curtains of her eyes.   15

But bondslave I know neither day nor night,
   Whether she murth'ring sleep or saving wake;
Now broiled i' th' zone of her reflected light,
   Then froze, my icicles not sinews shake.
      Smile then, new Nature, your soft blast   20
      Doth melt our ice, and fires waste;
      Whilst the scorched shiv'ring world new-born
Now feels it all the day one rising morn.

---

28. 9–15 According to the rhyme-scheme of sts. 1 and 3, a line is missing between ll. 9 and 10.

29

Love Enthroned

Ode

In troth, I do myself persuade
   That the wild Boy is grown a man,
And all his childishness off laid,
    E'er since Lucasta did his fires fan;
      H'as left his apish jigs,   5
      And whipping hearts like gigs;
    For tother day I heard him swear
That Beauty should be crowned in Honour's chair.

With what a true and heavenly state
   He doth his glorious darts dispense,   10
Now cleansed from falsehood, blood, and hate,
   And newly tipped with innocence;
      Love Justice is become,
      And doth the cruel doom:
    Reversèd is the old decree;   15
Behold, he sits enthroned with majesty!

Enthronèd in Lucasta's eye,
   He doth our faith and hearts survey;
Then measures them by sympathy,
   And each to th' other's breast convey;   20
      Whilst to his altars now
      The frozen vestals bow,
    And strict Diana too doth go
A hunting with his feared, exchangèd bow.

---

29. 6 *gigs*: whirligigs, tops.   22 *Vestals*: see G.   23 *Diana*: Roman goddess of chastity and the hunt.

Th' embracing seas and ambient air   25
   Now in his holy fires burn;
Fish couple, birds and beasts in pair
   Do their own sacrifices turn.
     This is a miracle
     That might religion swell;   30
   But she, that these and their god awes,
Her crownèd self submits to her own laws.

30

A Black Patch on Lucasta's Face

Dull as I was, to think that a court fly
   Presumed so near her eye,
   When 'twas th' industrious bee
Mistook her glorious face for Paradise,
To sum up all his chemistry of spice;   5
   With a brave pride and honour led,
   Near both her suns he makes his bed,
And, though a spark, struggles to rise as red;
     Then emulates the gay
     Daughter of day,   10
   Acts the romantic phoenix' fate:
When now, with all his sweets laid out in state,
   Lucasta scatters but one heat,
And all the aromatic pills do sweat,
And gums, calcined, themselves to powder beat,   15
     Which a fresh gale of air
     Conveys into her hair;
     Then chafed he's set on fire,
And in these holy flames doth glad expire;
   And that black marble tablet there,   20
     So near her either sphere,
   Was placed: nor foil nor ornament,
But the sweet little bee's large monument.

---

30. *Black Patch*: a cosmetic beauty-spot. 1, 3 *court fly . . . industrious bee*: stock metaphors for parasitic courtiers and productive country-folk, here literalized. 11 *phoenix*: see G. 22 *foil*: something that serves by contrast of colour (here, black) or quality to adorn or set off another thing (in this case, Lucasta's complexion).

31

The Ant

Forbear, thou great good husband, little ant;
    A little respite from thy flood of sweat.
Thou, thine own horse and cart, under this plant,
    Thy spacious tent, fan thy prodigious heat;
Down with thy double load of that one grain;   5
    It is a granary for all thy train.

Cease, large example of wise thrift, a while
    (For thy example is become our law),
And teach thy frowns a seasonable smile:
    So Cato sometimes the nak'd Florals saw.   10
And thou, almighty foe, lay by thy sting,
    Whilst thy unpaid musicians, crickets, sing.

Lucasta, she that holy makes the day,
    And 'stils new life in fields of feuillèmorte,
Hath back restored their verdure with one ray,   15
    And with her eye bid all to play and sport.
Ant, to work still, age will thee truant call;
    And to save now, th' art worse than prodigal.

Austere and Cynic! not one hour t' allow,
    To lose with pleasure what thou got'st with pain, 20
But drive on sacred festivals thy plough,
    Tearing highways with thy o'erchargèd wain.
Not all thy lifetime one poor minute live,
    And thy o'erlaboured bulk with mirth relieve?

31. 1 *husband*: (1) head of household (with connotations of thriftiness); (2) tiller
of the soil.   7–9 Lovelace refers to the humourless and unceasing puritan
industriousness.   10 *so Cato*, etc.: not quite so; since Cato's gravity would have
been spared the disrobing of the 'Florals' if he had stayed, he habitually left
the theatre rather than prevent the practice of a popular custom.   14 *feuille-
morte*: of the colour of dead leaves (pronounced 'föy[è]mort').   19 *Cynic*:
member of an ancient Greek sect of philosophers conventionally characterized
as contemptuous of knowledge and of current morality.   21 *drive on sacred
festivals thy plough*: in effect, to work on Sunday, the Lord's sabbatical day of
rest, when labour was forbidden.   22 *wain*: waggon.

Look up then, miserable ant, and spy   25
    Thy fatal foes, for breaking of her law,
Hovering above thee—Madam, Margaret Pie,
    And her fierce servant, meagre Sir John Daw:
Thyself and storehouse now they do store up,
And thy whole harvest too within their crop.   30

Thus we unthrifty thrive within earth's tomb
    For some more ravenous and ambitious jaw:
The grain in th' ant's, the ant's in the pie's womb,
    The pie in th' hawk's, the hawk's i' th' eagle's maw:
So scattering to hoard gainst a long day,   35
Thinking to save all, we cast all away.

32

The Snail

Wise emblem of our pol'tic world,
Sage snail, within thine own self curled,
Instruct me softly to make haste
Whilst these my feet go slowly fast.
    Compendious snail! thou seem'st to me   5
Large Euclid's strict epitome,
And in each diagram dost fling
Thee from the point unto the ring;
A figure now triangular,
An oval now, and now a square;   10
And then a serpentine dost crawl,
Now a straight line, now crook'd, now all.
    Preventing rival of the day,
Th' art up and openest thy ray,

27–8 *Madam, Margaret Pie . . . Sir John Daw*: the magpie and the jackdaw.
30 *crop*: gullet, with a turn on the sense related to 'harvest'.   33 *womb*: i.e.
stomach.

32. See 'On "The Snail" by Richard Lovelace' by Randolph L. Wadsworth, Jr.
in *MLR* lxv (1970), 750–60.   6 *Euclid*: Greek mathematician and 'father' of
plane geometry.   13 *preventing*: coming before.

And ere the morn cradles the moon, 15
Th'art broke into a beauteous noon.
Then when the sun sups in the deep,
Thy silver horns ere Cynthia's peep;
And thou from thine own liquid bed,
New Phoebus, heav'st thy pleasant head. 20
   Who shall a name for thee create,
Deep riddle of mysterious state?
Bold Nature, that gives common birth
To all products of seas and earth,
Of thee, as earthquakes, is afraid, 25
Nor will thy dire deliv'ry aid.
   Thou thine own daughter, then, and sire,
That son and mother art entire,
That big still with thyself dost go,
And liv'st an aged embryo; 30
That, like the cubs of India,
Thou from thyself a while dost play,
But, frighted with a dog or gun,
In thine own belly thou dost run,
And as thy house was thine own womb, 35
So thine own womb concludes thy tomb.
   But now I must, analysed king,
Thy economic virtues sing:
Thou great staid husband, still within,
Thou thee, that's thine, dost discipline; 40
And when thou art to progress bent,
Thou mov'st thyself and tenement;
As warlike Scythians travelled, you
Remove your men and city, too;

18 *Cynthia*: the moon personified. 20 *Phoebus*: the sun personified. 31 *cubs of India*: the mother of the species—obviously some kind of marsupial, in modern terms—was said by some to 'shut up her cubs in a depending scrip' (1615; Wilkinson, p. 301). The lore concerns a beast that John Stephens calls a 'su' (in *Satyrical Essayes, Characters, and Others*, 1615) and Edward Topsell—who claims the su carries its young on its back—calls a 'semivulpa or apish fox' (*The Historie of Foure-Footed Beastes*, 1607). 35-6 *womb . . . tomb*: the Platonic σῶμα σῆμα. 39 *great staid husband*: dignified, reserved, and thrifty head of household. Cf. 'The Ant' (L-31). 43-4 *Scythians*, etc.: Herodotus refers to the tented Scythians by a term that Hesiod uses of the snail, 'house-bearing' (Wilkinson, p. 301).

Then, after a sad dearth and rain,   45
Thou scatterest thy silver train;
And when the trees grow nak'd and old,
Thou clothest them with cloth of gold,
Which from thy bowels thou dost spin,
And draw from the rich mines within.   50
   Now hast thou changed thee saint, and made
Thyself a fane that's cupola'd;
And in thy wreathèd cloister thou
Walkest thine own Grey Friar, too;
Strict, and locked up, th'art hood all o'er   55
And ne'er eliminat'st thy door.
On salads thou dost feed severe,
And 'stead of beads thou dropp'st a tear,
And when to rest each calls the bell,
Thou sleep'st within thy marble cell,   60
Where, in dark contemplation placed,
The sweets of nature thou dost taste;
Who now with time thy days resolve,
And in a jelly thee dissolve
Like a shot star, which doth repair   65
Upward, and rarefy the air.

---

52 *fane*: temple.   54 *Grey Friar*: strictly, a Franciscan.   56 *eliminat'st*: cross the
threshold of, pass out of (a usage apparently unique to Lovelace).   58 *beads*:
i.e. of a rosary.   64–5 *jelly . . . shot star*: it was a common superstition that
fallen stars dissolved to jelly; cf. e.g. Suckling, S–25: 11–15.

33

Another

The centaur, siren, I forgo;
Those have been sung, and loudly, too;
Nor of the mixèd sphinx I'll write,
Nor the renowned hermaphrodite:
Behold, this huddle doth appear   5
Of horses, coach, and charioteer,
That moveth him by traverse law,
And doth himself both drive and draw;
Then, when the sun the south doth win,
He baits him hot in his own inn.   10
I heard a grave and austere clerk
Resolved him pilot both and bark,
That, like the famed ship of Trevere,
Did on the shore himself laveer.
Yet the authentic do believe,   15
Who keep their judgement in their sleeve,
That he is his own double man,
And, sick, still carries his sedan;
Or that, like dames i' th' land of Luyck,
He wears his everlasting huke.   20
But, banished, I admire his fate,
Since neither ostracism of state
Nor a perpetual exile
Can force this virtue change his soil;
For wheresoever he doth go,   25
He wanders with his country, too.

---

33. 1 *centaur, siren.* The centaur was a male human above the waist and a
stallion below; the sirens, birds with the heads of women, could lure men to
destruction by their song.   3 *mixed sphinx.* The mythical sphinx had a human
head, a lion's body, and a bird's wings.   4 *renowned hermaphrodite*: see Ovid,
Met. iv. 347–88.   5 *huddle*: confused mass.   11 *clerk*: scholar.   13–14 *the famed
ship*, etc. Wilkinson (pp. 302–4) conjectures that it is a land-boat and that
Trevere is Vere, Holland; the reference is clearly to a ship that 'landed itself'.
14 *laveer*: tack, beat to windward.   17–18 *double man . . . sedan.* A sedan was a
closed vehicle for one borne on two poles by a bearer each at front and rear.
19 *Luyck*: Liège.   20 *huke*: a hooded cape or cloak.   25–6 *wheresoever he doth go*,
etc.: possibly alluding to the Flying Dutchman.

L

34

A Loose Saraband

Nay, prithee dear, draw nigher,
   Yet closer, nigher yet;
Here is a double fire,
   A dry one and a wet:
True lasting heavenly fuel   5
Puts out the vestal jewel,
When once we twining marry
Mad love with wild canary.

Off with that crownèd Venice,
   Till all the house doth flame;   10
We 'll quench it straight in Rhenish,
   Or what we must not name:
Milk lightning still assuageth,
So when our fury rageth,
As th' only means to cross it,   15
We 'll drown it in Love's posset.

Love never was well-willer
   Unto my nag or me,
Ne'er watered us i' th' cellar,
   But the cheap buttery: 20
At th' head of his own barrels,
Where broached are all his quarrels,
Should a true noble master
Still make his guest his taster.

---

34. *Saraband*: originally a slow and stately Spanish dance in triple time, but the
'Loose Saraband' is something quite different, like 'the bawdy saraband' in
Jonson's *Staple of News* (v. iii). 8 *canary*: a wine from the Canary Islands
popular from the sixteenth to the eighteenth century. 9 *Off with*: toss off,
quaff. *crowned Venice*: Venetian drinking-glass, with a turn on 'Venetian
crown' as the crown or cap of state worn by the Doge of Venice. 11 *Rhenish*:
Rhine wine or hock. 13–16 *milk lightning . . . love's posset*: the tenor here is
sexual; for the vehicle of 'posset' see G. 19–20 *cellar . . . buttery*: the wine-cellar
as opposed to the place (in colleges and elsewhere) where ale, bread and butter,
etc., are dispensed. 22 *broached*: a commonplace pun on *broach*, 'to tap a
barrel' and 'to begin (a quarrel)'; cf. *Rom.* i. i. 111.

See all the world how 't staggers,   25
   More ugly drunk than we,
As if far gone in daggers
   And blood it seemed to be:
We drink our glass of roses,
Which nought but sweets discloses,   30
Then, in our loyal chamber,
Refresh us with love's amber.

Now tell me, thou fair cripple,
   That dumb canst scarcely see
Th' almightiness of tipple,   35
   And th' odds 'twixt thee and thee:
What of Elysium's missing?
Still drinking and still kissing,
Adoring plump October,
Lord! what is man and sober?   40

Now is there such a trifle
   As Honour, the fool's giant?
What is there left to rifle,
   When wine makes all parts pliant?
Let others glory follow,   45
In their false riches wallow,
And with their grief be merry:
Leave me but love and sherry.

---

32 *love's amber*: the tenor is sexual; the vehicle is probably either oil of amber
or ambergris, a substance used in perfumes. *OED* cites Sir Thomas Blount,
Natural History (1693): 'Great variety of opinions hath there been concerning
amber. Some think it to be a gum that distils from trees; others tell us it is
made of whale's dung, or else of their sperm or seed (as others will have it),
which being consolidate and hardened by the sea is cast upon the shore.'
37 *Elysium*: see G.   40 *Lord! what is man and sober?* Cf. Ps. 8: 4: 'What is man,
that thou art mindful of him?'; Byron's *Don Juan*, 'Man, being reasonable,
must get drunk; / The best of life is but intoxication' (II. clxxix); and
Housman's 'Malt does more than Milton can / To justify God's ways to man'
(*A Shropshire Lad*, lxii, ll. 21–2).   42 *Honour, the fool's giant*: cf. Carew, C–28: 3,
and Suckling, S–24: 35.

35

The Falcon

Fair princess of the spacious air,
That hast vouchsafed acquaintance here
With us are quartered below stairs,
That can reach heaven with nought but prayers,
Who, when our activ'st wings we try,   5
Advance a foot into the sky;

Bright heir to th' bird imperiäl,
From whose avenging pennons fall
Thunder and lightning twisted spun;
Brave cousin-german to the sun,   10
That didst forsake thy throne and sphere,
To be an humble prisoner here,
And, for a perch of her soft hand,
Resign the royal wood's command:

How often wouldst thou shoot heaven's arc,   15
Then mount thyself into a lark;
And after our short faint eyes call,
When now a fly, now nought at all;
Then stoop so swift unto our sense,
As thou wert sent intelligence!   20

Free beauteous slave, thy happy feet
In silver fetters varvels meet,
And trample on that noble wrist
The gods have kneeled in vain t' have kissed.

35. Raymond A. Anselment reads this poem allegorically in ' "Griefe
Triumphant" and "Victorious Sorrow": A Reading of Richard Lovelace's
"The Falcon" ', *JEGP* lxx (1971), 404–17. On literary falconry see ref. cit. in
L–24 n.   7 *bird imperial*: i.e. Jove's bird, the eagle. (*LP 59* reads 't" for 'to'
here.)   12 *pennons*: used by Milton and others for pinions, 'wings', possibly here
with some of the force of *pennons* as ensigns or banners (of the type carried by
the Roman legions).   10 *cousin-german*: first cousin.   19 *stoop*: descend on prey
or to the lure (falconry).   22 *varvel[s]*: a metal ring connecting a hawk's jess
(leg-strap) with the leash.

But gaze not, bold deceivèd spy,   25
Too much o' th' lustre of her eye;
The Sun thou dost outstare, alas!
Winks at the glory of her face.

Be safe then in thy velvet helm:
Her looks are calms that do o'erwhelm;   30
Than the Arabian bird more blest,
Chafe in the spic'ry of her breast,
And lose you in her breath, a wind
Sours the delicious gales of Ind.

But now a quill from thine own wing   35
I pluck, thy lofty fate to sing;
Whilst we behold the various fight,
With mingled pleasure and affright,
The humbler hinds do fall to prayer,
As when an army 's seen i' th' air,   40
And the prophetic spaniels run
And howl thy epicedium.

The heron mounted doth appear
On his own Peg'sus a lancier,
And seems on earth, when he doth hut,   45
A proper halberdier on foot;
Secure i' th' moor, about to sup,
The dogs have beat his quarters up.

And now he takes the open air,
Draws up his wings with tactic care,   50
Whilst th' expert falcon swift doth climb
In subtle mazes serpentine;
And to advantage closely twined
She gets the upper sky and wind,
Where she dissembles to invade   55
And lies a pol'tic ambuscade.

27 *the Sun*, etc.: proverbial (Tilley E 3).   29 *helm*: hood.   31 *Arabian bird*: the
phoenix (see G).   32 *chafe*: (1) fret, or show anger; (2) rub, as spices are chafed
for the resulting fragrance.   42 *epicedium*: funeral ode.   43 *The heron*: 'a flight
at the heron [is] . . . the most noble and stately flight that is, and pleasant to
behold' (from Turberville's *Falconrie*, 1611, quoted by Wilkinson, p. 306).
45 *hut*: hide.

The hedged-in heron, whom the foe
Awaits above and dogs below,
In his fortification lies
And makes him ready for surprise,   60
When rousèd with a shrill alarm
Was shouted from beneath, they arm.

The falcon charges at first view
With her brigade of talons, through
Whose shoots the wary heron beat   65
With a well counterwheeled retreat.
But the bold general, never lost,
Hath won again her airy post,
Who, wild in this affront, now fries,
Then gives a volley of her eyes.   70

The desperate heron now contracts
In one design all former facts;
Noble he is resolved to fall,
His and his en'my's funeral,
And, to be rid of her, to die   75
A public martyr of the sky.

When now he turns his last to wreak
The palisadoes of his beak,
The raging foe impatiënt,
Racked with revenge, and fury rent,   80
Swift as the thunderbolt he strikes
Too sure upon the stand of pikes;
There she his naked breast doth hit,
And on the case of rapiers's split.

62 *Was*: i.e. that was.   77–8 *When now he turns*, etc.: Wilkinson quotes a passage
which says that a heron, being stooped upon (usually on the ground) by a hawk,
will turn its 'long bill upwards, upon which the hawk, not being able to stop,
runs itself through, and so both often drop down dead together' (p. 307).

But even in her expiring pangs 85
The heron's pounced within her fangs,
And so above she stoops to rise
A trophy and a sacrifice;
Whilst her own bells in the sad fall
Ring out the double funeral. 90

Ah victory unhapp'ly won!
Weeping and red is set the sun,
Whilst the whole field floats in one tear,
And all the air doth mourning wear;
Close-hooded all thy kindred come 95
To pay their vows upon thy tomb;
The hobby and the musket, too,
Do march to take their last adieu.

The lanner and the lanneret
Thy colours bear as banneret; 100
The goshawk and her tercel, roused,
With tears attend thee as new boused;
All these are in their dark array
Led by the various herald-jay.

But thy eternal name shall live 105
Whilst quills from ashes fame reprieve,
Whilst open stands renown's wide door,
And wings are left on which to soar:
Doctor Robin, the prelate Pie,
And the poetic Swan shall die, 110
Only to sing thy elegy.

87 *she stoops to rise*: a conventional paradox, here involving the technical sense of the falcon's descending on her prey (cf. *She Stoops to Conquer*). 89 *her own bells*: the bells fastened to the rings on the falcon's feet. 97, 99, 101 The *hobby* is a small species of falcon; the *musket* is the male sparrowhawk; the *lanner* and *lanneret* are the female and male of the same species; the *tercel* is any male hawk, but especially a peregrine falcon or a goshawk. 102 *bouse[d]*: to drink much (falconry).

36

Love Made in the First Age

To Chloris

In the nativity of time,
Chloris, it was not thought a crime
    In direct Hebrew for to woo.
Now we make love as all on fire,
Ring retrograde our loud desire,   5
    And court in English, backward, too.

Thrice happy was that golden age,
When compliment was construed rage,
    And fine words in the centre hid;
When cursèd No stained no maid's bliss,   10
And all discourse was summed in Yes,
    And nought forbad, but to forbid.

Love, then unstinted, Love did sip,
And cherries plucked fresh from the lip;
    On cheeks and roses free he fed;   15
Lasses like autumn plums did drop,
And lads indifferently did crop
    A flower and a maidenhead.

Then unconfinèd each did tipple
Wine from the bunch, milk from the nipple;   20
    Paps tractable as udders were;
Then equally the wholesome jellies
Were squeezed from olive-trees and bellies,
    Nor suits of trespass did they fear.

A fragrant bank of strawberries,   25
Diapered with violets' eyes,

36. 3 *direct Hebrew*: Hebrew was thought to have been the original language, as
Gen. 11: 1 seemed to suggest.   6 *court in English backward*: presumably because
Hebrew is written from right to left.   8 *rage*: natural passion, not mannered
artifice.   26 *diapered*: patterned geometrically, like the linen called diaper.

Was table, tablecloth, and fare;
No palace to the clouds did swell:
Each humble princess then did dwell
  In the piazza of her hair.   30

Both broken faith and th' cause of it,
All-damning gold, was damned to th' Pit;
  Their troth, sealed with a clasp and kiss,
Lasted until that extreme day
In which they smiled their souls away,   35
  And in each other breathed new bliss.

Because no fault, there was no tear;
No groan did grate the granting ear,
  No false foul breath their del'cate smell;
No serpent kiss poisoned the taste;   40
Each touch was naturally chaste,
  And their mere sense a miracle.

Naked as their own innocence,
And unembroidered from offence
  They went, above poor riches gay;   45
On softer than the cygnet's down
In beds they tumbled of their own,
  For each within the other lay.

Thus did they live, thus did they love,
Repeating only joys above;   50
  And angels were, but with clothes on,
Which they would put off cheerfully,
To bathe them in the Galaxy,
  Then gird them with the heavenly zone.

Now, Chloris! miserably crave   55
The offered bliss you would not have,
  Which evermore I must deny;
Whilst ravished with these noble dreams,
And crownèd with mine own soft beams,
  Enjoying of myself I lie.   60

37

The Duel

Love, drunk the other day, knocked at my breast,
    But I, alas, was not within:
My man, my ear, told me he came t' attest
    That without cause h'ad boxèd him,
And batterèd the windows of mine eyes,   5
And took my heart for one of 's nunneries.

I wondered at the outrage safe returned,
    And stormèd at the base affront;
And by a friend of mine, bold Faith, that burned,
    I called him to a strict accompt.   10
He said that, by the law, the challenged might
Take the advantage both of arms and fight.

Two darts of equal length and points he sent,
    And nobly gave the choice to me,
Which I not weighed, young and indifferent,   15
    Now full of nought but victory.
So we both met in one of 's mother's groves,
The time, at the first murm'ring of her doves.

I stripped myself naked all o'er, as he,
    For so I was best armed, when bare;   20
His first pass did my liver raise, yet I
    Made home a falsify too near,
For when my arm to its true distance came,
I nothing touched but a fantastic flame.

This, this is Love we daily quarrel so,   25
    An idle Don-Quixotery:
We whip ourselves with our own twisted woe,
    And wound the aïr for a fly.
The only way t' undo this enemy
Is to laugh at the Boy, and he will cry.   30

---

37. 1 *Love*: Cupid, Eros. 6 *nunneries*: convents (and, by ironical transference,
brothels); places of resort. 20 *falsify*: feint (fencing).

38

Cupid Far Gone

What so beyond all madness is the elf,
  Now he hath got out of himself!
  His fatal enemy the bee,
  Nor his deceived artillery,
  His shackles nor the rose's bough   5
Ne'er half so nettled him as he is now.

See! at's own mother he is offering;
  His finger now fits any ring:
  Old Cybele he would enjoy,
  And now the girl, and now the boy.   10
  He proffers Jove a back caress,
And all his love in the Antipodes.

Jealous of his chaste Psyche, raging, he
  Quarrels the student Mercury,
  And with a proud submissive breath   15
  Offers to change his darts with Death.
  He strikes at the bright eye of day,
And Juno tumbles in her Milky Way.

The dear sweet secrets of the gods he tells,
  And with loathed hate loved heaven he swells;   20
  Now like a fury he belies
  Myriads of pure virginities,
  And swears, with this false frenzy hurled,
There's not a virtuous she in all the world.

---

38. 13 *Psyche*: the mortal paramour of Cupid who violated her trust never to look upon the young god by lighting an oil-lamp as he slept. Awakened by a drop of hot oil, Cupid fled, but continued to love Psyche; eventually the lovers were joined in marriage. This tale is told by Apuleius in his *Metamorphoses (The Golden Ass)*, and also by Shackerley Marmion (1637), for example. 14 *student Mercury*: Mercury was something of a pagan patron-saint of clever persons generally, and in astrology 'signifieth subtle men, ingenious, inconstant: rhymers, poets, advocates, orators, philosophers, arithmeticians, and busy fellows' (Jonson's masque, *Mercury Vindicated*). 18 *Juno tumbles in her Milky Way*: Jupiter's consort, the queen-mother of the gods, goddess of women and childbirth, who is given by Homer the epithet 'ox-eyed'.

Olympus he renounces, then descends   25
  And makes a friendship with the fiends;
  Bids Charon be no more a slave,
  He Argo rigged with stars shall have;
  And triple Cerberus from below
Must leashed t' himself with him a hunting go.   30

39

A Mock Song

Now Whitehall's in the grave,
  And our head is our slave,
The bright pearl in his close shell of oyster;

25 *Olympus*: a mountain in Greece whose summit was regarded as the residence of the gods.   27 *Charon*: the ferryman who conveyed the dead across the river Styx to Hades.   28–30 *Argo*, etc.: *LP 59* erroneously reads 'Argos'. What is surely intended—as a counterpart to Charon's ferry-boat—is the image of a ship, Argo, of the Argonauts who sailed for and won the Golden Fleece, and also of the constellation Argo Navis (hence 'rigged with stars').

39. Willa McClung Evans has written on 'Richard Lovelace's "Mock-Song" in *PQ* xxiv (1945), 317–28. This song of mockery is a Royalist satire on the Parliamentarian view of the Civil War, which is ostensibly represented by the poem's speaker (a little like Burns's Holy Willy), who thinks well of the defeat of the Royalists, the King's beheading (in 1649), the suppression of the Church of England ('Rome' to the Puritans), and the over-all ascendancy of the Puritan-dominated House of Commons. Tarquin—as often with the anti-monarchical journalists—is Charles II, after Tarquinius Superbus, a tyrannical Roman king; and 'Oliver-Brutus' is Oliver Cromwell, after Lucius Junius Brutus, who led the revolt against the Tarquins, liberated Rome, and became one of the first two consuls (of course, there are connotations of Caesar's assassin, the '*et tu* Brutus', too). Although the general sense of the poem is clear, obscurities remain. The metaphor of the body politic is reminiscent of the parable of the belly in Shakespeare's *Cor.* i. i. 94–153.   1 *Now Whitehall's in the grave*: may refer to the general overthrow of (monarchical) government or to the King's beheading in 1649, or both; Whitehall was the principal royal residence in London, and from it Charles I stepped to his execution in the street below.   2 *our head is our slave*: some take this to refer to the capture and imprisonment of the King (Charles surrendered to the Scots on 5 May 1646 and was beheaded on 30 January 1649), rather than to his beheading. 'Our head' is either the King himself or his head as 'our head', and thus the collective reason of the realm, which is now enslaved.   3 *The bright pearl*, etc.: could refer to the King's return, by death, to the earth whence he came; otherwise, to the King's imprisonment at Hampton Court.

Now the mitre is lost,
   The proud prelates, too, crossed,   5
And all Rome's confined to a cloister;
   He that Tarquin was styled
   Our white land's exiled,
      Yea undefiled,
Not a court ape's left to confute us: 10
   Then let your voices rise high,
   As your colours did fly,
      And flour'shing cry,
'Long live the brave Oliver-Brutus!'

Now the sun is unarmed,   15
   And the moon by us charmed,
All the stars dissolved to a jelly;
   Now the thighs of the crown
   And the arms are lopped down,
And the body is all but a belly: 20
   Let the Commons go on,
   The Town is our own,
      We 'll rule alone,
For the Knights have yielded their spent-gorge;

8 *Tarquin*: Charles II.   14 *Oliver-Brutus*: Cromwell; 'The Brave Oliver' was a
popular song of the time.   15–28 *Now the sun*, etc.: heraldic terms and conventional symbolism figure prominently in these lines. According to Willa
McC. Evans, sun = King, moon = Queen, stars = nobility (specifically the
House of Lords, I think), thighs = the crown's chief supports (Laud and
Strafford, according to Weidhorn), arms lopped down = 'the dismemberment
of the body politic as well as . . . the Parliamentary order, after the execution
of Charles, to remove the royal arms from public places' (Weidhorn, pp. 72–3).
17 *stars dissolved to a jelly*: a common superstition about falling stars, possibly
alluding here to the dissolution of the House of Lords.   20–3 *And the body*, etc.
The body politic is reduced almost to mere belly, or 'Commons', both in general
and in relation to the House of Commons, which dissolved the House of Lords.
23 *The Town*: London.   24–8 *for the knights*, etc.: perhaps knights in general,
certainly the Knights of the Garter in particular. ('Knights' is capitalized in
LP 59.)   24 *spent-gorge*: almost certainly a quibble on the 'full-gorge' of feeding
hawks (Wilkinson, p. 311); possibly also a collar supposedly worn by Knights of
the Garter (Evans, p. 326, n. 26), or, for 'gorget', a piece of armour for the
throat. The specific point is unclear. As Wilkinson suggests, 'Pride's Purge'—
the excluding from Parliament of persons sympathetic to the King—in
December 1648 may be alluded to.

And an order is ta'en,   25
  With *Honi Soit* profane,
    Shout forth amain,
For our Dragon hath vanquished the St. George.

40

A Fly Caught in a Cobweb

Small type of great ones, that do hum
Within this whole world's narrow room,
That with a busy hollow noise
Catch at the people's vainer voice,
And with spread sails play with their breath,   5
Whose very hails new christen Death.
Poor fly caught in an airy net,
Thy wings have fettered now thy feet;
Where, like a lion in a toil,
Howe'er, thou keep'st a noble coil,   10
And beat'st thy generous breast, that o'er
The plains thy fatal buzzes roar,
Till thy all-bellied foe (round elf)
Hath quartered thee within himself.
    Was it not better once to play   15
I' th' light of a majestic ray?
Where, though too near and bold, the fire
Might singe thy upper down attire,
And thou i' th' storm to lose an eye,
A wing, or a self-trapping thigh;   20

---

26 *Honi Soit*: 'Hony soit qui mal y pense' ('shame to him who evil thinks'), the
motto of the Order of the Garter.   28 *For our Dragon*, etc.: a significant
inversion of the conventional vanquishing of the dragon by England's patron
saint, a picture of which is encircled by the motto on the badge of the Order
of the Garter.

40. See 'Lovelace's "A Fly Caught in a Cobweb" ' by Lynn Veach Sadler in
Literatur in Wissenschaft und Unterricht (Kiel) vi (1973), 23–30.   13 *round elf*:
'round' clearly complements 'all-bellied', and Lovelace refers to the spider as
'elf' in 'The Toad and The Spider: A Duel', l. 120.   16 *I' th' light of a majestic
ray*: i.e. round a candle.

Yet hadst thou fall'n like him, whose coil
Made fishes in the sea to broil,
When now th'ast scaped the noble flame,
Trapped basely in a slimy frame;
And free of air, thou art become   25
Slave to the spawn of mud and loam.
    Nor is't enough thyself dost dress
To thy swoll'n lord a num'rous mess,
And by degrees thy thin veins bleed,
And piecemeal dost his poison feed;   30
But now, devoured, art like to be
A net spun for thy family,
And straight expanded in the air
Hang'st for thy issue too a snare.
Strange witty death, and cruel ill,   35
That, killing thee, thou thine dost kill!
Like pies—in whose entombèd ark
All fowl crowd downward—to a lark,
Thou art thine en'my's sepulchre,
And in thee buriest too thine heir.   40

21–2 *him whose coil*, etc.: Phaeton (see G).   23–6 *noble flame . . . mud and loam*:
the fly's ignominious descent is characterized by the conventional hierarchy
of the four elements.   27 *thyself dost dress*: (1) thou, thyself, dost dress; (2)
thou dost dress thyself.   37–40 These lines contain so many ambiguities
that no commentator has seen fit to paraphrase them; the sole usual gloss
explains 'pies' as 'magpies'. It seems to me likely that Lovelace had in
mind the large pies, often very elaborate, for which 'coffin' was the usual
term, pastries of the four-and-twenty-blackbird kind, which were tomb-like,
Noah's-ark-like, and sepulchre-like by obvious analogy and sometimes probably
in actual form. This requires one to take 'like pies . . . to a lark' for ordinary
usage's 'like a pie to larks', perhaps, but that seems no great strain. Cf. *Titus
Andronicus* v. ii. 186–91, where Tamora's sons baked in Titus' 'coffin' (l. 188,
there meaning 'crust') are referred to; also see *R 2* III. ii. 153–4. The intended
wit is perhaps as follows: you are not only a pie-'coffin' but a sepulchre for your
enemy-cum-heir. The first evident of coexistent senses is a statement of a double
loss for the fly: becoming his enemy's property and losing his posterity at a
blow. This sense leads to the mock-heroic compensation explained after 'Yet'
(l. 41). The 'secondary' but pre-eminent sense is that the spider is the loser, too,
as the fly's heir buried by the fly.

Yet Fates a glory have reserved
For one so highly hath deserved:
As the rhinoceros doth die
Under his castle-enemy;
As through the crane's trunk-throat doth speed   45
The asp doth on his feeder feed;
Fall yet triumphant in thy woe,
Bound with the entrails of thy foe.

41

A Fly about a Glass of Burnt Claret

Forbear this liquid fire, fly,
It is more fatal than the dry:
That singly, but embracing, wounds,
And this at once both burns and drowns.

The salamander, that in heat   5
And flames doth cool his monstrous sweat,
Whose fan, a glowing cake, 'tis said,
Of this red furnace is afraid.

43–4 More difficulties, although Wilkinson may have the explanation, from
Du Bartas (*Divine Weeks and Works Translated*, 1611, p. 145), in the 'traditional'
enmity between the elephant and the rhinoceros: 'his huge strength nor subtle
wit cannot / Defend him from the sly rhinocerot'. 'Castle-enemy' = elephant
because one sense of 'castle' is 'a tower borne on the back of an elephant'
(*OED* sb. 6); it may have come to Lovelace through chess (cf. L–47), since
such elephants are common figures for rooks.   45 *trunk*[–]: tube.   48 *Bound
with the entrails of thy foe*: 'The fly's death amid its enemy's entrails (the cobweb)
is . . . close to the epic description of the dying warrior's piercing his opponent's
belly and dying in the other's entrails' (Weidhorn, p. 43).

41. *Burnt Claret*: 'Burnt' = 'made hot' (Dr. Johnson) or 'the precise early sense
is doubtful' (*OED*); perhaps much like mulled claret.   5–8 *The salamander that,*
etc. The superstition was of long duration. Aristotle wrote that the salamander
'not only walks through fire, but puts it out in doing so.'   7 *fan's . . . 'tis*. LP *59*
reads 'fan . . . is' (Wilkinson corrected to ''tis').   *cake*: error for 'coke' (*OED*'s
earliest recorded use for this type of mineral coal is 1669), or an unusual use
of 'cake [of coal]'?   *OED* sb. 4: 'any solidified or compressed substance in a
flattened form, such as a cake of soap, wax, paint, dry clay, coagulated blood
tobacco, etc.'

Viewing the ruby-crystal shine,
Thou tak'st it for heaven-crystalline;   10
Anon thou wilt be taught to groan,
'Tis an ascended Acheron.

A snowball-heart in it let fall,
And take it out a fire-ball:
An icy breast in it betrayed   15
Breaks a destructive wild grenade.

'Tis this makes Venus' altars shine,
This kindles frosty Hymen's pine;
When th' Boy grows old in his desires,
This flambeau doth new light his fires.   20

Though the cold hermit ever wail,
Whose sighs do freeze, and tears drop hail,
Once having passèd this, will ne'er
Another flaming purging fear.

The Vestal drinking this doth burn   25
Now more than in her funeral urn;
Her fires, that with the sun kept race,
Are now extinguished by her face.

The chemist, that himself doth 'stil,
Let him but taste this limbec's bill,   30
And prove this sublimated bowl,
He'll swear it will calcine a soul.

---

10 *heaven-crystalline*: the crystalline sphere found between the firmament of fixed stars and the *primum mobile* in one version of the Ptolemaic universe (see NRC). 12 *Acheron*: a river in Hades; Lovelace meant Phlegethon, the infernal river of fire. 13 *snowball-heart*: an allusion to the contemporary method of cooling wine by snow (Wilkinson, p. 311). 18 *Hymen*: god of marriage, here identified with Cupid. *pine*: (1) torch (*OED* sb.². 3); (2) penis (cf. Carew, C–28: 85). 25 *Vestal*: see G. 29 *chemist*: i.e. alchemist. *'stil*: distil. 30 *limbec*: alembic, retort. *bill*: lip or edge of the alembic's opening. 31 *prove*: try, test. *sublimated*: technically (alchemy and chemistry), vaporized and then solidified again.

Noble and brave! now thou dost know
The false preparèd decks below,
Dost thou the fatal liquor sup,   35
One drop, alas, thy bark blows up.

What airy country hast to save,
Whose plagues thou'lt bury in thy grave?
For even now thou seem'st to us
On this gulf's brink a Curtius.   40

And now th'art fall'n, magnan'mous fly,
In, where thine oceän doth fry,
Like the Sun's son who blushed the flood
To a complexiön of blood.

Yet see! my glad auricular   45
Redeems thee (though dissolved) a star:
Flaggy thy wings, and scorched thy thighs,
Thou li'st a double sacrifice.

And now my warming, cooling breath
Shall a new life afford in death: 50
See! in the hosp'tal of my hand,
Already cured, thou fierce dost stand.

Burnt insect! dost thou reaspire
The moist-hot glass and liquid fire?
I see! 'tis such a pleasing pain,   55
Thou wouldst be scorched and drowned again!

---

40 *Curtius*: Marcus Curtius, a soldier who leaped armed and on his horse into a chasm that had opened in the Roman Forum, thus sacrificing Rome's 'greatest strength' (arms and valour) and causing the chasm to close. 41 *magnan'mous*: courageous, loftily ambitious. 43–4 *Like the Sun's son*, etc.: Helios' son, Phaeton (see G). 45 *auricular*: little finger (as the one most easily inserted in the ear). 46 *dissolved*: immersed. 53 *reaspire*: again be ambitious of (transitive).

42

A Mock Charon

Dialogue

Charon W.

W.	Charon! Thou slave! Thou fool! Thou Cavalier!
Charon.	A slave, a fool! What traitor's voice I hear?
W.	Come, bring thy boat. *Charon.* No sir. *W.* No, sirrah! Why?
Charon.	The blest will disagree, and fiends will mutiny
	At thy, at thy unnumbered treachery. 5
W.	Villain, I have a pass, which who disdains
	I will sequester the Elysian plains.
Charon.	Woe's me! Ye gentle shades! Where shall I dwell?
	He's come! It is not safe to be in hell.

Chorus

Thus man, his honour lost, falls on these shelves;   10
Furies and fiends are still true to themselves.

Charon.	You must, lost fool, come in. *W.* Oh let me in!
	But now I fear thy boat will sink with my o'erweighty sin.
	Where, courteous Charon, am I now? *Charon.* Vile rant!
	At th' gates of thy supreme judge, Rhadamant. 15

---

42. A much-exploited kind of dialogue in the seventeenth century, which was evidently of French origin (see Wilkinson, pp. 312–14). Heavy Royalist irony at the expense of the traitor 'W.' and of the Parliamentary party generally. Charon was the ferryman who conveyed the dead across the Styx to Hades. *W.*: identity uncertain; perhaps Philip, fourth Baron Wharton (1613–96) (Wilkinson, p. 314); certainly a lord who was a staunch support of the Parliamentary party, but one would suppose Lovelace's subject to have been actually dead.   7 *sequester*: confiscate.   *the Elysian plains*: see G ('Elysium').   15 *Rhadamant*: Rhadamanthus, one of the three judges of the dead and rulers of Elysium, with Minos and Aeacus.

Double Chorus of Devils
Welcome to rape, to theft, to perjury;
To all the ills thou wert, we cannot hope to be;
Oh pity us condemned! Oh cease to woo,
And softly, softly breathe, lest you infect us, too.

43

Advice to My Best Brother,
Colonel Francis Lovelace

Frank, wilt live handsomely? Trust not too far
Thyself to waving seas, for what thy star
Calculated by sure event must be,
Look in the glassy-epithet and see.

Yet settle here your rest, and take your state,　　　　5
And in calm halcyon's nest ev'n build your fate;
Prithee lie down securely, Frank, and keep
With as much no-noise the inconstant deep
As its inhabitants; nay, steadfast stand,
As if discovered were a New-found-land　　　　10
Fit for plantation here; dream, dream still,
Lulled in Dione's cradle, dream until
Horror awake your sense, and you now find
Yourself a bubbled pastime for the wind,
And in loose Thetis' blankets torn and tossed:　　　　15
Frank, to undo thyself why art at cost?

43. Col. Francis Lovelace (1618?–1678?) commanded Royalist troops at
Carmarthen in 1644 until the town was taken. In 1650 he was given a pass to
Long Island, in the Colonies; in 1652 a pass to go 'beyond seas'; and in 1657
a pass for Holland. In 1678 he is mentioned as Governor-General of the Duke
of York's territories in America (see Wilkinson, pp. 242–5). This poem may be
associated with Francis's departure for America. 4 *glassy-epithet* [*LP 59*
'-epithite']: 'glass-epitome' would make better sense to me, but the reference
s to a 'glass of skill' (crystal ball) and, presumably, the named characteristic
to be found there. 6 *halcyon*: see G. 8 *no-noise*: hyphen supplied. 12 *Dione*:
Hesiod makes her an Oceanid, but Homer has her as mother of Aphrodite
(Venus), whose father is always Zeus (Jupiter). She is commonly identified with
her daughter, almost certainly so here. Dione's cradle = ocean, whence
Aphrodite emerged. 14 *bubbled*: (1) beset with bubbles; (2) made a fool of.
15 *Thetis*: sea nymph and mother of Achilles.

Nor be too confident, fixed on the shore,
For even that too borrows from the store
Of her rich neighbour, since now wisest know
(And this to Galileo's judgement owe)   20
The palsy earth itself is every jot
As frail, inconstant, waving as that blot
We lay upon the deep, that sometimes lies
Changed, you would think, with's bottom's properties;
But this eternal strange Ixion's wheel   25
Of giddy earth ne'er whirling leaves to reel
Till all things are inverted, till they are
Turned to that antique confused state they were.

Who loves the golden mean doth safely want
A cobwebbed cot, and wrongs entailed upon 't;   30
He richly needs a palace for to breed
Vipers and moths, that on their feeder feed;
The toy that we (too true) a mistress call,
Whose looking-glass and feather weighs up all;
And clothes which larks would play with, in the sun,   35
That mock him in the night when's course is run.

To rear an edifice by art so high
That envy should not reach it with her eye,
Nay, with a thought come near it—wouldst thou know
How such a structure should be raised? Build low.   40
The blust'ring wind's invisible rough stroke
More often shakes the stubborn'st, prop'rest oak,

20–3 *Galileo*: Lovelace probably refers to Galileo's *Dialogue on the Ptolemaic and Copernican Systems* (1632), in which Galileo defended the Copernican theory of the diurnal and annual motion of the earth and of the stability of the sun. 25 *Ixion*. When Ixion attempted to make love to Hera, Zeus formed a cloud (Nephele) to look like her; through this union the centaurs were begotten; as punishment for his crimes, Ixion was bound upon a wheel that turned forever. 26 *ne'er whirling leaves to reel*: whirling, never stops reeling. 30 *cot*: cottage. *wrongs entailed*: converted into 'fee tail', settled on a number of persons in succession, so that there is no one absolute owner (here as one person who endures all the adversity). 33 *(too true) a mistress*: 'mis' meant to be taken here in the sense 'bad, wicked, amiss'? 35 *clothes*: pieces of scarlet cloth used for 'daring' (bewildering and dazzling) larks, so they could be shot or taken down with a net (Wilkinson, p. 318; *LP 59* reads 'Cloaths').

And in proud turrets we behold withal,
'Tis the imperial top declines to fall.
Nor does heaven's lightning strike the humble vales,   45
But high aspiring mounts batters and scales.

A breast of proof defies all shocks of fate,
Fears in the best, hopes in the worser state;
Heaven forbid that, as of old, Time ever
Flourished in spring so contrary, now never: 50
That mighty breath which blew foul winter hither
Can eas'ly puff it to a fairer weather.
Why dost despair then, Frank? Aeolus has
A Zephyrus as well as Boreas.

'Tis a false sequel, solecism, gainst those   55
Precepts by fortune giv'n us, to suppose
That, 'cause it is now ill, 'twill e'er be so;
Apollo doth not always bend his bow,
But oft uncrownèd of his beams divine
With his soft harp awakes the sleeping Nine.   60

In strictest things magnanimous appear,
Greater in hope, howe'er thy fate, than fear:
Draw all your sails in quickly, though no storm
Threaten your ruin with a sad alarm;
For tell me how they differ, tell me pray,   65
A cloudy tempest, and a too fair day.

47 *of proof*: well armed, invulnerable.   53–4 *Aeolus* [god of winds] *has a Zephyrus* [mild west wind] *as well as Boreas* [fierce north wind].   58 Apollo is generally represented as holding either a bow or a lyre, since he was god of both archery and music.   60 *Nine*: the Muses.

44

An Anniversary on the Hymeneals of My
Noble Kinsman, Thomas Stanley, Esquire

The day is curled about again
To view the splendour she was in,
    When first with hallowed hands
The holy man knit the mysterious bands;
When you two your contracted souls did move,   5
        Like cherubims above,
            And did make love,
As your un-understanding issue now,
In a glad sigh, a smile, a tear, a vow.

    Tell me, O self-reviving Sun,   10
        In thy peregrination
        Hast thou beheld a pair
Twist their soft beams like these in their chaste air?
As from bright numberless embracing rays
        Are sprung th' industrious days,   15
            So when they gaze,
And change their fertile eyes with the new morn,
A beauteous offspring is shot forth, not born.

---

44. Thomas Stanley (1625–78), poet, translator, and scholar, was a distant
cousin of Lovelace. Wilkinson has a longer note on him (pp. 318–19), and see
The Poems of Thomas Stanley, ed. Galbraith Miller Crump (1962). This poem
owes a good deal to Donne, especially to 'The Sun Rising' and 'The Ecstasy',
and also to analogies drawn from the Christian-Platonized Ptolemaic cosmology (see NRC). The etymology of 'Anniversary' figures prominently in the
conceits of the poem, Latin *versare* meaning 'to keep turning', 'wind', 'twist'
(cf. 'curled about', l. 1). *Hymeneals*: nuptials, after Hymen, god of marriage.
4 *bands*: and 'bonds' (interchangeable spellings and, often, meanings at the
time). 13 *Twist their soft beams*: cf. Donne, 'The Ecstasy', ll. 7–8. 16–18 *So*
when they gaze, etc.: a complicated conceit involving the hyperbolic identification of eyes with suns, the phenomenon of shooting stars, and the notion of
'looking babies', with reference to persons' seeing themselves reflected in each
other's eyes.

Be witness then, all-seeing Sun,
Old spy, thou that thy race hast run   20
    In full five thousand rings;
To thee were ever purer offerings
Sent on the wings of faiths? And thou, O Night!
        Curtain of their delight,
            By these made bright,   25
Have you not markèd their celestial play,
And no more peeked the gaieties of day?

Come then, pale virgins, roses strew,
Mingled with *Io*'s, as you go;
    The snowy ox is killed,   30
The fane with pros'lyte lads and lasses filled;
You too may hope the same seraphic joy
        Old Time cannot destroy,
            Nor fulness cloy,
When, like these, you shall stamp by sympathies   35
Thousands of new-born loves with your chaste eyes.

20–1 *thou that thy race hast run*, etc.: alluding to the traditional notion that the world would end in or before its 6,000th year, having been created somewhere between 5200 and 3760 B.C.   29 *Io's*: from the Greek word for an exultant shout or song.   30 *snowy ox*: an expiatory sacrifice.   31 *fane*: temple.   35–6 *you shall stamp*, etc.: multiply by weeping. Cf. Donne, 'A Valediction: of Weeping', ll. 1–3.

45

Painture

A Panegyric to the Best Picture of Friendship,
Master Peter Lely

If Pliny, Lord High Treasurer of all
Nature's exchequer shuffled in this our ball,
Painture, her richer rival, did admire,
And cried she wrought with more almighty fire,
That judged th' unnumbered issue of her scroll　　　5
Infinite and various as her mother soul,
That contemplation into matter brought,
Bodied ideas, and could form a thought:
Why do I pause to couch the cataract,
And the gross pearls from our dull eyes abstract?　　10
That, powerful Lely, now awakened, we
This new Creation may behold by thee.
　　To thy victorious pencil all that eyes
And minds can reach do bow; the deities
Bold poets first but feigned you do, and make,　　15
And from your awe they our devotion take.
Your beauteous palette first defined Love's Queen,
And made her in her heavenly colours seen;
You strung the bow of the bandite her son,
And tipped his arrows with religion.　　20
Neptune as unknown as his fish might dwell,
But that you seat him in his throne of shell.

---

45. 'Painture', the art of painting, is analogous to 'sculpture'. *LP 59* has two older spellings, 'Peinture' (Old French) and 'Pincture' (from Latin *pingere* 'to paint'). On Peter Lely see L–13 n. Lely's later and best-known work was in portraiture, and the 'half-dozen mythological pictures by Lely which Lovelace here describes are not easy to trace' (Wilkinson, p. 319); there is a *Venus* at Penshurst, a *Susanna and the Elders* at Burghley House, and a *Magdalene* at Kingston Lacy, according to John Buxton. 1 *Pliny*: Pliny the Elder (A.D. 23–79), whose *Natural History* made him an important scientific authority in the Middle Ages. 5 *th' unnumbered*: *LP 59* has 'the'. 9 *couch*: remove. 13 *pencil*: artist's paint-brush. 17 *Love's Queen*: Venus. 19 *the bandite her son*: Cupid; the spelling is evidently phonetic for the pronunciation 'bandeet' (cf. Italian *banditto*). 21 *Neptune*: Roman god of the sea.

The Thunderer's artillery and brand
You fancied, Rome in his fantastic hand.
And the pale frights, the pains and fears of hell,   25
First from your sullen Melancholy fell.
Who cleft th' Infernal Dog's loathed head in three,
And spun out Hydra's fifty necks? By thee
As prepossessed w' enjoy th' Elysian plain,
Which but before was flattered in our brain.   30
Whoe'er yet viewed air's child invisible,
A hollow voice, but in thy subtile skill?
Faint-stamm'ring Echo you so draw that we
The very repercussiön do see.

Cheat hocus-pocus-Nature an essay   35
O' th' spring affords us, presto! and away;
You all the year do chain her, and her fruits,
Roots to their beds, and flowers to their roots.
Have not mine eyes feasted i' th' frozen zone
Upon a fresh new-grown collation   40
Of apples, unknown sweets, that seemed to me
Hanging to tempt as on the fatal tree,
So delicately limned I vowed to try
My appetite imposed upon my eye?

You, sir, alone, Fame and all-conquering Rhyme   45
File the set teeth of all-devouring Time.
When Beauty once thy virtuous paint hath on,
Age needs not call her to vermilion;
Her beams ne'er shed or change like th' hair of day,
She scatters fresh her everlasting ray;   50
Nay, from her ashes her fair virgin fire
Ascends, that doth new massacres conspire,

---

23 *The Thunderer*: Jupiter *tonans* (Jupiter as the sky-god of thunder).   26 *Melan-choly*: a personification, like Albrecht Dürer's 'Melancholia' (1514).   27–8 *Who cleft*, etc.: Hercules, as two of his Twelve Labours, subdued Cerberus, the three-headed watchdog of Hades (12th), and the hydra (2nd).   29 *Elysian plains*: see G ('Elysium').   45–6 *You, sir, alone, Fame*, etc. Archaic usage probably accounts for the minor difficulties: understand 'for you' (ethic dative) and either 'Fame and all-conquering Rhyme' as a compound singular (Abbott, sec. 336) or 'Files' as third-person plural in -s (Abbott 333).   49 *th' hair of day*: sunbeams.   51–2 *Nay, from her ashes*, etc.: that is, 'though dead through nature, she lives through art, and is still unique', with reference to the phoenix myth (see G).

Whilst we wipe off the num'rous score of years,
And do behold our grandsires as our peers;
With the first father of our house compare   55
We do the features of our new-born heir;
For though each copiëd a son, they all
Meet in thy first and true original.
  Sacred luxurious! what princess not
But comes to you to have herself begot?   60
As when first man was kneaded, from his side
Is born to's hand a ready-made-up bride.
He husband to his issue then doth play,
And for more wives remove th' obstructed way:
So by your art you spring up in two moons   65
What could not else be formed by fifteen suns;
Thy skill doth an'mate the prolific flood,
And thy red oil assimilates to blood.
  Where then, when all the world pays its respect,
Lies our transalpine barbarous neglect?   70
When the chaste hands of pow'rful Titiän
Had drawn the scourges of our God and man,
And now the top of th' altar did ascend,
To crown the heavenly piece with a bright end;
Whilst he who to seven languages gave law,   75
And always like the sun his subjects saw,
Did, in his robes imperial and gold,
The basis of the doubtful ladder hold:

57–8 *each copied a son*, etc. Art is made the original of nature here.   59 *luxurious*:
lustful (one).   61–4 *As when first man*, etc.: alluding to the account of the creation
and succeeding events in Genesis, esp. 2: 21–2.   70 *transalpine barbarous*: something of a pleonasm; in transalpine Gaul lived (from the Roman perspective) the
barbarians. There is allusion here to Titian's journey across the Alps to join
Charles V at Augsburg in 1548.   71–80 *Titian*. Titian (*c.* 1477–1576), the great
portrait-painter of the Venetian school, also painted religious pictures as well
as mythological, poetical, and allegorical subjects. There is a story that
Charles V once asked several of his courtiers to hold a table on their shoulders
for Titian to stand on while he raised a picture higher up on the wall (Wilkinson, p. 321). Charles V (1500–58) was Emperor of the Holy Roman Empire
and (as Charles I) King of Spain.   72 *the scourges of our God and man*: perhaps
one of his paintings of 'The Mocking of Christ', as Wilkinson suggests (p. 321).
79–80 *a nobler monument*, etc.: with reference (perhaps) to Charles's attempt to
preserve the medieval ideal of the empire, his lifelong effort.

O Charles! a nobler monument than that
Which thou thine own executor wert at.   80
When to our huffling Henry there complained
A grievèd earl, that thought his honour stained,
'Away', frowned he, 'for your own safeties, haste!
In one cheap hour ten coronets I 'll cast;
But Holbein's noble and prodigious worth   85
Only the pangs of an whole age brings forth.'
Henry! A word so princely saving said,
It might new raise the ruins thou hast made.
    O sacred Painture, that dost fairly draw
What but in mists deep inward poets saw!   90
'Twixt thee and an Intelligence no odds,
That art of privy counsel to the gods;
By thee unto our eyes they do prefer
A stamp of their abstracted character;
Thou that in frames eternity dost bind,   95
And art a written and a bodied mind;
To thee is ope the Junto o' th' Abyss,
And its conspiracy detected is;
Whilst their cabal thou to our sense dost show,
And in thy square paint'st what they threat below.   100
    Now, my best Lely, let 's walk hand in hand,
And smile at this un-understanding land;
Let them their own dull counterfeits adore,
Their rainbow-clothes admire, and no more;
Within one shade of thine more substance is   105
Than all their varnished idol-mistresses:
Whilst great Vasari and Vermander shall
Interpret the deep mystery of all,

---

81 *huffling*: blustering. *Henry*: Henry VIII (1491–1547). 85 *Holbein*: Hans Holbein the Younger (1497–1543), an artist of extraordinary versatility and accomplishment who came to Henry VIII's notice in the mid-1530s 86 *only*: alone; i.e. 'only Holbein's'. 88 *the ruins thou hast made*: i.e. in confiscating and despoiling the monasteries (1536–9). 91 *Intelligence*: see NRC. 97 *Junto*: in general, a clique, faction, or 'cabal' (l. 99), as a variant form of junta; by topical allusion, the Junto were members of the Rump Parliament, those submissive to Cromwell who survived 'Pride's Purge' of moderate and Presbyterian Members (1648). Here, the fallen-angel inhabitants of hell. 107 *Vasari and Vermander*: Giorgio Vasari (1511–74), Italian painter, architect, and biographer of artists; and Karel van Mander (1584–1606), Dutch painter and writer on art.

And I unto our modern Picts shall show
What due renown to thy fair art they owe,   110
In the delineated lives of those
By whom this everlasting laurel grows.
Then if they will not gently apprehend,
Let one great blot give to their fame an end;
Whilst no poetic flower their hearse doth dress,   115
But perish they and their effigiës.

46

To My Noble Kinsman, Thomas Stanley, Esquire,
on His Lyric Poems Composed by Master John Gamble

What means this stately tablature,
    The balance of thy strains,
Which seems, instead of sifting pure,
    T' extend and rack thy veins?
Thy odes first their own harmony did break,   5
For singing troth is but in tune to speak.

Nor thus thy golden feet and wings
    May it be thought false melody
T' ascend to heaven by silver strings;
    This is Urania's heraldry: 10
Thy royal poem now we may extol,
And truly Luna blazoned upon Sol.

---

109 *Picts*: painted or tattooed inhabitants of ancient Britain, hence barbarians
(from Latin *pingere* 'to paint'). 112 *this everlasting laurel*: i.e. Lovelace's
panegyric.

46. Wilkinson prints this poem from John Gamble's first book of *Ayres and
Dialogues* (1656). On Thomas Stanley see L–44 n. 1 *tablature*: musical
notation; specifically, a form of notation used for the lute and other stringed
instruments. 2 *strain[s]*: melody, tune; technically, a definite rhythmical
section of a piece of music, divided from what follows by a double bar (1575).
5 *break*: reveal, disclose, utter (*OED* v. 22). 7–8 That is, nor may it be thought
false melody for the golden feet and wings of your poem to be thus set to music
and performed. 10 *Urania*: the Muse of Astronomy. 12 *And truly Luna
blazoned upon Sol*: alchemical and heraldic terminology; *Luna* is silver and a
name for 'argent' in blazoning (describing or depicting) the arms of sovereigns;
Sol is gold and 'or'; the terms of course mean 'moon' and 'sun' in Latin.

As when Amphion first did call
　　Each listening stone from's den,
And with the lute did form his wall,　　　　　　15
　　But with his words the men;
So, in your twisted numbers now, you thus
Not only stocks persuade, but ravish us.

Thus do your aïrs echo o'er
　　The notes and anthems of the spheres,　　　　20
And their whole consort back restore,
　　As if Earth too would bless Heaven's ears:
But yet the spokes, by which they scaled so high,
Gamble hath wisely laid of *ut re mi*.

17 *twisted numbers*: the intertwining of lines of verse set to music.　18 *stocks*: Orpheus' power to charm trees is here lent to Amphion (see G).　19–22 *Thus do your airs*, etc.: with reference to the music made by the motions of the spheres (see NRC).　23 *spokes*: rounds or rungs of a ladder.　*scaled*: (1) climbed; (2) 'harmonized'; a 'scale' is a definite series of sounds ascending (or descending) by fixed intervals.　24 *ut re mi*: the first three signs of the 'gamut'.

47

To Dr. F. B. on His Book of Chess

Sir, now unravelled is the Golden Fleece:
Men that could only fool at fox-and-geese
Are new made politicians by thy book,
And both can judge and conquer with a look.
The hidden fate of princes you unfold,   5
Court, clergy, commons, by your law controlled.
   Strange, serious wantoning: all that they
   Blustered and cluttered for you *play*.

47. Wilkinson conjectures that 'F.B.' may be Francis Beale, who signs the
'Epistle Dedicatory' and speaks of himself as publishing the book from which
this poem is taken, *The Royall Game of Chesse-Play* (1656), or 'Dr. Budden, to
whom the third, anonymous, set of commendatory verses is addressed' (pp.
326–7). 1 *unravelled is the Golden Fleece*. Jason won the Fleece by performing
apparently impossible tasks, such as sowing a dragon's teeth, from which armed
men arose; there may also be (through 'unravelled') an allusion to the thread
by which Theseus was able to make his way through the Labyrinth. 2 *Fox and
Geese*: 'a game played with seventeen pieces called geese and a larger piece
which represents the fox. The player with the geese tries to enclose the fox so
that he cannot move, his opponent to take so many pieces that he cannot be
blocked' (Wilkinson, p. 327, from Strutt's *Sports and Pastimes*, 1845, pp. 318–19).
5–6 *princes . . . Court, clergy, commons*: i.e. the king, queen, knights, bishops, and
pawns. 7–8 *Strange, serious wantoning*, etc.: a paradoxical cross-examination of
the work and play of the world and of chess. 8 *cluttered*: the sense compounds
'clustered' and 'clattered'.

CHRONOLOGICAL TABLE

Robert Herrick (1591–1674), Thomas Carew (1594/5–1640), Sir
John Suckling (1609–42), Richard Lovelace (1618–57)

1591   **Herrick** baptized (28 Aug.) at St. Vedast's, Foster
Lane; seventh of eight children of Nicholas Herrick, the
first of his family to come from Leicestershire to London,
where he became a goldsmith and banker. Herrick's
mother was Julia(na) Stone, daughter of a London
mercer.

1592   **Herrick**'s father makes his will on 7 Nov. and dies
about two days later; on 29 Nov. his mother and her
children are granted the estate (£5,068).

1594/5   **Carew** born the younger son of Sir Matthew Carew
(aged *c.* 57 or 58, ktd. 1605), a well-educated Master in
Chancery descended from a landed Cornish family, and
Alice Ryvers, daughter of a Lord Mayor of London,
possibly at West Wickham, Kent; family moves to
Chancery Lane, London, in 1598.

1607   **Herrick** apprenticed (25 Sept.) to his uncle, Sir
William Herrick, a goldsmith.

1608   **Carew** enters Merton College, Oxford (June); B.A.
31 Jan. 1611.

1609   **Suckling** baptized (10 Feb.) at Goodfathers, Whitton,
in Twickenham, Middlesex; born the elder son and
second of six children of Sir John Suckling *père* (ktd.
1616), at the time Receiver of Fines on Alienations
(1604) and later Master of Requests (1619) and
Member of the Privy Council (1622), and Martha
Cranfield, daughter of a prosperous London merchant.

1612   **Carew** incorporated B.A. of Cambridge and admitted
to Middle Temple (6 Aug.).

1613   **Carew** goes to Italy with Sir Dudley Carleton, a
relative by marriage; Carleton's embassy returns to
London in December. **Herrick** enters St. John's
College, Cambridge, as a fellow commoner, along with
John Wickes (fellow) and Clipsby Crew (student): B.A.
1617 and M.A. 1620 from Trinity Hall. **Suckling**'s
mother dies (28 Oct.) when he is four-and-a-half years
old.

1616   Carleton employs **Carew** for embassy to the Nether-
lands; Carew offends Carleton and his Lady (his
father's niece) and is sent back to London (Aug.).
Active and successful at court as a squire 'of high degree
for cost and bravery'.

1618   **Lovelace** born, possibly in Woolwich but more likely in
Holland, the eldest of four sons and three daughters of
Sir William Lovelace, of Woolwich, Kent, and Anne
Barne. **Carew**'s father dies (2 Aug.) aged *c*. 85.

1619   **Carew** leaves (13 May) on the embassy to Paris with
Sir Edward Herbert (later Lord Herbert of Cherbury),
who refers to him in his *Autobiography* as 'that excellent
wit'.

1623   **Suckling** matriculates at Trinity College, Cambridge,
in Easter Term; apparently stays three or four years but
takes no degree, as was not uncommon with gentlemen.
Herrick ordained, with John Wickes, at Peterborough:
deacon 24 Apr. and priest 25 Apr.

1625   Richard James, in *The Muses' Dirge* for James I, groups
'some Jonson, Drayton, or some **Herrick**'—'the most
flattering public compliment that Herrick is known to
have received' (Martin, p. xvii).

1627   **Suckling** admitted to Gray's Inn (23 Feb.) but leaves
almost immediately, upon his father's death (27 Mar.);
on the unsuccessful expedition to the Isle of Rhé, as
Herrick was as a chaplain to the Duke of Buckingham.
Lovelace's father killed, aged 44, at the siege of Groll;
Lovelace becomes his mother's ward.

1629   **Lovelace** admitted a 'boarder' at Charterhouse, prob-
ably on the King's nomination and at the same time as
Richard Crashaw. **Suckling** licensed to join Lord
Wimbledon's regiment in the Low Countries (22 Oct.).

1630   **Carew** becomes a Gentleman of the Privy Chamber
Extraordinary (6 Apr.) and Sewer in Ordinary to the
King. **Suckling** remains on the Continent probably
until September, when he is knighted at Theobald's
(19th); for a short time a student at Leyden (admitted
26 Feb.). **Herrick** installed vicar of Dean Prior
(29 Oct.).

1631   **Lovelace** becomes a Gentleman Waiter Extraordinary
to the King (5 May). **Suckling** with Sir Henry Vane's
embassy to Gustavus Adolphus until spring 1632; in

London on 10 Apr., from which time he lives the life of a courtier-wit and prodigal heir. Said to have invented cribbage, to have introduced marked cards into England, and to have been 'the greatest gallant of his time, and the greatest gamester, both for bowling and cards, so that no shop-keeper would trust him for 6*d*' (Aubrey).

1633   **Carew**'s elegy, apparently first written soon after Donne's death in 1631, published before *Poems of J.D.*

1634   **Carew**'s masque, *Coelum Brittanicum*, performed by the King and his gentlemen (18 Feb.) in a setting designed by Inigo Jones. At Oxford—matriculated at Gloucester Hall (now Worcester College) on 27 June—**Lovelace** is 'accounted the most amiable and beautiful person that ever eye beheld' (Anthony Wood); his comedy *The Scholar(s)* is produced at the Hall and later at White-friars 'with applause'.

1635   **Suckling** wins nearly £2,000 at bowls from Viscount Dunluce (Sept.).

1636   On a visit to Oxford by the King and Queen, **Lovelace** is created an honorary M.A. (31 Aug.).

1637   **Suckling** writes the tragedy *Aglaura*, *An Account of Religion by Reason*, and 'The Wits'. **Lovelace** is incorporated M.A. at Cambridge (4 Oct.) and goes to Court, where he becomes a particular favourite of George Lord Goring, later a commanding officer in the Bishops' Wars.

1638   *Aglaura* staged by the King's Company at Blackfriars (7 Feb.), at a cost to **Suckling** of £300–400, and again, before the King and Queen, at the Cockpit (3 Apr.), this time as a tragi-comedy; the play is printed in an extravagant folio at Suckling's expense. Suckling is made a Gentleman of the Privy Chamber Extraordinary (20 Nov.), as **Carew** already was. Carew's mother buried at Little Middleton (7 Dec.); the poet is not mentioned in her will (10 Dec. 1637). Carew and Thomas Killigrew together are painted by Van Dyck (as **Suckling** also was, probably in 1637).

1639   **Suckling** equips his celebrated 'Hundred Horse', at a cost said to have been £12,000, for the first Bishops' War, which was aborted by the treaty of Berwick (18 June); **Carew** and **Lovelace**, as an ensign, also serve.

1640   **Carew** buried beside his father at St. Dunstan's-in-the-
West, 23 Mar.; *Poems* published, with a second edition
in 1642 and a third in 1651. Stationers' Register entry
(29 Apr.) for 'the several poems written by Master
Robert **Herrick**', indicating prospective publication of
a book.

1640   **Suckling** and **Lovelace** take part in the second
Bishops' War, which was concluded by a battle fought
at Newburn Ford (28 Aug.). Lovelace, an ensign in
Goring's regiment and commissioned a captain, writes
a tragedy, *The Soldier*, in 1640. After the opening of the
Long Parliament on 3 Nov., Suckling writes a polemical
tract, *To Mr. Henry Jermyn, in the Beginning of Parliament,
1640* (printed 1641).

1641   **Suckling** attempts, unsuccessfully, to rescue the Earl of
Strafford from the Tower and bring the army to the aid
of the King, and is forced to flee the country; arrives in
Paris on 14 May; alive as late as 23 July but dies a
suicide probably before autumn.

1642   For delivering a royalist petition to the House of
Commons, **Lovelace** is committed to the Gatehouse at
Westminster, where he is supposed to have written 'To
Althea, from Prison'; out on bail in three to four
months. Probably goes to Holland with Goring in
September to raise recruits for the King's cause.

1646   **Suckling**'s *Fragmenta Aurea* published, with a second
edition in 1648 and a third in 1658–9.

1647   **Lovelace** admitted to the freedom of the Painters'
Company (along with Peter Lely), presumably as a
connoisseur and expert critic. **Herrick** ejected from
Dean Prior for 'the affection that he bore to his late
Majesty of blessed memory', as he wrote in 1660
when petitioning Parliament for his reinstatement as
vicar.

1648   Publication of **Herrick**'s *Hesperides* with *Noble Numbers*.
Lovelace committed to Peterhouse Prison (warrant
9 June); discharged 10 Apr. 1649.

1649   **Lovelace**'s *Lucasta* published (licensed 4 Feb. 1648,
entered 14 May 1649).

1656   **Lovelace** writes 'The Triumphs of Philamore and
Amoret' for the marriage of Charles Cotton the younger
and Isabella Hutchinson.

1657   Probably the year of **Lovelace**'s death, in dire poverty as is generally thought. He is said to have been buried at St. Bride's, which was destroyed by the Great Fire.

1659   *The Last Remains of Sir John* **Suckling** published. **Lovelace**'s *Lucasta. Posthume Poems* published by the poet's youngest brother, Dudley Posthumus Lovelace.

1660   **Herrick** returns to Dean Prior.

1674   **Herrick** buried at Dean Prior, 15 Oct.

SELECT BIBLIOGRAPHY

LITERARY HISTORY AND CRITICISM: CAVALIER POETS†

*Bush, Douglas, 'Jonson, Donne, and Their Successors', ch. iv in *English Literature in the Earlier Seventeenth Century* (OHEL), 2nd edition revised (1962). The paperback reprint (1975) does not contain the still valuable bibliography.

Holliday, Carl, *The Cavalier Poets* (1911).

*Johnson, Samuel, 'Life of Abraham Cowley', *The Works of the Most Eminent English Poets, with Prefaces, Biographical and Critical* (1779–81). Much reprinted, as in **Johnson's Lives of the Poets: A Selection*, edited by J. P. Hardy (OPET, 1971), pp. 1–49.

Judkins, David C., 'Recent Studies in the Cavalier Poets: Thomas Carew, Richard Lovelace, John Suckling, and Edmund Waller', *English Literary Renaissance*, vii (1977), 243–55. An annotated bibliography of writings from 1945 through 1974.

*Keast, William R., ed., *Seventeenth-Century English Poetry: Modern Essays in Criticism*, revised edition (1971).

*Leavis, F. R., 'The Line of Wit', *Revaluation: Tradition and Development in English Poetry* (1947).

McKuen, Kathryn A., *Classical Influence upon the Tribe of Ben* (1939; rpt., 1968).

*MacLean, Hugh, ed., 'Criticism' section in *Ben Jonson and the Cavalier Poets* (1975), pp. 399–584.

Miner, Earl, *The Cavalier Mode from Jonson to Cotton* (1971).

*Skelton, Robin, *Cavalier Poets*, Writers and their Work, No. 117 (1960). Essays on Carew, Suckling, and Lovelace.

Skelton, Robin, ed., Introduction to *The Cavalier Poets* (1970).

Summers, Joseph H., *The Heirs of Donne and Jonson* (1970).

*Walton, Geoffrey, 'The Cavalier Poets', *From Donne to Marvell*, ed. Boris Ford, revised edition (1968).

† Since all the books listed are easily identified and available in both the U.K. and the U.S.A., I omit place of publication. The availability of paperback editions is indicated by an asterisk. Essays on individual poems are referred to in the notes.

THOMAS CAREW

Major Modern Edition
The Poems of Thomas Carew with His Masque Coelum Brittanicum, edited by Rhodes Dunlap (OET, 1949; corr. rpt., 1957).

Criticism and Scholarship
BLANSHARD, RUFUS A., 'Thomas Carew and the Cavalier Poets', *Transactions of the Wisconsin Academy of Arts, Sciences, and Letters*, xliii (1957), 214–27.
KING, BRUCE, 'The Strategy of Carew's Wit', *REL* v (1964), 42–51.
MARTZ, LOUIS L., 'Thomas Carew: The Cavalier World', *The Wit of Love* (1969), pp. 59–110.
RAUBER, D. F., 'Carew Redivivus', *TSLL* xiii (1971), 17–28.
SELIG, EDWARD I., *The Flourishing Wreath: A Study of Thomas Carew's Poetry* (1958).

ROBERT HERRICK

Major Modern Edition
The Poetical Works of Robert Herrick, edited by L. C. Martin (OET, 1956; corr. rpt., 1963).

Criticism and Scholarship
BERMAN, RONALD, 'Herrick's Secular Poetry', *ES* lii (1971), 20–30.
DELATTRE, F., *Robert Herrick: Contribution a l'étude de la poésie lyrique en Angleterre au dix-septième siècle* (1912).
DEMING, ROBERT H., *Ceremony and Art: Robert Herrick's Poetry* (1974).
DENEEF, A. LEIGH, '*This Poetick Liturgie': Robert Herrick's Ceremonial Mode* (1974).
MOORMAN, F. W., *Robert Herrick: A Biographical and Critical Study* (1910; rpt. 1962).
MUSGROVE, S., *The Universe of Robert Herrick*, Auckland University College Bulletin No. 38, English Series No. 4 (1950).
*PATRICK, J. MAX, notes in his edition of *The Complete Poetry of Robert Herrick* (1963; corr. rpt., 1968).
POLLARD, ALFRED, notes in his edition of *Robert Herrick: The Hesperides and Noble Numbers*, revised edition (1898).

REED, MARK L., 'Herrick Among the Maypoles: Dean Prior and the *Hesperides*', *SEL* v (1965), 133–50.

ROLLIN, ROGER B., *Robert Herrick* (1966).

SWARDSON, HAROLD R., 'Herrick and the Ceremony of Mirth', *Poetry and the Fountain of Light* (1962).

WHITAKER, THOMAS R., 'Herrick and the Fruits of the Garden', *ELH* xxii (1955), 16–33.

WOODWARD, DANIEL H., 'Herrick's Oberon Poems', *JEGP* lxiv (1965), 270–84.

RICHARD LOVELACE

Major Modern Edition

The Poems of Richard Lovelace, edited by C. H. Wilkinson (OET, 1930; corr. rpt., 1953).

Criticism and Scholarship

HARTMANN, CYRIL HUGHES, *The Cavalier Spirit and Its Influence on the Life and Work of Richard Lovelace (1618–1658)* (1925; rpt. 1973).

JONES, GEORGE FENWICK, 'Love'd I Not Honour More: The Durability of a Literary Motif', *CL* xi (1959), 131–43.

WEIDHORN, MANFRED, *Richard Lovelace* (1970).

SIR JOHN SUCKLING

Major Modern Edition

The Works of Sir John Suckling, two volumes (OET, 1971): *The Non-Dramatic Works*, edited by Thomas Clayton; *The Plays*, edited by L. A. Beaurline.

Criticism and Scholarship

ANSELMENT, RAYMOND A., ' "Men Most of All Enjoy, When Least They Do": The Love Poetry of John Suckling', *TSLL* xiv (1972), 17–32.

BEAURLINE, L. A., ' "Why So Pale and Wan": An Essay in Critical Method', *TSLL* iv (1962), 553–63.

HENDERSON, F. O., 'Traditions of "Précieux" and "Libertin" in Suckling's Poetry', *ELH* iv (1937), 274–98.

A NOTE ON RENAISSANCE COSMOLOGY

The Ptolemaic universe had a coherence, economy, and explanatory power that enabled it long to survive the discovery of Copernicus (1473–1543) that the earth revolves around the sun and that the rotation of the earth on its axis accounts for the apparent rising and setting of the sun, moon, and stars. It was spherical, stationary, and geocentric. The earth stood at the centre of a series of nested transparent spheres in which the planets moved, each guided by an angelic 'intelligence'. The revolving bodies (the seven 'planets') and their spheres, in order of their proximity to earth, were (1) the moon, (2) Mercury, (3) Venus, (4) the sun, (5) Mars, (6) Jupiter, and (7) Saturn. Beyond these moving bodies were two or three additional heavens: (8) the firmament of 'fixed stars', (9) a crystalline sphere (sometimes), and (10) the *primum mobile*, or prime mover. The stability, order, and symmetry of this cosmos gave it enormous appeal, and it has continued to afford a basis for myth-making even in the twentieth century.

The universe was supposed to be in a state of divine harmony, one expression of which was the 'music of the spheres', which could no longer be heard by man after the Fall of Adam and Eve. By an elaborate and persuasive system of deductions and analogies, a macrocosm hypothetically in a state of perfect and divine order and hierarchy was related doctrinally by theological, philosophical, political, and poetical thinkers to the other 'cosms' generally associated with man: the microcosm, or man himself; the politicosm, or the body politic; and the geocosm, the world of earth and of terrestrial nature. The relationships between the manifestations of creation in God's surrational world were such that they were capable of almost endlessly defining and vivifying each other.

A number of books have been written on Renaissance cosmology and related belief. See, for example, the books by J. B. Bamborough, Leonard Barkan, Hardin Craig, S. K. Heninger jun., John Hollander, C. S. Lewis, A. O. Lovejoy, Marjorie Nicolson, E. M. W. Tillyard, and Basil Willey. From one perspective, the whole of *Paradise Lost* (especially Books vii–viii) might be said to be an exposition of the *created* universe, which has

gained in appreciable myth what it lost in physics. As Raphael
the affable angel assures the inquisitive Adam (viii. 70–5),

> This to attain, whether Heav'n move or Earth,
> Imports not, if thou reck'n right; the rest
> From Man or Angel the great Architect
> Did wisely to conceal, and not divulge
> His secrets to be scann'd by them who ought
> Rather admire . . .

GLOSSARY

This brief and selective glossary allows a single source of reference for notes that would otherwise have to be repeated several times or cross-referenced within the text. I have made no attempt to list every occurrence in the poems of every word included in the glossary, but I give a selection of varied and important instances. References to a title are abbreviated as *t*.

AMPHION. Like Orpheus (q.v.) an archetypal poet. His skill at the lyre drew stones, and by exercising that power he raised the walls of Thebes. H–74: 6 and 90b: 13; L–46: 13–16.

BARLEY-BREAK. A country game, like prisoner's bars or tag, 'originally played by six persons (three of each sex) in couples; one couple, being left in a middle den termed "hell", had to catch the others, who were allowed to separate or "break" when hard pressed, and thus to change partners, but had when caught to take their turn as catchers' (*OED*). H–29 and 47: 118; S–1.

BAYS (and LAUREL). The Greeks gave a wreath of bay or laurel (*Laurus nobilis*)—sacred to Apollo—to the victor in the Pythian games, and victorious Roman generals were crowned with it; thus 'bay(s)' and 'laurel(s)' signify victory, whatever the kind of contest. C–28: 138 and 34: 84; H–34: 8 and 41: 36; L–15: 73; S–7: 23 and 16: 29.

CARLISLE, LUCY HAY, COUNTESS OF (1599–1660). Daughter of Henry Percy, ninth Earl of Northumberland, she married James Hay, first Earl of Carlisle, a Scottish lord who came to England with James I, in 1617 (he died in March 1636). At Charles I's court she was noted for her beauty and wit, kept a French-style salon for persons of elegance and fashion, had much influence with Queen Henrietta Maria, and 'affects [i.e. is fond of] the conversation of the persons who are most famed for [w]it' (Sir Toby Mathew's 'Character' of her, quoted by Patrick, p. 94; see S–26: 61 and n.). She was praised by many of the Court poets (including Carew) and other poets of the day (including Herrick), but not by all (Suckling, for example). C–22 and 40; H–53: *t*; S–7 and 26: 60.

COUNTRY-HOUSE POEMS. These express 'the values of a society conscious of its own achievement of a civilized way of living, and conscious also of the forces that threatened to undermine and overthrow that achievement', according to G. R. Hibbard in 'The Country-House Poem of the Seventeenth Century', *JWCI* xix (1956), 159, quoted in Richard Gill, *Happy Rural Seat: The English Country House and the Literary Imagination* (1972), p. 230. The owners are closely identified with their estates, which are typically seen as extensions and expressions of human character. Ben Jonson, in 'To Penshurst', introduced the genre into England, on the models of Martial's epigram iii. lviii and Horace's epodes ii and xvi. Another notable example is Marvell's 'Upon Appleton House'. Charles Molesworth has written on 'Property and Virtue: The Genre of the Country-House Poem in the Seventeenth Century', *Genre*, i (1968), 141–57. Also see ch. ii, 'The Peerage in Society', in Lawrence Stone, *Crisis of the Aristocracy*: 'a by-product of this cult of reputation was an insistence upon the aristocratic virtue of generosity. Though contemporaries lamented the decay of hospitality—and it undoubtedly did fall away during this period—this is less remarkable than the vigorous persistence of the ideal, and in some measure the practice, in direct opposition to Calvinist ideals of frugality and thrift. The prime test of rank was liberality, the pagan virtue of open-handedness' (abr. edn., 1967, pp. 25–6). C–19 and 39; H–32 and 116.

CROFTS, SIR JOHN (1563–1628), and his family figure in a number of Carew's poems (C–19, 21, 32, 38, and 48). The Crofts estate, Little Saxham, is celebrated in C–19. Carew wrote epitaphs on Sir John's grand-daughter, Mary Wentworth, when she died at eighteen in 1633 (32), and a 'Hymeneal Song' on her sister Anne when she married John Lord Lovelace in 1638 (48). If one may judge by Carew's poems, Crofts evidently perpetuated the ideals of open house and open hand of an earlier age (see note on 'Country-House Poems').

DANAE. Confined in a tower by her father, Acrisius, she was loved by Zeus and visited by him in the form of a shower of gold. The offspring of their union was Perseus. C–4: 8 and 28: 84; H–99: 144 and 101: 4.

DELPHI. A very ancient oracular shrine and precinct of Apollo, and for Renaissance poets a symbolic academy of poets. C–22: 24 and 34: 22.

ELYSIUM. References in Renaissance poetry to 'Elysium', or the 'Elysian Fields' or 'Plains', range from the reasonably specific to the very general idea of 'heaven', any place or any kind of happy afterlife. In Greek mythology Elysium, or the Isles of the Blest, were the place where those favoured by the gods enjoy a bountiful life after death. In earlier mythology Elysium was situated (often) in the west, a meadow by the stream Oceanus; in later mythology it is part of the nether world (Virgil). C–28: 2 and 47: 16; L–34: 37, 42: 7, 45: 29; S–16: 19.

EPITHALAMY (-ION, -IUM). A wedding-song, originally conceived as any song or poem sung outside the bridal chamber on the wedding night. It is of very great antiquity, going back to Homer, Hesiod, Sappho, Aristophanes, and Theocritus, and, in Rome, to Ovid, Statius, and Claudian. The most important for literary history are the epithalamia of Catullus (lxi, lxii, and lxiv). The classical form was revived at the Renaissance and given extraordinary treatments both on the Continent and, in England, by Spenser, Sidney, Donne, Jonson, Herrick, Crashaw, Marvell, and Dryden, and in a rusticated burlesque form by Suckling. Spenser's 'Epithalamion' on his own wedding is customarily regarded as the greatest of English poems in the genre. Many of the conventions of the form are the situational and narrative characteristics of H–99, in which the speaker gives lyric celebration to the wedding day of the knight and his lady of the poem's title. C–48; H–47 and 99; S–27.

FATES. The *Parcae* (Greek *Moirai*) were usually represented as old women of forbidding appearance spinning and thus determining the course of human lives; Clotho held the distaff, Lachesis drew off the thread, and Atropos cut it short. By contrast, Herrick's Fates are 'dainty'. H–8 and 47: 161.

GENIUS. In Roman religion the *genius* was a tutelary spirit that attended a man from cradle to grave, governed his fortunes, and determined his character. In H–47 Herrick uses the *genius* as a god of nature, or child-bearing, a male equivalent of Juno; this use is consonant with the *genius* as an indwelling spirit or *numen* that conferred the power of generation and had the marriage-bed as its sphere (*lectus genialis*, the 'genial couch'). H–47: 43, 111: 128, 116: 4, 166: 7.

HALCYON. Usually identified with the kingfisher; 'anciently fabled to . . . breed in a nest floating on the sea, and to charm the wind and waves so that the sea was then specially calm' (*SOED*); hence 'halcyon days' are calm and peaceful, as though stilled by the halcyon. C–35: 22; H–78: 4; L–43: 6.

HYMEN. The god of marriage in Greek and Roman mythology; he is represented as carrying a torch (hence the phrase, once in popular use, for being in love) and veil. C–48: *t*; H–47: 9 and 99: 31; L–41: 18; S–28: 2.

LAR(ES). Herrick's 'Lares' are identified with the Roman *Lares Familiares*, the spirits who had the special care of the house and household, and were worshipped at the domestic hearth on special occasions. They are viewed by some authorities as having been originally rustic spirits, guardians of the farm and of crops and wine, who were only later transferred to the house. Herrick's 'Lares' have a peculiarly English and personal character. H–32: 106, 110: *t*, 111: 124, 116: 4, 174: 12.

LAWES, HENRY (1595/6–1662). Lawes became a gentleman of the Chapel Royal in 1626 and a royal musician for lutes and voices in 1631. He set to music a very large number of poems written during the Caroline period, including a number written by the four poets of the present collection, and his settings were 'noteworthy' for the concern shown to keep 'just note and accent'; he is in fact the first English composer to make the sense of the poem of paramount importance. He also wrote the music for Carew's masque, *Coelum Brittanicum*, and Milton's, *Comus* (both 1634). Poems in the present collection set to music by Lawes are so identified in individual notes.

ODYSSEUS. The archetypal voyager and wanderer, in many of the poets' references to the hero of the *Odyssey*, whose cunning and resourcefulness were legendary (he is identified as 'a man of many ways' in the first line). After the ten years of the Trojan war, Odysseus was another ten years getting back to Ithaca, where his wife Penelope faithfully awaited his return. C–28: 130; H–67: 18; L–20: 43–6 (as Ulysses).

ORPHEUS. The archetypal poet, he was a legendary pre-Homeric Thracian able to charm beasts and even rocks and trees by his skill on the lyre. His wife, Eurydice (a dryad, or tree-nymph), died of a snake's bite she received when running from the lustful Aristaeus. Persephone, the queen of the lower world, was persuaded by Orpheus' music to let Eurydice return from the dead, on condition that he not look back as she followed him. As they approached the world of the living, Orpheus forgot the condition and looked back, whereupon Eurydice vanished forever. Orpheus was later torn to pieces by Thracian maenads (female votaries of Dionysus), either because he interfered with their worship or because, according to another explanation, he became a misogynist after he lost Eurydice. C–34: 40; H–176; L–6 and 7.

PHAETON. Ovid, *Met.* ii. 319–32. Son of Helios, the Sun. Given permission—with warnings—to drive his father's chariot for a day, he lost control of the horses, which bolted from their usual course and endangered the earth; Zeus intervened and hurled a thunderbolt at Phaeton, who fell into the river Eridanus. Phaeton is eponymous for self-destructive presumptuousness. C–24: 15–16; L–20: 33, 40: 21–2, 41: 43–4.

PHOENIX. In Brewer's succinct description, 'a fabulous Egyptian (Arabian, or Indian, etc.) bird, the only one of its kind, according to Greek legend said to live a certain number of years', usually five hundred, 'at the close of which it makes in Egypt (or Arabia, etc.) a nest of spices, sings a melodious dirge, flaps its wings to set fire to the pile, burns itself to ashes, and comes forth with new life' (*Dictionary of Phrase and Fable*, 1974). A recurrent sacred and secular symbol of renewal and immortality. C–40: 5, 44: 18, 47: 14; H–62: 17, 99: 25, 174: 8; L–30: 11, 35: 31, 45: 51–2.

POSSET. Spiced and sweetened hot milk curdled with ale, wine (often 'sack'), or spirits and drunk especially at bedtime. H–99: 136; L–34: 16; S–27: 122.

SACK. Kinds of white wine imported from Spain (sherry, the best sack), Galicia, Portugal, and the Canary Islands, and a fashion-

able drink in the Renaissance much favoured by Falstaff, who
apostrophizes it passionately in soliloquy in *2H4* IV. iii. 92–119.
The beneficence of wine is a Biblical commonplace in both the
Old Testament and the New (esp. 1 Tim. 5: 23). H–41: *t* and
67: *t*.

SHOWBREAD. The twelve loaves placed every sabbath 'before the
Lord' on a table beside the altar of incense and at the end of the
week eaten by the priests alone. A ready symbol for open display
and closed consumption. H–78: 69 and H–125.

SMALL-. Used in *ad hoc* compounds to denote 'minor rank, note,
or importance, in respect of some specified office, function, etc.'
(*OED* 17). S–26: 115, 'small-poets' (also Jonson, *Alchemist*, 1610,
I. ii. 50–2). The conventional compound 'small-wares' (see S–2:
t. and n.) is related but is less directly pejorative.

SPIRIT(s). Vapour(s) formed in the liver (natural spirits), refined
by the heart (vital), and further purified by the brain (animal:
anima 'soul'); they were responsible for mediating to the body the
vital animating heat generated by the four bodily humours
created in the liver (see E. M. W. Tillyard, *The Elizabethan World
Picture*, 1943, pp. 68–9, and C. S. Lewis, *The Discarded Image*, 1964,
pp. 165–74, for a detailed description of conventional Renaissance
physiology). Burton: 'spirit is a most subtle vapour, which is
expressed from the blood, and the instrument of the soul, to
perform all his actions; a common tie or medium [*tertium quid*]
betwixt the body and the soul, as some will have it' (*Anatomy of
Melancholy*, Part. I, sect. I, mem. ii, Subs. ii). See also Donne,
'The Ecstasy', ll. 61–4. C–8: 1; H–41: 2.

THYRSE. In Herrick's gloss, 'a javelin twined with ivy'; traditionally the staff of Bacchus, and for Herrick a kind of Baccha-
nalian caduceus. H–2: 7, 34: 8, 68: 32, 111: 135.

VESTA(L). Vesta is the Roman hearth-goddess. In her temple a
perpetual flame was tended and Vesta was served by two–six
Vestal Virgins, who could marry after their term of service (first
five, later thirty, years). L–29: 22, 41: 25.

INDEX OF TITLES AND FIRST LINES
(Titles are indicated in italic, first lines in roman.)

INDEX 349